Laoshi

Tai Chi, Teachers, and Pursuit of Principle

by Jan Kauskas

Via Media Publishing
Santa Fe, NM

Printed in the United States of America

The paper in this book meets the guidelines for permanence and durability of the Committee on Production Guidelines for Book Longevity of the Council on Library Resources.

Copyright © 2014 by
Via Media Publishing Company

Via Media Publishing Company
941 Calle Mejia #822
Santa Fe, NM 87501 USA
Tel: 1-505-983-1919 • E-mail: md@goviamedia.com

Book and cover design by
Via Media Publishing Company.

Edited by T. G. LaFredo, MFA

Cover illustration by
Chang Jungshan (張榕柵) and Jungshan Ink.

Background mountain illustration used on the cover
and throughout this book © elen/123RF.com

ISBN 978-0-615-96736-3 (alk. paper)

www.viamediapublishing.com

Dedication
To my teachers.

Acknowledgements
I would like to thank
Ai-Lien Banks for her
help in writing this book.
Without the many hours she
contributed to the process,
this book may well
have been written, but
certainly not widely read.
I also wish to thank
James Morrison of
Immediate Arts for his
encouragement, advice, and
technical assistance, which
I have greatly appreciated.
Mike DeMarco of Via Media
Publishing also receives
my gratitude for his
enthusiasm and encouragement,
matched only by his flair for
design. I could not have
wished for better hands
into which to place my
manuscript and my trust.
Finally, I must thank my
students, past and present,
at Autumn River Tai Chi,
with whom I was able to explore
many of the themes
presented in this volume.

contents

preface

One of my early tai chi[1] teachers was fond of saying to his students: "Study the kind of tai chi that will be useful when you don't have a body." At the time, the notion did not strike me as particularly bizarre since, like my teacher, I was intent on understanding spirituality through the medium of tai chi ch'uan. Implicit within the statement is the recognition that tai chi is more than just a physical exercise for the body.

I have spent more than twenty-five years exploring the question of what else tai chi is with a number of teachers—each of whom offered something of his own perspective on tai chi in general and on the tai chi of Zheng Manqing (Cheng Man-ch'ing) in particular. Some perspectives appealed to me more than others, but gradually a tapestry of ideas and principles took shape, resulting in the approach I find myself studying and teaching today.

Central to this approach is the importance of the *heart-mind*,[2] that indefinable aspect of ourselves that can only be known through inference and analogy. It is, for me, the greater part of us, and tai chi without it would be an empty wrapper. Like the Dao itself, it is impossible to "know" the heart-mind in the way we might know arithmetic. And, like the Dao, anything that can be said about it is, at best, incomplete—yet many of us feel a need to express the inexpressible in whatever way we can: through movement, voice, or art.

For me, tai chi is a way of expressing and exploring the notion of heart-mind in a physical form. However, I also recognize the desire in me to extend that expression to the written word. How, then, to write something *meaning-ful* about something *inexpressible*? The need is there to be expressed, but the tools are inadequate to the purpose. What is to be done?

One approach, and the one adopted extensively in the following pages, is to recount stories. The wonderful thing about a story is that it can function as an entertaining diversion while also hinting at a deeper meaning, a meaning that can comfort or inspire.

Dialogue between student and teacher is a well-established device, and with good reason: it is effective. The immature novice with energy and innocence on his side seeks the knowledge and wisdom of the one who has traveled the path ahead of him—a wisdom based on experience and maturity. This is the province of the teacher.

The relationship between teacher and student is a recurring theme in martial arts stories, as is the fruit of that relationship. The Japanese idiom *ishin denshin* means it is a heart-to-heart transmission. Therefore, a major theme of our story is the deepening heart-to-heart communication between the teacher (*laoshi*) and his student.

The conversations between Laoshi and the student, as well as the stories recounted by each of them, have elements of fact and fiction embedded within, but they are all true in the sense that they speak of the genuine challenges both teachers and students encounter on the Way. It is my feeling that a story-telling approach (as compared with pure reportage of given incidents) leads us deeper into the land of *truth*—a "pathless land," as Jiddu Krishnamurti might say—not least because the heart-mind can better relate to truth at a metaphorical or visceral level. A list of technical details and bald facts may satisfy the rational within us, but such an approach will likely make little impact on the heart-mind, which has the capacity to grasp the most fragile of figurative ideas and, from them, construct an entire universe.

The two main characters, Laoshi and the student, are not based upon any particular individuals, but are rather an amalgam of ideas and events, as well as teachers and students I have encountered throughout forty years of study, first in Japanese martial arts, and then in the tai chi boxing art of Zheng Manqing.

Other characters who appear, especially Laoshi's former teachers, are likewise an amalgam of those individuals who have been my own teachers during those forty years. Some fulfilled the role of teacher for a single day, others for a decade. Some excelled in form, others in push-hands, sword, or philosophy. Thus, I have endeavored to weave together the various strands of wisdom and experience gleaned from these teachers into a vivid portrait of the tai chi that resonates most closely with me.

The following pages, then, are a kind of semifictional memoir. They reflect my own experiences gained in the pursuit of tai chi and other martial arts. They also reflect ideas on form, energy (*qi*), push-hands, sword form, and fencing, which developed from that study.

I hope they are of some value to you.

---

[1] There are many systems used to transliterate Chinese to the Latin alphabet, but the academic standard and official phonetic system in China used today is known as Pinyin. All should be using this method, but we have a few hundred years of familiarity with older, awkward systems that persist in common usage today. We have decided to keep the familiar "tai chi" spelling for this book because it is widely recognized, but to put all other Chinese names and terms into Pinyin.

[2] In Chinese, the word *xin* translates both to "heart" and to "mind." It is often written in combination as "heart-mind" to expresses the unity of thoughts and feelings.

Exploring

the various

facets of

learning,

studying,

teaching,

and playing

tai`chi.

Photographs of
Jan Kauskas by David Paton.
Background © elen/123RF.com

Photography
by David Paton.

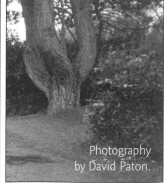

Photography
by David Paton.

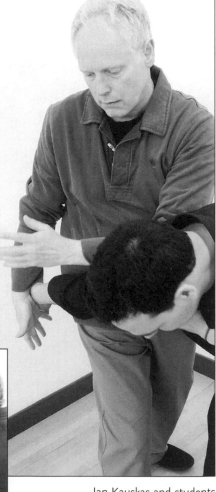

Jan Kauskas and students
from Autumn River Tai Chi:
Jamie Simpson, Anthony Johnston,
Dougie Blane, and Tom Wallace.
Photography by Dougie Blane.

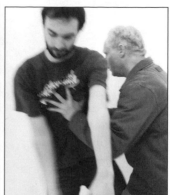

道可道非常道
名可名非常名
無名天地之始
有名萬物之母

I'm not sure I like Laoshi (老師), my teacher. I'm not sure he likes me. I'm not even sure you are supposed to like your teacher. In fact, I am not particularly sure of anything except he is the real deal or, at least, as real as it gets these days.

預
備
式

He is my tai chi (太極) teacher, a curious mix of martial artist, exercise coach, and spiritual guide. He is a mass of contradictions, sometimes challenging, sometimes gentle, but always teaching. And watching. It is not an altogether comfortable feeling being in class, even though he is always stressing the need for relaxation. You always have the feeling the word means something else to him, something hidden and hard to access. He has a presence, warm and inviting, but at the same time potent. He is not someone you take lightly, but he is someone you want to be around.

The senior students say he has done it all, but he is self-effacing. He studied a number of Japanese martial arts before devoting himself to tai chi, Zheng Manqing (鄭曼青) style, although he never refers to it as a "style."

I call him Laoshi, though he seems a little irritated by this. He does not like such titles, but tolerates Laoshi even though I clearly cannot pronounce it properly. It is a Chinese word meaning "teacher," but due to the vagaries of a tonal language, my attempts at pronunciation can seem laughable. Even perfect pronunciation but using different characters turn the meaning to "old corpse." Equally difficult is *shifu* (師父 teacher-father), which can sound like "washer woman." Although his mother was Chinese, he does not look Asian, but there again he does not seem to be particularly Western either. He is an even rarer breed: a martial artist.

Laoshi's credentials are impressive. He studied with at least three of Zheng Manqing's most notable students, one Chinese and two American, but also with several other less well-known teachers he sometimes mentions. So much about him is a mystery but I, in common with so many, am drawn to the mysterious and exotic. After so many years studying tai chi, I do not know if I could say I enjoy it, but I keep coming back just to be around the man and the things he does. It is a real education.

Take, for instance, the time I met him in a railway station. I had not been studying with him long, but by chance happened upon him while he was on his way to do a workshop. I noticed him sitting, reading a book on one of the metallic seats in a quiet corner of the station, if there can be such a thing.

At first I was inclined just to pretend I had not noticed him, as he seemed to be involved with his book. There was a feeling of unhurried peacefulness around him, which contrasted strongly with the hustle and bustle of a busy railway station. He appeared to be the epitome of stillness in the eye of a hurricane—a phrase one of my former teachers used a lot to describe being centered. I decided to approach him because I heard it was considered bad manners to see your teacher on the street and not greet him.

Laoshi was in his midforties at the time, more or less twice as old as me, and of average height, weight, and appearance. He did not make any effort to attract attention in his manner or clothing. There was, however, something about him that was a touch different. He stood out against his background a little. It did not shout out at you, it was more of a whisper, but when you looked for it, you could sense it.

As I approached, he looked up and smiled warmly. I had the distinct impression he had known I was there all along, deciding what to do. I told him I hoped I was not disturbing him, but he seemed genuinely pleased to see me and invited me to join him while we waited for our respective trains.

As we sat talking, mostly about tai chi, I felt a strong sense of respect for the man and his dedication to living the Way over many years. I had similar feelings of respect for my former aikido teacher, Billy Coyle, but had always felt deeply uncomfortable talking to him about anything other than aikido. I sensed a greater bond was growing with Laoshi, so I found myself trying to find words that would convey how I felt toward him.

I ended up saying, "Laoshi, I just wanted to say I really appreciate the classes you teach and how you have put up with so much suffering in order to follow the Way and to bring it to us." It sounds a little sycophantic, now in hindsight, but I did not mean it to be so. Words can be so inadequate sometimes.

His reply surprised me, a theme that would become common in the years to come.

He said, "Well, maybe, but I don't see it that way. Following my path has always seemed more of an adventure than a path filled with suffering. In fact, studying tai chi has shown me that suffering is another aspect of fear. As my old teacher Wang Lang used to say, there are only two emotions: happiness and fear. If you do not have a sense of well-being and joyfulness, then you are experiencing one of the ten thousand faces of fear."

That was such a bizarre thought that I found myself lost for words for a few moments, then finally asked, "But there is a lot of pain and hardship in life. Isn't that suffering?"

He nodded, acknowledging my point before continuing. "You might think so, and I suppose a lot of people think that way, but the path we follow offers another point of view. This view says pain and suffering are two different things. Pain may be a part of life, but suffering doesn't have to be. To a very great extent, this is why I study tai chi. It does not offer an end to pain, but it does offer us the chance to end our suffering."

I was beginning to realize how big a subject tai chi was for people like Laoshi. I have to admit, I was keen to hear more, so I asked him if he could elaborate a little on what he had just told me, especially how pain and suffering were different.

He spoke again. "Pain—physical, psychological, or emotional—will always be with us as long as we have pleasure. It is the yin to the yang of pleasure. They cannot be separated. Even if you could, by some miracle, manage to remove all pain from your life, leaving only pleasurable experiences, you would find that some would be more pleasurable than others and pretty soon, these less pleasant experiences you would regard as pain. You only know pain because of pleasure. They are, as the Daoists would say, 'mutually arising.'

"Suffering, however, has a lot to do with how we react to the pain and hardship life offers us."

"But how?" I interrupted. This was as interesting as it was disconcerting. It was not what I wanted to hear. As a young boy, I was fascinated by images of Buddhist monks self-immolating in protest of the Vietnam War. Their act impressed me, not because of the deep feeling for peace that prompted it, but because they were able to withstand such a terrible and painful death unperturbed. I wanted some of that kind of power. Laoshi seemed to be offering something else.

He continued, "You have heard me talk about the principle of investing in loss. Usually, invest in loss is mentioned in respect to push-hands, but like all of tai chi's principles, it can be applied at a deeper level to all aspects of life. Normally, it means when we 'lose' in push-hands and are pushed, we have the opportunity to see how the pusher managed to do it. It is not exactly the same as saying 'trial and error,' but similar.

"However, with time, the principle can become part of our being. We can begin to see that though we may have losses and failures, our deep selves are not fundamentally damaged by the loss or failing. A lot of stress and worry come from life not living up to what we expect or feel entitled to. If we can accept loss, we can learn from it and use it to make progress in much the same way we played games as children. At some point, we were contaminated by fear of loss and failure and learned to resist it. Then suffering entered."

He looked at me as if assessing how much I was taking in before adding, "I very much suspect you are looking for power, but I would ask you this question: would you rather be a man who could beat anyone, or a man who no one could beat?"

Laoshi was very intuitive and was uncannily accurate in sensing what people were thinking. My own intuition told me his question was asking something fundamental about how we approach this mystery of life. The question was about my need to feel in control of my life so I could stop bad things happening to me. I felt a little embarrassed about how transparent I was and felt myself to be like a scared little boy, looking for a way to stop life from hurting me.

He reassured me, saying, "Don't feel bad about wanting to be powerful. Life, one way or another, has wounded us all. How could I know that you are looking for power over life if I had not wanted it too? Life can be hard and we all seek some kind of protection or escape."

This conversation was getting deep and, as I looked up at the people milling about, I was struck by the discrepancy between the cold, impersonal space we were in and the deep, intimate conversation we were having. Perhaps because of the environment, I felt my reluctance to let go of the need for control that I had been nurturing most of my life. How could I abandon myself to the cold, harsh, unforgiving world as evidenced by the scene before my eyes?

I questioned him again. "But if I give up trying to control things, what will I be left with? I will be at the mercy of all the hateful things that are part of life, as well as the good. I don't know if I can do that."

I could feel the concern for me in his voice as he continued very quietly. "You may not have much choice. The more you try to control life, the more you imprison yourself. You will experience greater and greater tension and so, less and less joy, happiness, and love.

"Once you understand the only way to control the universe is to realize you can't, there is a wonderful freedom. It takes away the pressure that goes with trying to force things to your will. When that happens, something strange happens. Have you ever heard the expression, 'To a hammer, everything looks like a nail'?"

"No, but I think I understand what it means," I replied.

He nodded and continued. "When you seek to make things happen, to control everything, a tight, grasping mindset takes over. This inevitably leads to fear because you separate yourself from the flow of life. It is like spinning lots of plates on rods. You have to go around keeping them all spinning. You cannot stop even for a moment or else they will fall. Pretty soon all that matters is that you keep the plates spinning. You have even forgotten why you are spinning them in the first place.

"The hammer creates its own reality because everything becomes a nail and needs to be hammered down. If you live fearful of failure, life will reflect to you evidence of the need to be fearful. This is not some cosmic intervention; it is only a result of perception. You see what you want to see, which confirms that you were right in the first place."

"But, if we don't try to control the world," I asked again, "aren't we just being fatalistic? Aren't we just puppets with no free will?"

"Think about breathing," he said. "Do you control it, or does it control you?"

"A bit of both," I answered.

"Quite right," he added. "You can hold your breath, but not forever. You control it partially, but not fully. It is the same with your will. Life is partly what you will and partly what life wills. You control your breath to some extent, but there comes a point where it controls you. This is what free will is like. You may think about doing something, but the question is, where did that thought come from?"

I must admit, the question took me aback. Surely it was obvious where thoughts came from.

"They come from me." I answered hesitantly, beginning to realize for the first time that I did not know how thoughts entered my head. All kinds of thoughts come to mind continuously through the day. Some seem to be related, but then a totally unrelated thought will enter at random. It is true I can decide to think about something, but what made me decide in the first place? I would have had to decide to decide. It could regress endlessly. I then had another thought, origin unknown, that I was not all that sure what "me" was either. I blurted out, "Where do thoughts come from, then?"

All he did was laugh and say, "Now, that is a very, very good question!"

With that he got up and went for his train, while I sat there trying to make sense of what he told me.

At that point, the story of a young judoka on his way to a competition in postwar Japan came to mind. Getting on the train, he took the empty seat next to an old man and closed his eyes to get some sleep. He wanted to rest before the competition. The old man, however, kept on talking and asking questions. The judoka, several times, respectfully asked the old man to be quiet so he could rest before he competed. The old man, nevertheless, kept on talking. Eventually, he was more direct and told the old man to shut up. The old man replied, "If I am an old man and you are such a great judo champion, then perhaps you can break my finger. I will be quiet if you can break my little finger."

The judoka thought if that is what it would take, he would do it. As he grabbed the old man's finger and twisted it, rather than the sound of a dry twig snapping, he was thrown in the air, slammed down on his back on the train floor, and immobilized.

"Who are you?" he asked in amazement.

"I am Ueshiba, founder of aikido."

The judoka was, in fact, Kenshiro Abbe. He became Ueshiba's student and stayed with him for ten years before becoming the first man to teach aikido in the United Kingdom.

What Laoshi did that day in the train station was metaphorically the same thing. Thankfully, I did not end up slammed onto the floor next to him, but I was from that point captivated and really became his student. From then on, "I harmonized with my teacher," as Zheng Manqing would say. I let his influence into my life and became the better for it. I began to find my heart-mind and trust it to guide my actions. In short, Laoshi changed my life.

Chapter 2: Ward Off Doubt and Fear

起
勢

There are those in the martial arts community who frown on something as sordid as teaching for money. For them the art is sacred and not to be bought with anything as squalid as money—blood, sweat, and tears, maybe, but not money. Laoshi was not wholly dismissive of critics who complained that his actions both cheapened himself and the art he taught. He was sensitive to the problems commercializing martial arts can bring, but was not persuaded by their argument. Once, when confronted by such a critic, he said, "There is always exchange; only the currency varies."

I once asked him what he meant when he said "only the currency varies."

"Almost everything we do is done for payment of some kind," he said. "Payment for teaching martial arts has changed over the years. It can be money, as is the norm today in an industrial age, or some form of work, as in a more agrarian society, or by the flattery of our ego, which is a timeless currency. The totally selfless act is something illusory. Nobody does something for nothing, but sometimes our motives are hidden to us. Even the apparently noble ambition of maintaining the art for future generations is merely subtle ego. The Way does not need to be defended. It is the Way. How can you and I save it? This is gross arrogance. It saves us. This is like those who would save Mother Earth. She does not need to be saved. We do. When she is tired of our folly, she will eradicate us and start again."

It is not surprising then, that by the time I met Laoshi he was earning his living as a tai chi teacher, although he did not teach full time until he was about forty. He was not from a wealthy family and so had to build up his school over the years before it was stable enough to support him.

"Even in this, there is a lesson," he once told me. "When the idea began to form in my mind that the way forward was to dedicate my life to the Dao and pursue my real work, the consequences of throwing away secure but unsatisfying work weighed heavily.

"When throwing ourselves on the mercy of the Dao by leaving the world of paid work, the thought of a financial cushion becomes very attractive. The trap is then formed. The Dao allows the accumulation of such a cushion, in my case £1,000. I thought with such a sum I would be confident in taking the step into the unknown. My rational mind then introduced doubt by asking, 'Are you sure £1,000 is enough?' Suddenly, I was sure it was not; I needed £3,000. Soon I was convinced I needed £5,000, then £10,000, then £15,000. I caught myself in time. In service of the Dao, no guarantees are given. It is a big lesson to learn: to the rational mind, no guarantee can ever be enough; to the heart-mind, none is necessary."

Laoshi was talking about himself, but his message was clear for us all. Some of us are fortunate enough to actually find out what our life's work is— but, consumed by doubt and fear, we fail to make it a reality.

Even before meeting Laoshi, I had felt the urge to write about martial arts, but I persuaded myself I did not have anything to say and, even if I did, I would never find the right words. I told myself that it was pointless even to start.

I remembered hearing about a well-known and highly respected Japanese aikido expert who was asked why he had not written a book. He replied, "There is already a book."

I said to myself, "There are already plenty written about tai chi. Why does the world need any more?"

Hearing Laoshi's words, however, I began writing with no thought of where it would lead, how much money it would bring, or, indeed, if it would be any good. I began writing because I wanted to write and realized all those petty doubts were crushing any creativity before it had a chance to flourish.

When our doubts cause us to abandon our true Way because we fear failure, we can only live a shallow, unfulfilled life. The heart-mind does not care about being good enough, or doing something special. As Laoshi used to say, "The water does not care how beautiful the cup is. It fills the shape without judgment."

The notion that everything we do has to be purposeful, or have a saleable value, is a fiction I was brought up with. Educated to fit in and be a good consumer unit, I had unwittingly "bought in" to the whole tyranny. I had stifled any creativity, believing myself to be untalented, and allowed my doubts to persuade me not to risk trying, in case I could not live up to my expectations. There are many of us who come to the conclusion that it is better not to try than to try and be a failure.

The Way is at its most powerful when it dispels illusions such as these.

Chapter 3: Life-Giving Sword

Laoshi loved to fence—tai chi fencing, that is. He still practiced the Japanese sword routines (*kumitachi*) he learned in aikido, but tai chi fencing and push-hands were his real loves. He always stressed the importance of the form,

左
挒

but it was clear to all of us that fencing and push-hands kept his interest vibrant and alive.

He once said, "The kumitachi are useful to understand timing, rhythm, balance, and distance—the real skills in fighting—but tai chi fencing reveals the fusion of yin and yang in a more direct way, if you know how to look."

He thought the great Morihei Ueshiba, the founder of aikido, was talking about this fusion of yin and yang when he said, "In order for someone to defeat me, he must change the order of the universe." Similarly, he thought Zheng Manqing meant much the same thing when he advised his students to "first study the yin, then study the yang, then put them together."

For Laoshi, this was a profound principle, the depths of which he mined continually in his own practice. His thinking on the idea gradually evolved as he considered how yin and yang could be used against another swordsman or in push-hands. I began to have a flavor of the direction of his study when he said, "I used to think Zheng Manqing meant we should be soft and hard as necessary, applying each to our surroundings as needed. Over time, I have come to sense a deeper meaning. A possibility that permits the fusion of yin and yang into something different: something unique, something that does not divide yin and yang."

Laoshi would often quote his teacher Wang Lang on his experience fencing with Professor Zheng. "Contact with his sword sometimes felt full, but when you tried to disconnect, you found you couldn't. His contact did not exhibit the normal characteristics of hardness." Laoshi would usually add, "This is where the secret lies."

The goal for Laoshi was a connection with the other person's sword, a feeling that has none of the characteristics we associate with hard or soft. It is something different. They say great swordsmen can "magnetize" your sword so it becomes stuck fast to theirs. No matter what you do, you cannot separate from it once it has control of you. This is what Laoshi was looking for when he fenced, while the rest of us were, childishly, trying to emulate Toshiro Mifune or Errol Flynn.

For this reason, no doubt, Laoshi did not spend much time tantalizing us with these mystical and esoteric ideas. He would always return to the simplest ideas when he watched us in our attempts to master the sword. Laoshi's method for teaching fencing began with five basic but fundamental ideas, which we had to understand before we even began to talk about yin and yang.

"First you have to understand that you have no shield to defend yourself. The irony is that the weapon you hold in your hand is primarily not for inflicting damage to your opponent; it is, first and foremost, to protect yourself."

This is one of Laoshi's teachings on *katsujinken*—a Japanese word meaning "life-giving sword." He seemed to believe it is important how we think about the sword. He would stress its value as a positive force in life rather than just a tool for killing people. The idea that weapons are anything but killing implements may seem strange to us. It is even stranger to think the sword has a nature or character for good or evil, but in some martial arts, swords are more than just swords.

There is a story of two master swordsmiths in ancient Japan who made swords of the highest quality. One was called Masamune, who was said to be a spiritual, pure, and benevolent man. The other was Muramasa, who they say was violent, brutish, and evil. According to the legend, each of these two masters imbued his swords with his own character: one essentially peaceful and kind, the other violent and aggressive. Because of this, it was very easy to tell which man had made which blade. All you had to do was place them hilt down in a small stream with the cutting edge upstream, and then sprinkle flower petals on the water and watch while they floated toward the swords. As the petals approached Masamune's sword, they would magically be repelled from the edge and float past safely on their journey. The petals nearing Muramasa's blade would all be drawn in and cut.

It is hard to say if Laoshi believed in this sort of superstition, but he would always warn new students to the sword class never to touch another person's sword without asking first. He would explain by saying, "Some people believe their spirit goes into the sword, and they don't need you contaminating it."

He also once told me a rather curious tale, the authenticity of which he could not verify, but considered significant anyway. "One of my former teachers, Don, had not practiced his saber form for many years and had given away his saber. At some point he decided to reacquaint himself with the saber, but since he did not have one, he used an antique katana he had acquired as an investment years before. He took the katana from its stand and began swirling it around and cutting in the manner you would with a saber. It was a passable replacement, if a little cumbersome because of the longer handle.

"As it happened, his senior student at the time, a woman named Janice, came by for a visit. She picked up the Japanese sword to examine it and swung it around in a light-hearted and flippant manner, until Don told her to put it down and treat it with some respect. A few days later, Don received a phone call from Janice. She told him shortly after getting home, she began to feel ill and had to take to her bed. The illness lasted for a few days before she eventually recovered. It was an unusual illness, unlike any she had experienced before, arriving without reason and leaving equally suddenly. According to Don, the illness was the sword taking its revenge on her for her lack of respect."

"Do you think that is possible?" I asked Laoshi, clearly skeptical.

"It doesn't matter whether it is true or not," he answered. "What matters is people may think it is true. The sword has a powerful effect on the imagination."

Back in sword class, he would elaborate on the first of the five principles.

"You must, first of all, maintain the discipline of keeping your blade between you and the other person's sword. He must get past your sword to kill you. If you begin by pointing the sword at the enemy, you automatically open the lines of attack to yourself. This is another of the marvelous ironies of martial arts."

Laoshi loved the ironic in martial arts. He used to smile when he commented on how life often confounds our expectations. "Martial arts contain so many paradoxes. For instance, people come to martial arts fearing they will be hurt by others, but injure themselves far worse by fighting or by crippling themselves in senseless ascetics." For Laoshi, the admonition against fighting in martial arts had nothing to do with morality. It was pure common sense not to needlessly damage yourself for any reason.

While the first principle is partly practical and partly philosophical, his second is almost exclusively practical. It is also crucial in making our fencing tai chi rather than Shaolin. He referred to it as "the cone."

Typically, he would begin his explanation of the cone by saying, "You must learn to make your defense impeccable." He always liked using the word "impeccable" in this context. None of us really knew if there were some subtle meaning he ascribed to the word or if he just liked saying it. "When you can defend without even the merest hint of the opponent touching you with his sword, then you can attack." He would explain that, in fencing, attack was really not much more than defense going forward. To demonstrate the impeccability of his defense, he used to sit on a chair and fence with us, yet nobody could find a way to get past his sword.

"The secret," he would say, "is in maintaining a defensive cone with the sword. To do this, you move the arm, not the wrist." In Western-style fencing, the wrist and fingers move the sword, but in tai chi fencing, the arm moves relative to the body. It traces a circle in the air, close to the body. By keeping the tip, or more usually the middle of the sword, relatively still and moving the hand in an arc, the shape of a cone can be traced in the air. Crucially, the broad end is toward you, not the opponent. When done as an exercise, it looks to the observer as if the tip is fixed in place and the sword is floating.

It is a difficult skill to master and all who begin to practice with the sword instinctively favor using the wrist to manipulate the blade, which is not what tai chi is about. It takes a long time to take the wrist out of fencing and—much like the temptation to resort to strength in push-hands when we find ourselves under pressure—the wrist creeps in.

Laoshi's third basic idea is about keeping the spot where the swords cross between your center and the other person's center. "We must understand," he would explain, "that what we are doing is not sword fighting. You are not likely to find yourself in a sword fight at the bus stop. We do not even have real swords."

Usually we used wooden swords for form and fencing. We were all aware that sword fighting was not the real aim of our practice, but we enjoyed the element of musketeer or flashing-blade action that sword class sometimes offered. Laoshi also told us a real *jian* (劍 Chinese straight sword) was nearly impossible to come across. According to Laoshi, even the antique jian that could be bought as investment pieces by collectors were just cheap militia swords, weighted incorrectly. A real jian that could be used for tai chi fencing was a very rare thing indeed. He would occasionally say, somewhat cryptically, that the true swords of old picked you, not the other way around. "When you are ready, the knowledge of where your soul's sword is will come to you in a dream. When this happens, you must stop at nothing to acquire it." I imagined an old, dusty antique shop hidden in an unlikely part of town, run by a dithering old relic of a man—complete with fingerless gloves and small, wire-rimmed half-moon glasses—guarding my sword until it sensed enough maturity in me to call me to its side. Needless to say, I am still waiting.

So if we were not learning how to fight with a sword, what were we learning? Laoshi would say, "Most fundamentally, you are learning to move your feet to gain positional advantage, specifically, how to close distance. As you know, fighting distance is of crucial importance. If you control distance, you are safe. Closing with the enemy is a dangerous time, whether he is attacking you or vice versa. You must learn to control this coming together. Make no holes in your defense and take advantage of the holes in his. On a basic level, stick to your opponent's sword so the point at which they cross is between you. When the point of contact moves to the side, this is crisis. Remember what we mean by crisis: danger and opportunity."

Laoshi was referring to the Chinese character for *crisis*, which contains the characters for *danger* and *opportunity*. When the point at which the swords cross is no longer between the two fencers, there is a hole or an opening into which one or the other can enter. It must be borne in mind that entering into the opening created by our opponent is very dangerous. It is like overtaking while driving a car. There will be an opportunity for the opponent to counter-attack because we create an opening in our own defense as we advance. It should also be borne in mind that it is not a question of who can first get into the opening left by the other. The skill is in recognizing the smallest and subtlest glimmers of openings as they arise and being able to take advantage of them before the moment passes. Against a skilled fencer, you might even be aware of a slight opening, but on those few instances, if you have to think about advancing, it is already too late. The master senses the opening and enters without thought.

Laoshi's fourth principle has to do with strategy. "When fencing in a room like this, we drive our opponent to the side of the room, where he has less space to maneuver; then, when he is stuck, we can cut him. We can also chase him into the path of other people and take advantage of the clash as they collide with each other. An experienced fencer, however, will not retreat in a straight line. He knows he has limited room to maneuver and will use it wisely by circling. You must circle even if there is limitless space, as the attacker can run faster going forward than the defender can going back."

Laoshi had a habit of stating the obvious as if unveiling a great truth, probably because in the heat of battle we seemed unable to adhere to even the simplest of ideas. I used to smile inwardly when he would "reveal" to me that "by going backward, you cannot see where you are going."

"Really?" I would say sarcastically to myself before he would follow up with, "When you circle, you can see where you are going with your peripheral vision."

With practice, though, we began to make straight-line retreating a thing of the past. So much so that one of the students, who often taught his five-year-old daughter sword principles in play, told us of her exasperation while watching a cartoon sword fight, saying, "Look, Daddy, they don't know anything about sword fighting. They are going straight back."

Laoshi's insistence on circling reminded me of boxing trainers who teach their fighters to circle away from the power hand. I also noticed how we could retreat skillfully to create angles to counterattack. This led to the last of his basic principles and the one that really needs practice: learning angles.

He would often say, "In learning angles, there is no substitute for time on the court." This was another of those phrases he liked to use, even though we did not practice on a tennis court, or indeed, any other type of court. The idea is that when swords cross, the angle at which they connect could be neutral, or give an advantage to one or the other swordsman. The only way to learn the angles is to fence, and then fence some more. What is remarkable is that although fencing is so free and unprescribed, the same positions keep coming up again and again. Gradually, it becomes clear that some positions are better than others, giving a slight positional advantage.

"Learn the angles," Laoshi insisted, "so you are a danger to the opponent, but he is not a danger to you. When he seeks to escape to a neutral position, adjust so you maintain the pressure until he is defeated." This was very much in tune with Laoshi's view on martial arts. Once you have the opening, you swarm all over the opponent, not letting him recover or regain his balance. One student said it felt like he took your breath away when he demonstrated tai chi as a fighting art. When he heard that, he said, "Of course. You steal the qi." Qi is often translated as breath, and Laoshi was happy with the pun. "You take away the opponent's breath, balance, mind, and will. And, if necessary, his life."

Chapter 4: Step Back to Repulse Boredom

At my first class, I was a little disappointed to find I would have to start 右
out by learning the form, a sequence of slow-motion movements repeated the 挒
same way every time, lasting about ten minutes. I was more interested in push-hands and getting the feel of the art with a partner. I was certain the form would be really boring, not particularly good exercise, and certainly not useful as a martial art. This impression is easily arrived at, and I would guess it's the reason most people view tai chi as mainly for old people. If it were not for the promise of push-hands and fencing, I probably would never have started, preferring a little more robust approach to exercise. This attitude was transformed very quickly by Laoshi's teaching method.

One of the limits to the success of tai chi, as it is normally taught, is the crushing boredom of continual repetition of the same movements, followed by more of the same. In the really strict schools, there is very little explanation and questions are not encouraged. I remember meeting a woman at a party who used to do tai chi with another teacher in town.

"Why did you stop?" I asked her.

"I was almost pulling my hair out with the boredom," she said.

There are some teachers who would shrug, saying, "She did not want it badly enough." The implication being that you have to endure the boredom as part of the price of reaping the rewards later on. Laoshi did not follow this approach.

"We study energy here, not sedation," he said once, commenting on a group of students who came from a nearby meditation teacher. They were a little disconcerting at first sight because they were very still and measured, both in movement and speech. Laoshi told me there is a class of teacher who brings relief to students by numbing them to the sharp reality of life. He, on the other hand, taught the opposite.

"We do not want to become immune to life. Life is not a disease to be cured. It is a celebration. This requires energy, not anesthetic, be it physical, chemical, or meditational."

As a result, Laoshi's classes were not boring. He employed a curious mix:

formal instruction; stories, usually tai chi related, sometimes funny, sometimes thought provoking; anecdotes about his teachers and tai chi luminaries; and digressions into related subjects as diverse as Chinese medicine and Weiqi (also known as Go, an Oriental board game).

He taught five or six form classes a week, as well as weapons class and several push-hands and fencing classes, but always seemed to enjoy what he was doing. His approach reminded me of the ideal attitude as advocated by an old aikido teacher. "Approach each class as if it were the first you have ever done, and also as if it will be the last you will ever do." Good advice, but not easy to follow. How did Laoshi do it?

One evening, after a new beginners' class, Laoshi was talking with some of the senior students nearing the time when they would teach their first classes. It was part of the training for senior students, even for those who harbored no ambition to teach. Laoshi firmly believed teaching is another way to improve understanding.

"In order to teach well, you must really inhabit your understanding. It must become like your own flesh and bones."

He began by posing a question. "How many times do you think I have taught the form to new students in the last twenty years? Sixty? Eighty? More? How can someone teach the same thing so many times and still remain fresh? It means nothing to the newest student that I have given the same instructions a hundred times before. It is the first time for him, and it must be said as if it were the first time. If not, it is rotten fruit. Would you serve rotten fruit to your guests? How do you maintain the freshness? How do you, as they say now, keep it real?"

It is indeed a challenge for the long-time teacher. Wang Lang solved this problem by taking a month off in summer and one in winter, letting his students run classes for him during this time of recharging. Chun Rong, someone I studied with for a couple of months at the initial stages of my study, would get bored during class and wander off for coffee, leaving the most experienced student to take over. I heard John Kellerman, one of the very first teachers in Britain, would only teach a small group, who would then teach the beginners. It is alleged, mind you, that he made time for some of the young women, who were honored, from time to time, with his variation of a qi injection.

Laoshi did none of these things, but he remained fresh.

"At first," Laoshi said, "we will be energized by the novelty of teaching and the status of being the teacher, but these thoughts only please the ego for a short time. To maintain freshness over time, you must become the instrument of the Dao and allow it to teach through you. You will then not only become good teachers, but will learn along with your students. There is also the added benefit of dispensing with lesson plans, learning outcomes, and other modern obstacles to learning."

"That sounds very mystical, Laoshi. How do we commune with the Dao?" asked one of the students.

"Not mystical, just mysterious," Laoshi replied. "Do not fear the mysterious in life. Dao, energy, mystery, joy, and love are all connected. None of them is the province of the rational mind or what passes for thinking, so they are labeled as 'mysterious.' The modern world shies away from the mysterious because it is unpredictable and uncontrollable. You can say the same for Dao, love, and joy. Because it cannot be controlled, it is mistrusted. This is the result of fearful and muddy thinking. When you rely on the mysterious, it does not betray you, even at the very instant your thinking mind tells you it already has."

"But shouldn't we be scientific, Laoshi, so we don't lurch into superstition?" the student asked.

"Of course," Laoshi replied. "The Dao does not see these two ideas as incompatible, though the thinking mind, and some of its champions, may wish it so. A man who is tired of the mystery in life is tired of life itself."

"So how do we learn to teach from the mysterious?" the questioner continued.

"I stumbled across the method many years ago, by chance, long before I taught martial arts. I was employed for a short time as an outdoor instructor, introducing urban youth to the wonders of the natural world. I was obliged to cram into unwilling minds the subtleties of map reading and navigation. As with today, the young men had no attention span to speak of and even less interest in the dust I poured into their minds. They were bored and quarrelsome, disruptive and distracting, in spite of my best efforts to inspire.

"It was dull, and I too was bored by this waste of time and energy, but did not know how to fix it. I only continued out of a sense of duty to the boss, whom I respected.

"One day, I had enough of forcing the learning upon them and just started to make whatever comment came into my mind. The lesson changed from a one-sided monologue into a multi-sided discussion. I did the lesson to entertain myself, with throwaway remarks, witty asides, and tangents of thought, which I felt free to not only indulge, but to present aloud. I began to have a good time and the bored youth began to listen. On considering the situation later, I realized a great truth. If you enjoy what you are teaching, so will everybody else. Joyfulness releases great energy and enthusiasm, no matter what activity you are engaged in, even map reading.

"It is not quite, as Oscar Wilde has said, that the best speech is directly proportional to the shortest time between the jokes, but the quality of lightness a joke brings helps to access the heart-mind, where the wonder in life resides. If you can find a way to the heart-mind, teaching is easy and fruitful. If not, it is like grinding away your soul with steel wool."

The concept of heart-mind would crop up regularly in Laoshi's classes. It was never explicitly defined, only hinted at through stories and metaphors. The point Laoshi seemed to be driving home constantly was that while the rational mind—logical, reasoned thought—may have made life easier to live, it is the heart-mind that makes it worth living.

Chapter 5: The Martial Sparrow

履   I love push-hands. I know this to be true because I could not continue otherwise. It is a practice that reaches down inside and cleans out the debris accumulated by arrogance, fear, and doubt. This deep spiritual cleansing is not always welcomed by our fragile egos, and I have left push-hands class many times, vowing never to return. Such is the frustration and confusion it can provoke. Then, usually, the following day when the dissatisfaction has abated slightly, I say to myself, "I'll, maybe, have one more go."

Is that not love?

The quality of our love is measured through the hard times when it is easier to give up than to go on. Even as the darkness of our despair and distress gathers, love still shines and refuses to abandon us in spite of the pain.

In a similar vein, I came to realize the quality of our *gongfu* (功夫)—deep, visceral understanding—is not tested when we are at our strongest, but when we are at our weakest. The lesson was brought home to me one morning when my girlfriend, also a tai chi student, was visiting for a few days to help me recover from an operation on my spine. I could only walk gingerly, not very fast and not very far. Both legs were fairly numb and I could not feel my right foot at all. I was nervous about how strong my back was going to be in the future and, at times, feared the worst.

To help with my rehabilitation, we went out for walks in the park. It was spring and the feeling of renewal was all around in the budding trees, singing birds, and warm air.

Near an abandoned riverside mill close to my house, I stopped for a few minutes, resting by sitting on one of the stone blocks of the ruined building. My girlfriend decided to do a form on a flat piece of ground close by. It was a lovely morning and a few people were taking advantage of the weather by walking along the riverside. The sun was shining through the trees, which offered some shade as the day was beginning to warm up.

Midway through her form, three teenagers, no doubt skipping school, came by. Noticing my girlfriend, they began shouting at her, "Hey, missus, are you all right? You want us to call an ambulance?"

We ignored them. They then started shouting at me, "Hey, mister, what's wrong with her?" and other such witticisms. They stood about twenty yards away and were not going to be ignored.

"She's just doing some exercise," I said eventually, hoping this would satisfy their curiosity, or whatever, but it did not. They began throwing stones at us— stones the size of half bricks. This was getting out of hand.

In days gone by, I could have handled, and did handle, such situations decisively. I have chased after such tearaways, caught them, and applied the kind of justice that caused a lot of pain but left no permanent damage. I realized, how- ever, I was severely limited in what I could do. I shouted a few obscenities at them, hoping either to scare them off or bring them close enough for me to hit; my arms still worked well enough. They did not, however, take the bait. It was pretty sober- ing to confront the weakness I felt in myself and realize the illusion I had of myself, as capable of dealing with whatever life threw at me, was breaking down.

Eventually, some of the people walking by the river chased the youths away and peace was restored near the old mill, but not in my mind. I thought about this incident long after it happened, as I recovered my strength, both physical and mental. I was irritated by what had happened and I told Laoshi about it a couple of months later.

"Did you survive the attack uninjured?" he asked.

I was perplexed. It was not the response I expected. When I answered that I had, he asked, "Did your companion survive the attack uninjured?"

"Well, yes, Laoshi," I responded, "but that is not the point. I felt unable to defend myself."

"You are mixing up self-defense with ego defense," he admonished. "You are annoyed that you were not able to emerge the victor from your encounter with your tormentors, but this is simply ego. It is enough to survive without physical loss."

When I thought about it, I realized he was right, of course, but it still annoyed me that I was not able to prove myself superior to them, force them to submit, or scare them off.

Laoshi then added, "If you were so helpless, and they wished to do you harm, why did they not close in and really hurt you?"

In all the time since the attack, the thought had not entered my head. Why did they stay out of reach?

Laoshi answered for me, "The truth is they feared you and your companion. You may have been physically weak, but the energy you were projecting was not. If they had sensed your weakness, they might have approached. It was your spiritual strength they felt and kept their distance."

He added, "It is not helpful to think of yourself as strong or weak. These are not absolute states of being in the same way that up and down are not absolute directions. Up is only up when compared to something below it. Strong is only strong when compared to something weaker. All is in comparison, as Laozi says:

When people see some things as beautiful,
Other things become ugly.
When people see some things as good,
Other things become bad.

"You were not weak. You were weaker than before, and as your life proceeds, and if you survive similar encounters, you will get physically weaker and, eventually, die. There are no exceptions to this rule, but the Dao must always reestablish balance. It takes away, but at the same time gives. Remember, Laozi [老子] also says:

As it acts in the world,
the Dao is like the bending of a bow.
The top is bent downward;
the bottom is bent up.
It adjusts excess and deficiency
so that there is perfect balance.
It takes from what is too much
and gives to what isn't enough

"You can, if you wish, develop your spiritual strength even to the moment of death."

It was a comforting thought. Our physical strength may weaken, but within that weakness there can be strength. The inevitable decline into old age is not all bad news. There is a compensation: as the Dao takes away, it also gives. Physical strength gives way to spiritual strength.

I remembered hearing how Zheng Manqing talked of the master being able to throw someone with a look. Is that what Laoshi was getting at?

"How do we develop this spiritual strength?" I asked.

"You have already begun with your martial arts training before meeting me, but with your practice of push-hands, you can develop even more. Push-hands is like a forge where steel is made, only this steel is of the spirit. The stripping away of ego, fear, doubt, and arrogance, reveals your true being, which brings you to your true strength, 'the tower of the spirit,' as Zhuangzi [庄子] would say. He describes it as 'an impregnable tower, which no danger can disturb.' You can call it spirit, heart-mind, original mind, greatness of the qi, love, Dao—whatever you like, but its power is unlimited."

Moments like these made me feel blessed in having found a Way, a path in life. These moments made up for so many of the hard times, but if I understood Laoshi correctly, he was saying that enduring these hard times was part of the process, part of the forging.

The Chinese phrase is to "eat bitter," *chiku* (吃苦), put up with hardships and endure. Up to that point I had approached "eating bitter" as a necessary evil, a type of jumping through hoops to get a gold star at the end of it. The process itself was something I resented and did reluctantly. It held the same appeal to me as scraping dog shit off my shoes. I wanted the power that came at the end of it and the process was just a means to that end.

I began to recognize that Laoshi was saying something subtler: you have to embrace the bitterness to be transformed. It is not an enemy. The bitterness is a friend. In approaching the Dao, thinking of getting rid of the bitterness is as much a mistake as it is impossible.

No doubt seeing the faraway look in my eye as I contemplated the mystical inherent in what he was saying, Laoshi then gave me another lecture on the basics of push-hands.

"All this talk of the miraculous is well and good, but its foundation is still in the physical, and we must study the basic principles of push-hands before entertaining thoughts of the sublime.

"You must first learn the *peng-lu-ji-an* [掤, 履, 擠, 按] sequence until you can do it without thought. At this point you must guard against it becoming an empty ritual. This is because the form by itself is well balanced, with neither partner having an advantage. Nothing can happen until one partner tries to gain advantage by pushing beyond the limits of the form; that is, he tries to take more than he is entitled to. His partner can then take advantage of the imbalance this greed causes. If you remain balanced, you are 'standing on the ground of victory,' as Wang Lang used to say.

"Bear in mind also that, just as push-hands can fall into the trap of being an empty ritual, it can, at the other extreme, descend into fighting. To take some of the 'heat' out of the process, it is more sensible if you agree to take turns being greedy and cooperate in being uncooperative. One person pushes; the other develops skill in neutralization."

Laoshi was talking about our standard method in push-hands. The peng-lu-ji-an sequence, as it is sometimes called, consists of four postures from the beginning of Zheng Manqing's thirty-seven-posture form, collectively known as grasp the sparrow's tail. Although occasionally we did free pushing, which dispenses with any form, normally we restricted ourselves to studying the exchanges that went on within the peng-lu-ji-an method.

The method has its critics, but it was the one employed by Professor Zheng in New York. If that were not endorsement enough, it does tend to take some, if not all, of the venom out of a practice that easily descends into the strong dominating the weak.

Although Laoshi says the form is balanced with neither side having an advantage until one or other becomes excessively yang, I see it another way. Standing so close and not being allowed to escape by moving our feet, the bigger, stronger, or heavier person has all the advantages. There is only so far back a person can go before running out of room, and only so much he can turn before becoming stuck. The skill is to use the right amount of each of these two ingredients to deflect even fast and hard pushes. The only advantage the soft player has is in sensing the direction and speed of the push, "catching" it at its weakest point, and leading to its own destruction. It is a bit like moving a huge fridge by tilting it onto its corners and then "walking" it where you want it to go. It is an exercise in understanding balance and the tipping point. Get it wrong, and the fridge can fall on top of you; get it right, and even really heavy appliances can be controlled without a lot of grunting and sweating.

Grunting and sweating in push-hands are to be avoided, but it is staggering how many of us find ourselves in their grasp as we exert ever more physical force to push or not be pushed.

Laoshi continued, "Once you know the form and take turns in pushing and neutralizing, you begin to see the influence of circles. As you are pushed, you must withdraw a little and feel the force and direction of the push. Then, by using the waist, turn left or right to deflect the push to the side."

This is the standard instruction given to all push-hands students. Where Laoshi differed from many was in advocating the use of a vertical circle as well. He would often say, "While a circle is useful in defense, a sphere is better. Using just the horizontal circle, you are like a door opening when pushed. When you combine the horizontal and vertical circles, you become like a greased ball. Just when they think they have you, you slip out, letting them slide off and leaving them vulnerable to your counterpush."

The vertical circle he advocated involved rotating the pelvis forward and upward, giving the feeling of rolling under the incoming push, but without leaning back. In so doing, we not only drop the lower spine so the root is secured in the foot, but, combined with the turn of the waist, we are like the ball in the nib of a pen, able to revolve in all directions.

Laoshi often quoted Zheng Manqing's advice: "First study the yin. Then study the yang. Then put them both together." To a great extent, in neutralizing, Laoshi thought of learning the horizontal circle as studying the yin and learning the vertical circle as studying the yang.

In pushing, the learning of the circles is reversed. In order to push in a tai chi way, the legs, body, and arms must connect using the ligaments, not the muscles. Studying the yin in pushing means identifying and discarding the unhelpful muscular force that interferes with the sinews. It is often aptly described as drawing a longbow, with the limbs and body forming an arc capable of releasing the "arrow" of the push with remarkable power. Crucially, this power comes from the sinews, not the muscles.

Once the skill of pushing is learned, study of the yang allows us to use the same principle to "shoot the arrow" from the hands, forearms, elbows, shoulders—indeed, any part of the body, including the back. The horizontal circle here is like having an infinite number of longbows all around us, ready to fire an arrow in any direction. This skill is sometimes called receiving energy and is used to explain why the bicycle rickshaw driver who crashed into the back of Yang Chengfu (楊澄甫) was bounced back ten feet or more, depositing his passengers onto the ground.

Taken together, using horizontal and vertical circles in push-hands provides the basis for all-around defense and offense, using a power that comes out of softness. As Laozi would say, "The soft overcomes the hard. The weak overcomes the strong." Comforting words for the aging tai chi player.

Chapter 6: Tales of the Repulsive Monkey

Although studying the form was not my primary focus when I started tai chi, I nevertheless attended beginners' classes with Laoshi as often as I could, even after I completed the form and revision classes. Laoshi did not see the value in boring the students with repeating movements ad nauseam. His classes were so much more. As I have written, from time to time he would say, "We study energy here, not sedation." He often followed up with, "This is not the Mogadon School of Tai Chi." To Laoshi, if the class did not leave us elated, albeit tired, then he considered what we were doing as simply dulling the senses.

Watching someone do the form can be soporific. Laoshi once told us of an early experience in his teaching career.

"When I first started teaching tai chi, I was paid to give a lesson to the wives of some businessmen at a conference. For them, it passed some time before lunch. For me, I needed the money," he admitted. "The conference hotel gave us a squash court to use: no windows, no ventilation, and no temperature control. It was too warm and too stuffy. Around that time it amused me to finish the form by noisily slapping my foot in the turn-to-sweep-the-lotus posture. The movement was quite dramatic and dynamic, simulating a kick to the kidneys. It was a flourish, which I thought quite impressive. After my talk and demonstration, one of the wives said to me, 'That was marvelous, the way you gradually sent us to sleep, then woke us all up at the end with that almighty slap! I feel really refreshed. I can see now why tai chi is so relaxing.' This was not quite the effect I had in mind."

To equate tai chi with a catnap was not the lesson Laoshi wished to impart, but he felt it could have been worse. He believed some teachers of the meditative arts merely succeeded in dulling the senses of their students. This leads to a deadened energy, which, while appearing to be stillness, has no life in it. "A corpse cannot meditate," was Laoshi's pronouncement when I wondered if there might not be some benefit to dulling the senses, reasoning that the more desensitized we become, the less painful the world is. This, however, was the opposite of Laoshi's approach. We were training to become more sensitive to ourselves and the world around us—perhaps limited only by how much reality we could take before it all became too much for us to handle.

Being in class I felt alive, relaxed physically, but mentally alert. Although there was a structure that almost never varied, within that structure there was a mixture of practice, philosophy, stories, instruction, and jokes—mostly, though not exclusively, about tai chi. As we relaxed, we learned not by fixating on increasingly minor points of technique, but rather by some form of osmosis, a mysterious and wonderful gift of the heart-mind.

It seemed ridiculous to Laoshi that tai chi, the art of relaxation, should be learned in a tense, angst-filled atmosphere. It was better to model the feeling we were aspiring to than be told what it should be. His refrain was, "Don't be intimidated by what you don't know. Be encouraged by what you do know." It took the grind out of learning and put enjoyment in its place, making a lifelong approach to learning seem eminently possible. He also liked to say, "When you are cheerful, you are qi-ful."

As part of this way of teaching, he would talk to us about the psychological and philosophical implications of the posture as we rested between bouts of technical instruction. I would often become so engrossed in what he was saying that I forgot what those technical points were. Nevertheless, I returned to practice again and would somehow find improvement. "Learn and forget, learn and forget; that is the secret," he used to say, although you never really forgot; you just remembered in a different way. This seemed to move learning more into the province of the heart-mind.

In particular, I used to like to hear him talk about the step-back-to-repulse-monkey sequence, or the "repulsive monkeys," as he liked to call it.

He would often start by saying the form could be considered a journey beginning with the early postures and moving toward "immortality" in the Daoist sense, by achieving something other people might call "enlightenment" or "liberation."

He would typically say, "Repulse monkey is near the middle of the form and represents the chattering mind, like the chattering of monkeys. We must step back to repulse this chattering in order for us to reside in the company of the heart-mind. It is not to say the chattering has no value. It does, but it is like a secretary who reminds us of appointments, deals with travel arrangements, or replies to correspondence. It is there to support you, not control you. If you didn't have this capacity, then you wouldn't have gotten here. You have to remember the time, know the bus route, and remember your shoes and class fees. But when you are here, you should not be thinking about the bus ride home, or what is on TV, or about buying milk for your cocoa tonight.

"Once it has completed its job of logistics, it should be silent, but here is the problem: it cannot be silenced. All we can do is turn our attention away from it and let it play like a recording at the back of our minds, which we tune in to from time to time to make use of whenever we wish."

The repulse monkey talk often included Zheng Manqing's thoughts on its martial application. As the waist is turned, the front hand is extended forward at eye height to simulate a strike to the eyes of the attacker. Zheng Manqing did not advocate this response lightly, but considered it necessary under extreme circumstances, such as when life is threatened or the attacker is armed.

The defenses against knife attacks I learned in aikido made Laoshi uncomfortable. He did not consider them realistic. "If you try that, you will get killed," he told me once, while I was showing one of the other guys the *kote geashi* technique I had learned. "Better to run away, or, if you cannot, then improvise a weapon, or, if you cannot do that, then attack the eyes. You may be lucky—he may be incompetent."

There is one other time an eye attack might be justified. Laoshi told us Zheng Manqing talked of the old days in China, where strange men could do amazing things, such as walk around the rim of a wicker basket without tipping it. Others practiced "orange sand hand," a method whereby, if they managed to touch your body with their hands, your insides would rot. The distinguishing feature of such fighters was that their palms were bright orange. According to Laoshi, Zheng Manqing advised striking the eyes of such people before they could lay hands on you.

I loved these tall tales. Their value lay less in their veracity and more in the manner in which they contributed to the overall portraiture of the postures. I came to realize that each posture is located at the center of a web of concepts, including martial application, imagery, philosophy and psychology, health matters, and metaphor. To truly get the feel of the posture, an exploration of this web was as invaluable as it was enjoyable. Like a maestro, Laoshi would draw together diverse strands to create a masterpiece in the imagination. The result was a memorable symphony of ideas.

Chapter 7: The Swallow Leaves the Nest

It was something that happened, periodically, and I wondered how Laoshi felt about it: a student would leave the school to go study with another teacher or in another style of tai chi.

Although Laoshi publically stated, "You must study whatever you feel is right for you, with whoever inspires you," I wondered if his real feelings were so casual. Many teachers take the loss of a student personally, feeling unappreciated and, perhaps, even used. For some, there is also the loss of income they suffer when students move on.

"Yes, there can be problems when people feel they must leave a teacher," Laoshi said when I asked one morning about the challenges of students leaving. The question seemed to make him a little ill at ease, but he answered anyway. Maybe I was right and he did have some raw nerves over the issue.

"I have not always managed the process of changing teacher very well, so I try to not make the same mistakes when my students leave me. There can be a bitter residue left in the aftermath of the breakup, with one or both sides feeling cheated or disrespected. Most of this is, of course, nonsense—nonsense comprised of the ego combined with the corrosive effects that money brings to a relationship.

"I remember when I left Don and his school to study with Wang Lang. I presumed there would be no problem, as other teachers were going to regular workshops with Dr. Chen. Indeed, I myself endured a weekend with Dr. Chen and his brand of qi-development exercises before concluding he had little to offer, but that is another matter.

"I phoned Don and told him of my intention to travel to the US to see Wang Lang, who had come to my attention some years before through articles he had written. To me, Wang Lang's approach seemed just the right blend of martial arts, qi development, and philosophy. I was not ready for Don's reaction. He told me I could not go as a teacher representing his school. 'Why?' I asked.

"'How will it look?' he growled. 'It will look as if there is something missing in my school if you have to go off and see someone else.'

"I was surprised, since he had offered no objection to me seeing Dr. Chen, along with half of the teachers in the school. When I pointed out the anomaly, he replied, 'That's different. He is doing something else.' I was not convinced. Rather, I thought he felt threatened by Wang Lang, a senior member of the

'Zheng Manqing family of teachers.' Even though they had never met, Don knew of Wang Lang by reputation and was, I suspect, intimidated.

"There was also the matter of the money he would lose. At the time, Glasgow, Birmingham, and Cardiff were the three biggest centers for his school in the UK, each with about a hundred students. From these students he would receive a membership fee each year amounting to several hundred pounds. As a teacher of the school, I was also obliged to sell his merchandise bearing the school logo. In addition, I was obliged to 'invite' him to teach two weekend courses per year in Scotland, and I had to financially guarantee both of them. Furthermore, my senior students and I were expected to attend courses he ran from his base in England. These obligations represented a significant loss of income, should he lose control of me and my students.

"Over the next few days he phoned me several times, once at eight in the morning, telling me how his night's sleep had been disturbed by my 'lack of manners.' He sent patronizing mail, saying, 'It's not what you do; it's the way you do it,' and he had other teachers contact me to tell me I was making a big mistake. All these pressure tactics, ironically, made my decision to leave the school easier.

"When he finally realized I was not going to be deterred from my course, he wrote to all my students, telling them to move to a nearby teacher, as I was misguided and leading them off in a dangerous direction. Sending such a letter made him look foolish in the eyes of my students and most simply ignored it and its sentiment. He then forbade the other teachers and students in the school from speaking to me or coming to any of my classes. He demanded I hand over all my students, halls, and classes to another teacher and start again from scratch. Finally, he accused me of stealing from him because I once accepted a fifteen-pound discount to one of his courses to help offset the cost of two days' missed work and travel from Scotland to the south of England.

"As you can see, these are serious matters to some.

"In the East, some schools still maintain the traditional practice of discipleship, with formal ceremonies and binding obligations on both the teacher and student. These disciples are sometimes known as 'inside the door' students and are given special instruction by the master. Even then, the traditional teacher must also make a distinction between those inside the door and his sons, who have a right to the deepest level of his teaching, if their interest leads them to the art. Zheng Manqing had a number of disciples in this sense, but it is debatable how much of the 'good oil' these people received, since Ben Lo, one of his best students, never became a disciple. Seen in this context, going to see another teacher might be perceived as breaking an oath.

"We in the West can feel aggrieved by this issue too. Like you, I once asked Wang Lang how he felt about two of his long-term students going off to see other, more senior teachers in the Zheng Manqing lineage. He made out that he understood their motives, but certainly his wife did not. She told me later how disgusted she felt with their betrayal, 'after all he had done for them.'"

"So, do you feel betrayed, Laoshi," I asked, "when someone like Danny goes off to study *qigong* [氣功] with Chun Rong, and then joins the Wu-style guys? Or when Maurice went off to do aikido?"

"It can be difficult," Laoshi admitted. "Our expectations of our students often lead us into trouble. It is most difficult when they go off to study with someone who is either not very good or not wholly ethical. We must resist the urge to control, however, and let them go their own way.

"Ultimately, it comes down to faith in principle. When we believe totally in what we are doing, a herd of horses cannot hold us back, but when we lose faith, we need a herd of horses to take one step. Once faith is lost, all is lost.

"Of course, our faith will be tested, as it should be, by doubts, illness, or some kind of loss. When this happens, some cannot resist the urge to change teacher, or more radically, the very art they study. There is also the notion these days that we can add to our art by cross-training to compensate for the perceived deficiencies in one art with the strengths of another.

"There are others whose faith is unshakable. They stay loyal to their teacher and redouble their search for understanding by exploring more deeply their own art. These people change within the system, rather than change to another system. They understand the problem is with the singer, not the song.

"In the end, the teacher cannot make this choice for the student, and, in one sense, the student cannot even make the choice for himself. What, after all, is faith and where does it grow? All you know is this: it is there, or it is not."

In talking to Laoshi, I came to realize how much he regretted the strained relations with some of his teachers that resulted from his crises of faith. However, the experience benefited us, his students, as we underwent our crises and sought resolution. Perhaps his loss in this matter was our gain.

Chapter 8: Punch the Big Toe

單
鞭
    The Zheng Manqing form contains a few postures that break the usual rules. One of them is low punch, although some jokingly call it "punch the toddler," because on completion, the fist is at about knee height, punching downward. The spine is bent like a cat stretching its back, breaking the rule about keeping the back straight, not leaning forward or back or to the side. The supposed martial applications are problematic as well. One application suggests punching an opponent's thigh. This can be done, as recently demonstrated by

Benson Henderson in the UFC, but it puts the head in a vulnerable position. Another application is a defense against an oncoming attacker shooting for a takedown. This too is potentially risky and seems not particularly effective.

Laoshi placed the value of the posture in flexing the middle of the back in preparation for the final third of the form, which he saw as being more focused on the relaxation of the spine. Although the form is holistic (in that all the postures are good for all of the body), Laoshi explained that the first third of the form, up to cross hands, places more emphasis on relaxing the arms. The second part of the form, up to and including the kicking section, focuses more on the legs. The final part of the form is for loosening the spine.

Crucial to executing this posture correctly is the idea that in spite of flexing the spine, the lower back must still be vertical and connected through the legs into the ground. Most students have significant difficulty with this notion, as it is easier to lean forward than fold from the middle of the back. As a result, very few people do this posture well—at least in the initial stages of learning.

To help us get a feel for the right shape in the spine, Laoshi would comment on some of the mistakes students make as they get to grips with the position. One mistake in particular staggered me. Laoshi told us of the way one of Wang Lang's students regularly performed this movement. She punched so low that the posture could have been called "punch the big toe," her fist finishing about an inch from the ground.

Thinking that Laoshi was exaggerating for effect, I asked him if the story was true and, if so, why Wang Lang, who was a good teacher, did not bother to correct her.

"It is a good question," he replied. "I used to wonder myself. There was another student who was very keen but, for some reason, would not ever have his back foot flat on the ground in front posture. It was so bad that his ankle almost touched the floor. As you know, even the slightest lifting of the outside of the foot when it should be flat is a grave error and can injure the joints. Both of these faults were visible to all, but I never heard Wang Lang say anything. Then I found the answer. Wang Lang did occasionally make the correction, but the result was always the same. It was as if nothing had been said."

Laoshi continued, "I found this most bizarre: a fault is obvious for all to see, but when it is pointed out, the student remains oblivious and the teacher gives up, at least for a while. How can that be? I thought about it a lot at that time, and then witnessed the same with some of my own students. I would correct a person three or four times for the same fault, yet it resulted in no change. Why does this happen?"

"Eh, I don't know, Laoshi," I said, wondering if it was supposed to be a rhetorical question.

"I realized," he went on, "that my students have many reasons for coming to class. Some, like yourself, really want to study the details of the art in depth. Is that not correct?"

"Yes, indeed, Laoshi. It means a great deal to me to get it right."

"Of course," he said, nodding. "Very good, but not all people who come to class are the same. Very few come out of true dedication to the art. Some come to bathe themselves in the gentle atmosphere of class; others come to meet their friends; still others come because they did pottery last year. Each person gains something from class, and each has a different level of commitment. Accordingly, they all have a different view on what constitutes progress.

"Some leave form class elated, even though they are heavily flawed technically. Others leave disappointed because some subtlety evades them, even though their form is technically superior. There is nothing wrong with this. There are no good or bad reasons for coming to class and, often, as with any lifetime endeavor, the degree of commitment depends on the challenges life presents at any given time.

"What is more interesting, however, is the manner in which teachers differ. It has been my good fortune to study with a number of very good teachers, each of whom had a unique approach, which I analyzed closely. I was often surprised and sometimes dismayed by the seemingly poor judgment they demonstrated in organizing their schools and in dealing with their students. I wondered how so many smart and capable teachers could be so foolish.

"Some teachers charged too little, some too much. Some would encourage talentless and divisive students and let them lead class; others would severely limit the scope of the school, discouraging progress even among the most senior students who, after years of study, effectively remained novices. Don even admitted that for fifteen years he had not taught the 'real deal' in push-hands.

"What was I missing? Later, as I began teaching, it became clearer to me. Just as students have a variety of reasons for attending class, so do teachers for teaching. As a student, like you, I was a tai chi purist. It was all about the art for me. All that mattered was technical competence in form, even more so in push-hands and fencing, all arising from a deep base of Daoist philosophy. But when I became burdened with the responsibility of organizing and teaching, I became aware of all the factors a teacher needs to take into account in even a small class.

"I realized while some teachers are purely about perfecting their art, others are about making money, and still others are about building empires. So being a teacher is about balancing tai chi the art, tai chi the business, and tai chi the school.

"Each teacher balances these three competing tendencies within the school. Some, like an aikido teacher I knew, focus almost exclusively on the art itself. He lived and breathed aikido the art, shunning matters of money and disdaining those who would attempt to politick in his school. He is an honorable exception, as most teachers are partly students of the Way, partly concerned with making money, and partly concerned with managing the politics of a school.

"When you come to teach, you will have to make these decisions, weighing up each of these competing pressures. Will you teach for money or just charge enough to pay for your expenses? Teaching to make a living gives you more time and energy to practice, but you will have to tend to the needs of the less committed, as they will make up the bulk of your students.

"Will you encourage your students to become teachers themselves? If so, you will have the headache of deciding how and when this happens, and also have to act as referee when disputes arise over who can teach, when, and where. How will you deal with the jealousy that results in promoting one person over others? How will you deal with dissatisfied students who form cliques and poison the atmosphere of your class?

"If you are only concerned with the art, you will have very few students to work with and might fail because you cannot attract sufficient people willing to put up with the rigid standards you will have to impose.

"Given the conflicting pressures, you can maybe see how difficult this aspect of teaching is and why teachers apparently make such bad choices."

I was grateful for this insight into Laoshi's world. I did not realize how much of a juggling act running a school is, since his classes seemed to run so smoothly. It was sobering and dismaying.

"Why do you bother to teach?" I asked. "It seems like a lot of hassle for not much gain."

After a pause, Laoshi answered, saying, "Student and teacher are in a delicate relationship. Without teachers, there would be no students. Without students, there would be no teachers. As student and teacher, we are mutually dependent, but there will always be a tension of sorts between us. It is one of life's little jokes.

"You became a student because there is a need in you to learn. This is your Dao. In the same way, I teach because there is a need in me to teach. This is my Dao. We are, as they say, like two wheels connected by an axle. Connected, we can carry a greater load than alone. The teacher, however, can only go at the speed the student can manage. The students must go in the same direction as the teacher. Maintaining this balance is challenging for both; if it cannot be maintained, the axle will be strained and break."

Hearing Laoshi, I understood why he would sometimes not correct faults, but, more important, I understood my own responsibility in not putting a strain on the axle. It was a truly collaborative approach: he determined the direction; I determined the speed.

"Here is an interesting dilemma I will leave you with," Laoshi said. "Would you rather be a great master of tai chi or be a great teacher?"

It was quite a shocking question. It implied that you could not be both. I could not answer, but it makes me think from time to time: what good is a master without students? What good is a student without a master? A great master who cannot teach leaves very little to the world—but a teacher who cannot master the art leaves very little either.

Chapter 9: Waving Hands in Confusion

提
手

Almost every class Laoshi taught made mention of Zheng Manqing, a most remarkable man who influenced so many people even after his death. Laoshi was one of these people who, never having met the man, still lived his life with Zheng Manqing's teachings firmly in mind.

If you were to ask Laoshi who he would most like to meet in his life, he would, without question, reply Zheng Manqing. Studying with such a man, however, can have unforeseen consequences, as the surviving senior students of Professor Zheng have found out. They have become tai chi celebrities, with all the good and bad that follow.

The more sincere, like Wang Lang, took the role seriously and saw themselves as promoting the legacy of the great man. To have a purpose in life is a wonderful blessing, but for those fortunate enough to have been so rewarded, there are a number of downsides. One drawback is the virtually impossible task of refuting the naysayers who would slander the reputation of the great man, either through misinformation or plain jealousy.

As a representative of Zheng Manqing's approach, Laoshi found himself a legacy holder amid doubters when he used to teach European workshops arranged by teachers of other styles of tai chi. Often, as a result of years invested in studying a more physical tai chi, some students in mainland Europe were seeking an approach more in line with the "soft overcomes the hard" dictum they felt lacking in their own practice. They retained a certain skepticism about Zheng Manqing, however, because a common opinion on the Continent, usually among Yang- and Chen-style students, was that the Professor had descended into alcoholism, and, bereft of any real skill, made his way to the United States to con the gullible Americans with his brand of fairy stories.

Naturally, our beliefs in these matters hinge greatly on the views of our teachers, and tai chi, like other martial arts, encourages the notion that our own teachers and our own style are second to none. In the absence of evidence to the contrary, we, as Robert Smith says, tend to make swans out of pigeons when it comes to our teachers.

Zheng Manqing, being sincere in his beliefs, was no stranger to controversy. According to Douglas Wile, "The two words that appear repeatedly in balanced articles on Zheng in the Taiwan press are 'crazy' [狂 *kuang*] and 'arrogant' [傲慢 *aoman*]." However, the most interesting "slander" of Professor Zheng I have come across is the story Laoshi told me of his meeting with the infamous qi master Dr. Chen, who was plying his trade in London a few years ago. He was gaining quite a reputation as a master of qi, using his abilities for healing and martial arts. Hearing of Dr. Chen's powers, Laoshi felt the need to see for himself by attending one of the regular courses.

"I attended a weekend with Dr. Chen in London," Laoshi explained. "I had heard of him from Andy, a fellow teacher of the Still Lotus School. I had always liked and respected Andy for the clarity of his approach and his personal integrity, neither of which I could fault. Many of the school's teachers were a bit 'happy-clappy,' but Andy seemed to be well rooted, skilled, and sincere.

"He first mentioned Dr. Chen at one of the numerous weekends I was obliged to attend. He told me of his decision to take some instruction from Dr. Chen. When I asked why, he told me that said doctor was a master of qi."

Laoshi added for clarity, "Up to that point, in the seven years I had studied with the Still Lotus School, qi was only mentioned on a handful of occasions. The implication was that we were pursuing a spiritual path, and qi was something less sophisticated. In spite of this, almost half the school's teachers were taking courses with Dr. Chen.

"'How do you know he is a qi master?' I asked Andy. He then proceeded to tell me this story. 'Dr. Chen was giving a lecture on qi in a church hall one day. Halfway through his talk, his niece, who was in the audience, came running up onto the stage. "Uncle, Uncle," she said, "my balloon has gotten away." True enough, when he looked up, her helium-filled balloon had escaped her grasp and had risen up the rafters of the church hall. Dr. Chen said something to the effect that he was busy and she should not bother him. She implored him, saying, "But Uncle, you are a qi master; you must help me!" No doubt reminded of his obligation as a qi master, he agreed to get her balloon, now bobbing gently against the wooden joists twenty feet above the assembled group.

"'Dr. Chen obviously could not reach the balloon,' Andy continued, 'as it was so high, but he stretched out a hand and sent up his qi to grasp the balloon. As you know, however, balloons are round and he could not get a grip with his qi. Not to be defeated, he used both hands and directed his qi upward and over the top of the balloon and brought it down and gave it to the little girl. The audience was stunned.'

"The story was absolutely amazing," Laoshi said. "I was captivated, thinking I'd have to meet this man. I then asked Andy, 'Did you actually see this?' 'No,' he replied, unfazed. 'I heard it from someone who heard it from someone who was there.' What a letdown. I knew Andy to be honest and sincere, but I suspected a case of Chinese whispers.

"Nevertheless, I went along to a weekend and booked an individual session with Dr. Chen so he could do some healing work on my back, which was giving me some trouble at the time. All in all, it was an expensive weekend, but a small price to assess the quality of a qi master.

"The course was very busy. The hype had traveled far, and many students from all over the country were there. We mostly did holding postures and some push-hands, Dr. Chen style, which I will tell you about later.

"At the end of day 1, I had my private meeting with Dr. Chen, who seemed surprised to see it was I who needed the treatment. He had earlier told me my tai chi was very good for someone who had only studied for eight years, as I had at the time.

"He asked me where I lived and if it was a humid country. Glasgow can be wet and cold, but not humid. He then said in his broken English, 'You teach in your country?' When I told him I did, he asked, 'How many students?'

"'About a hundred.' I lied a little for effect.

"'Ah, then you big mast',' he commented, as if weighing me up.

"Big Mast'," Laoshi said, smiling at the memory, "became my nickname for a while when I related the story to my students.

"After a little hands-on healing, which had no effect on my injury, he then began to give me his opinion of Zheng Manqing and his tai chi.

"'Zheng Manqing,' he pronounced, 'he no good. He cannot stand properly. You stand all wrong. That why you hurt back. Weight should be on front of foot. You should lean forward little bit.' He put me in a position where my weight was on the balls of my feet and I was tipping forward. He told me this was the right way to stand. I was beginning to smell a rat.

"'Zheng Manqing had mental illness,' Dr. Chen said. 'He not able to bend his hand at wrist. That why he always talk beautiful lady hand. All his Chinese student know this, but not tell Americans. They all lie to Americans so he not lose face.'"

Laoshi was smiling as he recalled this piece of nonsense. It brought to mind a student who asked him if he ever got angry with teachers who would appear on the scene claiming the outlandish. Laoshi replied, "No, I am used to it. I have met every stripe of tai chi dick there is." We all laughed, realizing there is not much more you can do than laugh at the claims of some of these "masters."

The Dr. Chen story continued because, even though Laoshi concluded Chen was not the teacher for him, he had paid for the course and gone along to see what other amusements Dr. Chen would serve up for the believers who were devoted students.

"Chen himself told the story of the church hall and the balloon," Laoshi continued, "followed by another tale of his sore arm; apparently he merely flicked it out a few times to get rid of the 'bad qi.' Farther down the street, he told us, a passerby started looking up and touching his head to see what was being sprinkled on him.

"More interesting though was the piece of theater that was the demonstration of *kongjin* [空勁], the empty force. You know of this, do you not? The ability to push people without even the necessity of touching them physically.

"Chen demonstrated this remarkable 'ability' on his senior student, who organized these courses, and practiced this brand of chicanery herself. Without touch he managed to 'push' her here and there. She was 'helpless' to do anything about it. As you may have guessed, he did not repeat the demonstration on any of us, no doubt for our own safety.

"This piece of circus did show me, though, how his push-hands practice contributed to the scam. It is a little more sophisticated than simply telling people to lie. The push-hands they do is also without touch. You stand six feet away from your partner and are supposed to feel for the qi of the other person coming at you, then catch it and return it. The clever bit is to suggest that if you do *not* feel the qi, then there is something wrong with you. You lack sensitivity and will not develop the kongjin until you do become sensitive. Students then try to feel for something coming at them and wind up believing they can feel the qi. In this case, if you remain unmoved when the master 'pushes,' the implication is that you are an insensitive clot. No one wants to be the one to reveal that the emperor has no clothes, as they are all so invested in it being true."

This reminded me of the story Robert Smith tells in his *Martial Musings* about the time he and Ben Lo went to see a tai chi master, recently arrived in California from China, who demonstrated the kongjin to an assembled audience. Like Dr. Chen, the master only demonstrated his skill on a familiar recipient, in this instance, his wife.

At the end of the show, Ben Lo and Robert Smith approached the master. Ben asked him, "Can you do that to me?" No doubt not knowing who Ben Lo was, the master responded, "No, because you have no qi." Instead of arguing about who has qi and who does not, Ben simply replied, "In that case, it is better not to have qi."

In defense of tai chi, this type of swindle is not just confined to one art. Nor are we in the West the only ones fooled by a good trickster. A while ago, while searching the internet, I happened across the footage of a master of kiai-jutsu, dropping dozens of his students as they attacked him, from all angles, without a single one getting close enough to even touch him. So confident was he in his abilities that he issued an open challenge, offering five thousand dollars to anyone who could defeat him. A passing MMA fighter accepted, and, once the formalities were over, he punched the kiai master full in the face before swarming all over him.

The master's attendants rescued their man before suggesting something had gone wrong and insisting on a restart. The result was similar the second time and the master got pummeled.

In a similar vein, Dr. Chen later ran into trouble of a comparable sort. Fortunately for him, he did not end up on the wrong end of a beating, but was humiliated, nonetheless, at one of his kongjin courses by someone who was not influenced by his mind tricks. The truly surprising thing is that, in spite of being declared a fraud by many, he still manages to ply his trade, selling his unique brand of snake oil. People still want to believe in the supernatural and can make unbelievable allowances for their heroes when they are found to have feet of clay.

Knowing this, a question began to intrude: "How do I know what they say about Zheng Manqing and his superior level of tai chi is true?" Am I, and more to the point, is Laoshi, blinded by our own desire to study the art of a swan rather than that of a pigeon?

While feeling uncomfortable about suggesting Laoshi was in an advanced stage of self-delusion, I felt I owed it to both of us to voice my concern. As tactfully as I could, I asked Laoshi if he was confident the remarkable abilities attributed to the late Professor were in fact true and not some kind of halo effect, which surrounds many deceased celebrities.

Laoshi took a little time to answer, and the hint of trepidation I had felt in asking him began to grow in the silence. There are some who regard even the slightest criticism of the Professor as blasphemous, and I began to fear Laoshi was one in their number. At last, after what seemed an age, he responded in a surprisingly uncritical tone.

"It is worth asking, though I would suggest you never ask Wang Lang. He knew Professor Zheng firsthand and had no doubts about his quality. So high was his regard for the Professor that when I once simply referred to the great man as 'Zheng,' he cut me down to size for my lack of respect, saying, 'It is Zheng Manqing, or Professor Zheng, never just Zheng. Never say that again.' I remember the lesson.

"Bear in mind that several of my teachers studied directly with Zheng

Manqing and tell the same story. In their minds there is no doubt. It is the same with Morihei Ueshiba. The stories surrounding him are, perhaps, even more fantastic than those surrounding the Professor. Once again, I have had the good fortune to have studied with a number of Ueshiba's students, none of whom were slouches in their own right, and none of whom claimed they were able to lace the boots of the master. In respect to Zheng Manqing, as someone once said, 'Better men than me have called him master.' The longer I study, the more his teachings have been proven true."

He looked at me for a while when he had finished speaking. I looked back blankly, not sure what to say, hoping my face was not betraying my feelings. To say, "Because they believed in Zheng Manqing, so I do," seemed a bit like saying, "We are all fools together." Surely, Laoshi had to have some greater evidence than the opinions of his teachers. I could feel a wave of disappointment swell around me. Maybe Laoshi had nothing else. Perhaps I had reached the end of his knowledge in this respect.

It was true his skills in push-hands and fencing dwarfed mine, and I would be able to drink from those wells for some years to come as I tried to narrow the gap between us. Nevertheless, there was a strange foreboding in me as I realized he could not answer all of my questions. How are we to react when we have reached the limit of our teachers' knowledge? I felt the slightest tingling of anger and immediately felt ashamed. One day, I might reach the point where he would have nothing left to teach. What would I do then?

Just at that point he said, "I can see you are not convinced. We maybe need to look at this problem from another angle, like the push-hands players we are.

"This is a debate between the heart-mind, on one hand, with its currency of faith, and, on the other, the rational mind, which specializes in doubt. Leaving aside the inability of any guarantee to assuage doubt, which reinvents itself with every mitigation, let us consider why the debate is joined in the first place.

"The rational mind, using the tools of reason and logic, is skilled in breaking things down. It is reductionist, analytical, taking things apart to see how they work. The heart-mind does the opposite; it sees the big picture. Its tendency is to make things whole, to emphasize the oneness of everything. It concerns itself with why, as reason concerns itself with how. The rational mind sees us as individuals; the heart-mind sees us as ecosystems.

"This is as it should be. They are the yin and yang of the mind. Each has its function, and when we are in balance, they work together, each in its place. The problem arises when the rational mind attempts to apply reason and logic to the heart-mind. It tries to quantify and measure that which lies beyond its scope, but the rational mind, in hubris for its diamond-sharp capacity for analysis, has forgotten it is born of the heart-mind as well. Its attempts to analyze the unanalyzable are, as the writer Alan Watts would say, like teeth trying to bite themselves or the eye trying to see itself. Do you understand?"

I had to admit, I did not. "How is the rational mind born out of the heart-mind?" I asked. "Surely, the point is that they are different."

"That is entirely the view of the rational mind," Laoshi said. "It is like a teenager who, in his desire for independence, asserts himself as an autonomous being while still staying with Mum and Dad, living on pocket money, and borrowing the car to take his girlfriend out to the cinema on the £20 he's borrowed from Dad. All the while, he is at great pains to tell everyone, even Mum and Dad, he is independent."

"I still don't get it," I stated, beginning to feel like the teenager in question being told off by Dad.

"OK," he continued, "when you gather the evidence in order to decide on what action to take, how do you decide when you have gathered enough evidence, and how do you decide which piece of evidence carries more weight than others?"

I thought for a moment and began to see where he was coming from. I related it to a recruiting process I had once been involved in. To be absolutely fair to all candidates, their application forms were to be assessed consistently by giving them a point for each key word they had written in their personal statements. I was shocked to find some of the assessors were not even reading the statements; they were just scanning for the key words, which were pretty much plucked at random from thin air by the management. Needless to say, it was a great success in hiring the wrong people.

I also remembered a televised religious debate on the topic of whether faith and reason were compatible. The staunchest advocate for the idea that religious faith was a result of emotion and "confirmation bias" stated, without irony, that he had "a lot of faith in reason."

When I mentioned that to Laoshi, he nodded adding, "Ah, this man with his 'faith in reason' highlights the very dilemma; reason does not exist in a vacuum. There is no yang without yin."

"So where does all this leave us?" I asked Laoshi. "What should we do and how do we judge what is true and what is not?"

"You rebalance heart and head," he replied. "You must become a skeptical believer or a gullible cynic. You must be like a cunning innocent."

That's a pretty good line, I thought. Perhaps I hadn't reached the end of Laoshi's knowledge after all. Like so much of Laoshi's teaching in push-hands and fencing, he was advocating a synthesis of yin and yang as an antidote to the experience of separation, which seems to be the price we pay for living together in a civilized way. Of course, this blending is not easy to attain and neither is it static. It is a dynamic process, continually adjusting itself, maintaining equilibrium in much the same way we make tiny adjustments just to remain standing upright. It is not simply knowledge; it is gongfu. It requires practice. The point is not to get overly invested in faith or reason. Both are there to balance each other as we walk the pathless path. Together they form our compass as we seek to make sense of a life in which we are simultaneously separate, individual beings, at one with all creation.

Chapter 10: Do a Form

A young woman came to class one evening, introduced herself, and asked if she could join the class. She had studied with another teacher and was now an "assistant teacher" looking to broaden her horizons. She also wanted to know how she could become accredited as a teacher within Laoshi's organization. 如封似閉

Laoshi suggested she take one thing at a time and, knowing her teacher taught twenty-four-step tai chi, said, "Why don't you sit down and watch what we do here and see if it suits you?"

"I could just join in," she replied.

"Maybe, but we do the Zheng Manqing form here," Laoshi explained.

"I am an assistant teacher, you know," she declared, a touch of irritation in her voice.

"As you wish," Laoshi said, shrugging his shoulders.

We began. After a few postures, she realized she could not follow the form and sat down. After class, she came up to Laoshi, saying sheepishly, "I didn't know there were different forms," before disappearing into the night.

Later Laoshi remarked, "Maybe she was never told there are different forms, or maybe she was and didn't listen, but it is common for people to think there is only one tai chi. Even the Chinese don't always understand this."

This reminded me of a chat I had with a Chinese girl at a Mandarin course I once attended. In conversation, she said, "Of course I know tai chi." When I asked what style, she became confused and just repeated "tai chi" several times. When I explained that there are different styles and approaches, she said, "Maybe someday you will go to China and do real tai chi."

Over time, I have observed that the difference in approach adopted by different teachers goes well beyond the style being taught. In my first year of tai chi study, I sought out a variety of teachers championing a variety of styles to get a feel for the art and how it was taught. One advocate of Zheng Manqing's tai chi, in stark contrast to Laoshi, placed heavy emphasis on exercises prior to starting work on the form. There were warm-ups, loosening exercises, self-massage, and entire sets of qigong routines to be performed before thoughts might turn to the form.

After I had settled on Laoshi's approach, I began to wonder why he did not teach any of the auxiliary exercises I had seen with other teachers. I began to wonder if we were maybe missing something, so I decided to ask.

"It is all in the form," he said.

"But what about stretching?" I persisted.

"It's all in the form," he repeated for the hard of comprehension—which would be me. He then relented a little and provided a response of more depth.

"The form has its own logic. We do not seek to stretch, in the sense of pulling a rubber band—for when you let go, the band resumes its original shape and sometimes it tears. Instead, the form encourages the body to progressively relax and loosen. This gradually increases the flexibility of the joints, but it is not the primary reason for our practice. Flexibility is a by-product of loosening the joints to allow energy to flow more freely—this is the real goal of the form.

"Remember too that 'flexibility' is not the same as 'looseness.' There are people who are very flexible, who can perform the splits and squat very low, but they are not loose. Their joints have permanent tension that manifests as rigidity—this too is a kind of stiffness. When they stretch, they force their bodies to bend, but there is no silkiness. This is not the body we train to develop."

"But shouldn't we warm up with some qigong or something?" I interrupted before wishing I hadn't. Laoshi sighed before continuing.

"You ask about warming up, but haven't you noticed the arrangement of postures? The first part of the form has no physically difficult movements. The turns are only at ninety degrees and there are no deep squats. It is only when the body has had a chance to warm up and the energy is flowing within that the first deep squatting posture makes an appearance. As you squat onto your right leg as deeply as possible, the hip joint is opened up considerably. Bear in mind, however, the posture is not primarily a stretch. It is for strengthening the body internally and has benefits for the stomach in particular. It is recommended that you do squatting single whip about fifteen times when your stomach is bothering you, or when you have eaten too much.

"In opening the joints, our goal is to gently ease out the tension; we do not pull them apart as you would tear the leg off a roast chicken. Follow Ben Lo's wisdom on this: 'If you feel you need a warm-up, do a form. Not warmed up enough? Do another form. When you have warmed up, do a form. If you need to warm down, do a form.'"

This was getting interesting, so I chanced a follow-up question.

"What about applications? Other schools practice them, believing if you don't know the fighting application, then you cannot do the right posture. Why don't we practice applications?"

"Yes, it is easy to be misled by this," he conceded. "When I studied with

Don in his Still Lotus School, I was desperate to know the applications. I thought the art would not be complete without them, so I persuaded him, reluctant as he was, to show me at least one application for each posture. In addition, I had somebody film the entire lesson. It took about an hour. Now, how many times do you think I have watched this piece of film?"

His manner clearly implied not many.

"It is like so many things: the desire to have the treasure blinds you to the fact that it is mostly useless. Once you acquire it, you realize you could have done without it in the first place."

"But, Laoshi," I interrupted, "doesn't it add to our overall knowledge if we know the applications?"

"That is probably true," he conceded, "provided the applications have enough tai chi in them. There was an occasional student of Zheng Manqing who practiced so many styles of martial arts that, for a time, he needed three hours a day to complete each of his forms just once. He decided to write a book on Zheng Manqing's form, including applications and breathing. In the book, however, the breathing is more in keeping with hard-style martial arts, as are the applications. It is very common that a history in another martial art will interfere, at least for a time, with our understanding of tai chi. This is the disadvantage of coming to tai chi from another art: after a while, it is common for people to think, 'Oh, this is just like karate,' or, 'I see a lot of aikido in this,' or, 'We did this in Shaolin.' While it is true to say the postures in our form come originally from Shaolin and other arts, tai chi postures have to be practiced with a different energy, or we risk getting Shaolin or karate or aikido in tai chi clothing.

"A famous *wushu* [武術] master, Pan Qingfu [潘清福], once said: 'Shaolin should be practiced like a tiger rampaging down the mountainside.' Such rampaging energy is quite unlike the energy of our form. At the same time, without this energy, Shaolin is not Shaolin in the same way boxercise is not boxing, no matter how much you want it to be.

"In applications, we must avoid blocking and grabbing; these are not tai chi concepts. They lock us in position, making us rigid and unable to feel what is going on. If the application has either of these two qualities, it should be discarded. Furthermore, every application has to be available to us from a neutral stance and without preparation; attackers seldom give us time to assume our best stance and do some limbering up."

I ventured one more question. "But don't we need to know how to punch and kick if we are attacked?"

"Possibly, yes," Laoshi allowed. "This is the benefit of previous experience in harder martial arts, but we must guard against thinking of tai chi in terms of responding to specific attacks with specific techniques. For many martial arts, this is the way it is, and it makes good sense. For us, however, it is not the way."

"Why not, Laoshi?" I asked.

"Because," he continued, "we train by placing emphasis on detecting the energy of the attack. As the Classics say: 'At the opponent's slightest stir, I have already anticipated it.' We train to feel if the attack is real or a feint, if it is solid or tentative, big or little, long or short, rigid or pliable, and if it is using inner strength or external force.

"One of the problems martial artists have is that, getting into a fight, they do not really listen to what is going on. Having been trained in a particular system, they will attempt to apply the techniques they are familiar with. Under stress, we revert to what we know, to what is comfortable. The opponent, naturally, is doing the same thing with a different system, resulting in things not going as either of them expected. If we approach a fight and imagine it will proceed as it does in the dojo, the sudden widening of parameters that comes with real life will confuse us. It is as if the rules have changed."

Up to this point Laoshi had appeared to be deadly serious, but the hint of a smile came to his lips as he continued. "Fortunately, as my student, you will not become confused if you cannot apply any techniques. You don't know any." He chuckled a little to himself before clarifying. "Maybe it is more correct to say you do not expect set responses to particular moves. In this respect your mind will be free to react to what happens without interference from the rational mind.

"I was once asked at a beginners' class," Laoshi recalled, still smiling, "what I would do if I were attacked. When I replied that I did not know, the questioner misunderstood, assuming I was saying I had no grasp of martial arts. I then explained that, in a fight, no one can 'know' what is going to happen. I told him one of my teachers, Don, was once attacked on the mean streets of Cardiff by a man armed with a bullwhip. No martial arts school practices defense against bullwhips—it is too exotic.

"The methods we practice here come from the belief that a fight is a dangerous, unpredictable affair, where an open, receptive mind and skill in interpreting strength may have greater validity in self-defense than specific counters to prescribed attacks."

Laoshi's countenance suddenly grew solemn. "Do you remember a young man who came to class for a short while? The lad who lived in Stirling and had practiced martial arts all his life? He wanted to learn tai chi to complement the kickboxing and aikido he had been studying for some time. He was a great example of what good martial arts training can do. He had a wonderful attitude, was humble and sincere. Physically, he was tough, but with a gentle energy. He was pleasant, unassuming, and instantly likable, but do you remember what happened to him?"

Laoshi told this story many times to his senior students as if to emphasize its lesson. Joe, the student in question, was planning to go to Australia with his girlfriend to teach fitness and martial arts. The girlfriend was just completing her qualification as a fitness instructor when disaster struck. At first, all we knew was that Joe suddenly stopped coming to Laoshi's class. This certainly disappointed Laoshi, who was very impressed with Joe's natural ability. Some weeks later, he came to speak with Laoshi to explain his absence. His arm was in a brace, his face was marked with injuries that still looked raw, and his eyes were tearful. Laoshi took him to a side room and Joe explained. It seemed when he and his girlfriend were returning home one evening, a junkie approached them looking for money. Somehow, the encounter turned nasty and the junkie attacked Joe, who, with his martial arts training, was managing the attacker without much trouble, knocking him down a few times. As a good martial artist and decent young man, he did not want to cause undue injury to his attacker, an attitude that was his undoing. Somehow his attacker managed to get hold of a bottle and smashed off its bottom in order to stab Joe repeatedly, not restrained by any sense of compassion for his victim. Joe's injuries were severe. He avoided being blinded by turning his head, but needed lots of stitches in his face and head. His index finger was almost severed, and tendons were damaged in his arm. At the time he did not know whether he would regain full capacity in that arm. Saddest of all, Laoshi said, was the pain in the lad's eyes. The observable injuries were nothing compared to the guilt, shame, loss of confidence, and the wrecking of his and his girlfriend's dream. Laoshi advised him to keep coming to class and rebuild himself physically and mentally—but he was never seen again.

"So what do we do then?" I asked, getting a little annoyed, in spite of myself, at Laoshi's habit of going around the houses before getting to the point.

"We respond in the moment with a clear mind," Laoshi said. "This is what Zheng Manqing meant when he said, 'In a fight, keep your mind in your legs and everything will turn out right.' This takes a lot of trust in your training. Your push-hands trains you to neutralize the attacker's energy by deflection and avoidance. If you can feel what he is going to do and when he will do it, you will be able to defeat it. Remember what they said about Zheng Manqing: he could 'hear' the intention to attack before it was initiated. He could detect the 'impendence,' as Wang Lang used to call it.

"Once they have attacked and are neutralized, you will be able to apply your response to their yin point. Whenever someone attacks, there will always be a weak point or soft spot. This is the universe's promise to us: if there is yang, there will always be yin. The very act of attacking exposes a weakness, if only we can see it and take advantage of it. Having avoided the force of the attack and being sensitive to the weakness created, you apply the principle of pushing.

Pushing, of course, can simply be a push—but it can also be a punch or palm strike. The body becomes a single unit that can deliver force generated from the legs and the ground. In effect, it is striking using gravity. When you train your *fajing* [發勁], your explosive force, in push-hands, you are training precisely this sort of strike. If, as is the case for most students, the fajing energy is not very powerful, then the strike should be to vulnerable parts of the body, like the eyes and throat."

Coming from a conventional martial arts background, I found myself struggling to give up the idea of self-defense as techniques applied in response to particular attacks. When I explained this to Laoshi, he told me the following story.

"As you know, in feudal Japan, the Yagyu family was celebrated for their martial arts, especially their sword-fighting style, the famous Shinkage Ryu. In fact, Yagyu Munenori was the fencing master to at least one of the Tokugawa shoguns.

"As you can expect, such a family exerted considerable pressure on their sons to learn the art and continue the family tradition. One of the lesser sons, Matajuro, did not seem to have the right stuff. He was considered lazy and was subsequently thrown out of the dojo—a considerable humiliation. Having awakened from his slothful ways, he decided to master the sword by finding another teacher. The question was where, since the Yagyus were considered best.

"As he searched for a teacher he heard of an eccentric old hermit named Banzo, who lived in the mountains near the Kumano Shrine and was reputed to be a supreme swordsman. Matajuro set out to become his student. Once he found Banzo, there was some discussion about how long it would take and some testing on the part of Banzo before he accepted Matajuro. The condition was that Matajuro must do as he was told without question. At the time, unquestioning obedience was expected from a student, and cooking and cleaning were part of the deal when learning from a master. In this case, however, Matajuro did nothing else. His daily routine consisted of household chores with no lessons in the sword whatsoever.

"After a year, or three years, depending on which version you read, Matajuro began to doubt the wisdom of his choice. He was on the point of leaving when Banzo crept up behind him and hit him, forcefully, on the back with a bamboo sword before walking away without explanation. From then on, Banzo would regularly sneak up on Matajuro as he was cooking or cleaning and strike him with the sword. From this training, Matajuro developed a strong sense of awareness and especially fast reflexes.

"Banzo then began to launch attacks at night, when Matajuro was asleep. As a result, Matajuro began to develop an instinct for the approach of his master and would wake up ready to defend himself. Eventually, after four years of this kind of training, or ten years, depending on which version you read, Banzo attacked the stooping figure of Matajuro as he was cooking. Matajuro deflected the sword with the lid of the rice pot without even looking up. Banzo then awarded him a certificate in swordsmanship. He never even picked up a sword."

"Very Japanese," I said, "but I get the point. The training is in awareness and spontaneous technique."

"That too," Laoshi replied.

"Well, what else?" I pursued.

"The story is as much about the expectation of what constitutes training. When training does not fit in with your expectations, you resist it. You have yet to grasp that tai chi is not just another form of karate or Shaolin; it is completely different. You need to approach it accordingly. You are like the drunk looking for his keys in the street when a passerby stops to help. After a while, the passerby asks him if he is sure he lost them there. 'No,' he replies, 'I lost them down that alley, but there is more light here.'"

As I pursued my tai chi studies, it often felt as if I were fumbling around in the dark, trying to find something to which I could relate from previous training. One of the most challenging aspects of studying with Laoshi was his unwillingness to compromise on authenticity. He did not—nor could he—simplify the core concepts to make us feel we "knew" what we were doing. He would often say, "Progress in tai chi creeps up and surprises you. As Zheng Manqing said, 'You only really know what you have when you are called upon to use it.'"

Later, reflecting on the young assistant teacher who came to class not knowing about other styles of tai chi, I came to realize we had much in common. She expected to learn some little flourish or other to add to what she already knew. Similarly, I had expected that learning tai chi would be similar to learning aikido or karate. I needed to abandon my expectations in order to open up to a new approach.

Chapter 11: Copy, Imitate, Steal

While still in full-time education, I began studying aikido with an exceptionally gifted teacher, Billy Coyle. He had studied with some of the real heavyweights in the aikido world, among them Sensei Masamichi Noro, Kazuo Chiba, Masatake Sekiya, and Morihito Saito. Not too long before I began studying with him, he had been injured quite badly—a car accident, I think. It meant he was reluctant to take *ukemi* (breakfalls) for a while and so developed a greater interest in Japanese sword. As a result, for a few years we were fortunate to practice Omori ryu iai in addition to traditional aikido.

Iaido is the art of drawing the sword, generally from the seated position—

白
鶴
亮
翅

the idea being the samurai could rise to his feet, dispatching his opponent en route. Initially, like everybody else, I began by using a *bokken* (wooden sword) during iaido, rather than a real sword. While this is fine for the beginner, the intricacies of unsheathing and returning the sword to the *saya* (scabbard) must not be overlooked, so after saving up for a while, I bought an *iaito*, a practice steel sword complete with saya.

It was secondhand and cost £60, a lot of money for me at the time, but it was quite beautiful. It looked just like a real sword, but without a sharp edge. Returning the sword to the saya is a stylish, elegant movement—one of the aforementioned intricacies—but it can result in fingers being sliced off the hand holding the saya. It is a good idea, then, to start with a blunt sword and work up to a sword with a cutting edge.

Although I was buying the iaito from a former classmate, one of the senior students, Charles, insisted on coming with me to make sure I wasn't being ripped off. After the deal was completed, Charles advised me to visit Billy so he could inspect the iaito and give his seal of approval. This I duly did one afternoon before class.

He looked over the iaito, shaking it from the very end of the hilt to see if the tang was in one piece. He checked to see if it was straight and that the *tsuba* and handle were tight before finally ensuring that the bamboo, or in this case wooden, *mekugi* (securing peg) was snugly in place. A broken tang or a loose peg could result in the blade flying out of the handle as a cut is made, which is not only embarrassing, but also highly dangerous.

Assuring me that I had bought well, we passed the afternoon in conversation before heading off to class. He told me of his injury and his decision to start doing breakfalls again. "We can't go on living like a half-shut knife," he said. His martial spirit was never in question as far as I was concerned, but the thought of a bad breakfall crippling him was enough to make me shiver. Later, when I had my own battle with a serious back injury, his words and spirit would often come to mind.

He then gave me some advice about studying the martial arts: "First you must copy your teacher; then you have to imitate; finally you will have to steal the art." It was a really curious piece of advice, which I thought about often in the years that followed. His words suggested there is a difference between copying and imitating—while the mention of stealing seemed suspect to me at the time. Billy did not elaborate further on the matter, however, and we moved on to talk of other things.

During one of the numerous tea-drinking sessions I enjoyed with Laoshi years later, I mentioned Billy's curious advice and asked Laoshi what he thought.

"It is a way of thinking about stages of development," he said, nodding his head as if in quiet approval. "It is also about the relationship you have with your teacher and the art. He was telling you how to relate to both him and your training while you were studying with him. He maybe sensed you were ready to move to the second level in your journey."

"What do you mean, Laoshi, the 'second level'?" I asked. I sensed Laoshi was going tell me something important about the art, but also about our teacher-student relationship.

He thought for a minute, then said, "The first level is that of merely copying. It is the basic level of commitment you must give to your teacher. At this point the teacher shows; you copy. You, as the student, are not permitted to question the method. Anything learned from other teachers is best disregarded. You voluntarily restrict yourself to your teacher's way of doing things. It is mechanical, learning by rote—and that is all that is required. 'Right way' and 'wrong way' are clearly defined and, to some extent, you surrender your ego to the teacher, who sets the agenda. At this time you may well owe your teacher a lot, but there is no deep connection between you. At this stage you may very well say, 'This is my teacher,' but it is unlikely your teacher would say, 'This is my student.'

"At some point, you move to the next level, where you imitate. The word itself is interesting. It sounds a lot like intimate. This may be a trick of the language, but to imitate implies a deeper level of copying. It is as if you get inside the skin of the teacher. As Zheng Manqing would say, you must 'harmonize' with your teacher. You must look at the art through your teacher's eyes. You must, to some extent, 'become' your teacher. This is a more involved relationship. It is where your intuition is of more value to you. You, with your teacher's help, begin to explore the heart-mind. It is the strength of feeling you have for your teacher that makes this possible. It is your respect, feelings of admiration, and even love for your teacher that begin to open your heart. At this point your teacher would say, 'This is my student.'

"Without this deeper relationship, it is very difficult to get to the finer points of the art. It is also very difficult to persevere with the demands of the training if you do not feel the teacher is on your side. A sense of place or belonging can help enormously until you reach the point where you are strong enough on your own.

"Used wisely, a good teacher utilizes this sometimes reverential respect to lead a student ever more deeply within himself. The sense of complete trust between teacher and student bypasses the normal ego defenses that inhibit advanced stages of learning."

Instinctively, I understood what he was saying. I could see how, as the art became subtler, I found myself resisting Laoshi and his teaching. There was a part of me in conflict with the process, especially when I felt demoralized by my lack of understanding. At times I doubted myself, at times I doubted Laoshi, and at other times I doubted tai chi itself; however, as the bond between us strengthened, I felt able to keep on going.

Laoshi used the feelings of respect his students had for him to help them persevere. Some were inspired by his presence and wanted to emulate him, while others did not want to disappoint him. A few of the seniors seemed to be going through a similar, sometimes stronger conflict, yet most of them kept on going, feeling a sense of belonging and comradeship.

Yet, the question of "stealing" still bothered me, so as Laoshi took a break to gather his thoughts, I asked, "But where does the stealing come in?"

"Near the end," he replied.

"The end of what?" I pressed.

"The end of your training, when you no longer need your teacher. When you grow beyond the discipline and reach the essence. Some people call this level ri. I shall explain. The Japanese martial tradition describes the levels we have been talking about as shu, ha, and ri. Shu, as we have seen, is the basic level where you copy what is put before you. You do not question it; you do not change it; you do not 'improve' it. It is slavish attention to the technique. The word itself means 'obey,' and that is all you are expected to do. You study the technique to get the structure and idea of an art. It can be repetitive and even uninspiring. It is to teach you the basic tools for learning the art.

"Then, if you persevere, the training begins to hint at something else within the structure. This is the level of ha. It is the element that is greater than the sum of the parts. The basics are not abandoned, but the narrow confines of the earlier stage are softened. The emphasis is on seeing something deeper in the practice of the basic ideas. It is not about more complicated technique—indeed, at this stage many teachers teach only the basics. For example, by the time I saw Master Lin, he was only teaching the first four postures of the form and a few other postures as specialized exercises. Yang Chengfu, latterly, did no form at all. His practice consisted of holding postures and doing endless repetitions of repulse monkey to work the qi up his spine.

"The final stage, and the one equated with stealing, as your teacher put it, is the level of ri. Ri refers to the essence of the art. Here there are no rules. There are no limitations. It is ultimate freedom of expression of the art. This level of mastery is impossible to describe and impossible to teach. It is the level beyond technique and teacher. This is the point where, having met the teacher along the road, you would have killed him—another metaphor for the same idea.

"At this level, the student must imbibe the very essence of the art directly from the master. An absolute commitment in the final stage is required—a commitment every bit as intense as a thief in the night who is alert to every sight, sound, and smell. This analogy has also been used before. Do you know Goso Hoen's story of the master burglar and his son?"

When I confessed I did not, Laoshi was pleased to put this right.

"When someone asked Goso Hoen what Zen is like, he told of a young man whose aging father was a successful burglar. As his father was getting older, he asked his father to teach him the art before he was too old and his skills lost.

"That night, the elder took the young man out to break into a house. After gaining entry, he told his son to open a large chest and look inside. When the youth obeyed, he pushed him in and locked the chest from the outside, then shouted and screamed, waking the whole house before escaping.

"Later that night the young man returned home furious, and demanded to know the meaning of this outrage. The father said, 'First tell me how you escaped.' The son explained that he had been petrified as he heard people search the house. He could just see a little, through a crack in the chest, but enough to see when only one of the servants was in the room. He hit on the idea of making scratching noises and meowing like a cat. When the servant opened the chest, he blew out his candle and ran into the garden. The servant called on the others and they gave chase. Once in the garden, he found a well and had the idea of throwing a large stone into it. As the servants came out, they heard the splash and went over, expecting to find the drowning burglar. Being so diverted, they did not see the young man slip away. On completion of his tale, the father simply said, 'You do not need me. You have already learned the art.'"

"That reminds me a little of the Johnny Cash song 'A Boy Named Sue,'" I added and was surprised to find Laoshi actually nodding in agreement. I was delighted.

"So, the penny drops," he said, smiling. "The final stage of learning cannot be taught. It comes about when the absolute essence of the art is ready to emerge. No situation ever happens twice; there are infinite variations. The master of ri is so in tune with the moment that he responds by doing just the right thing to the right degree at the right time. Does that remind you of anything?"

Indeed, it did. It was the meaning of Shr Jung (時中; pinyin: Shi Zhong), the name of Zheng Manqing's school.

He left me to ponder the idea of stealing from my teacher, arriving at a breakthrough by becoming as sensitive to ourselves and our surroundings as a thief who is on the point of getting caught.

It is a description of clarity of mind where the rational mind, being temporarily shocked into silence by the predicament, allows the heart-mind to break through and provide a creative solution.

We were back at heart-mind again—only by a different route. The rational mind consults with precedent in order to supply a ready-made answer to a problem, but nothing ever happens the same way twice. "You cannot step twice into the same river, for the waters are continually flowing," said Heraclitus. The heart-mind knows this, but the rational mind does not.

Chapter 12: Withdraw and Push the Yin

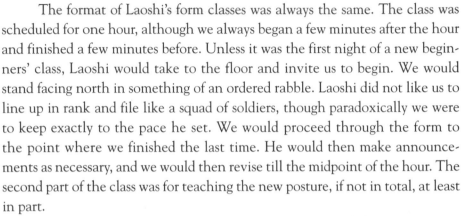

左
搂
膝
拗
步

The format of Laoshi's form classes was always the same. The class was scheduled for one hour, although we always began a few minutes after the hour and finished a few minutes before. Unless it was the first night of a new beginners' class, Laoshi would take to the floor and invite us to begin. We would stand facing north in something of an ordered rabble. Laoshi did not like us to line up in rank and file like a squad of soldiers, though paradoxically we were to keep exactly to the pace he set. We would proceed through the form to the point where we finished the last time. He would then make announcements as necessary, and we would then revise till the midpoint of the hour. The second part of the class was for teaching the new posture, if not in total, at least in part.

It amused me how often, after he had demonstrated the new posture, Laoshi would say, "This is one of my favorite postures of the form." This happened so regularly that a student once commented to those around him that it appeared every posture was one of his favorites. The touch of snideness I detected in the comment evoked in me a hostility in defense of my teacher, but I later came to understand Laoshi did not need defending from such remarks. Indeed, he seemed to welcome them. In time I came to relish observing how he dealt with some of the caustic comments from the floor. Often the merest twinkle would appear in his eye and he would turn the comment to his advantage.

Once when he was making a point about the importance of slight changes in the postures, Laoshi commented, "It is as small as a midge's eyebrow." One of the class wags, laughing, retorted, "I didn't know midges had eyebrows!" Laoshi smiled and said, "Ah, that's because they are so very small, you might have missed them when you last looked." There was general laughter and the mood was set for the rest of the class.

Interestingly, it was usually one of the beginners who would make, possibly unintentionally, "catty" comments or ask pointed questions, and, even though it only happened occasionally, I wondered aloud if it annoyed Laoshi.

"It used to," Laoshi replied, "when I first started teaching, but then I began to see things differently. Sometimes, I suspect 'attacking' questions come from those who are fearful, but who try to hide their feelings of vulnerability with a certain haughtiness. When the ego is threatened, people attempt to deal with negative feelings, which arise in many ways. For example, for professional people or those in academia, a 'smart' question is a way of asserting their knowledge or status. In a tai chi class, they are cast in the humble role of beginner and it does not sit well with them.

"The more important thing, however, is the opportunity even tricky exchanges offer for the teacher to play push-hands with the energy they represent. To the experienced teacher, there is an opportunity to practice deflecting the negativity in the question and to hijack its energy, for a sarcastic or rude comment carries energy that can infect the class with negativity—but the energy itself is not bad. It can be harnessed to advantage if we do not resist it or roughly try to subdue it. After all, it is better to have some energy coming back at you, even slightly negative, than none at all. It gives you something to work with.

"The skill of denying the barb its target and responding in the correct manner is the lesson of withdraw and push in the form—one of my favorite postures."

When it came to withdraw and push, Laoshi always showed its martial arts application. By contrast, he rarely demonstrated applications for other postures, and only when someone asked to see one might he agree. He explained that the essence of the posture was not only the quintessential expression of tai chi for self-defense, but also a way of dealing with all attacks, be they physical, verbal, or psychological.

In regard to withdraw and push, he once said: "This posture appears in the first part of the form, immediately after a punch. Is this an accident? I think not. The punch is the concentration of energy into a single point for a very short time; it is overwhelming force maximized in a small area for an instant. It is the epitome of yang in action. Withdraw and push is the very opposite. It is the epitome of yin in action. It receives with neither resistance nor rancor, allowing the excessive to peter out before replying, just on the spot that cannot be defended, thus precluding the need to overpower the attacker. It is victory without struggle.

"The form reminds us of the relative power of these two ways of looking at action. It does not hold one as superior to the other, but advises that we must understand them both.

"Always remember the postures are arranged with great care, and for a number of reasons: postures proceed from easy to more difficult, but they also offer a kind of narrative, as Gerda Geddes suggests in her book *Looking for the Golden Needle*. The form is interpreted as an allegorical journey from our first awakening through the various stages of development until we reach the level of mastery, the realm of the *xian* [仙]."

The xian Laoshi was referring to were the mythical immortals of Daoist folklore—sages or enlightened individuals who by the practice of secret breathing, meditational, and dietary techniques had reached the level of transcendent being, a kind of saint or bodhisattva. Some believed them to be physically immortal, while the more pragmatic regarded the immortality as more concerned with spirit.

I know Laoshi did not believe in the fairy stories surrounding immortals. His interest in Daoism was restricted to the philosophical approach, not the religious or folk varieties, well described in Goullart's *The Monastery of Jade Mountain*, another of the books Laoshi recommended to his students. To Laoshi, representing a journey from early spiritual and energetic awakening to the peak of mastery was a valuable way to consider the form.

He would sometimes quote Geddes as follows: "One enacts, through the body, the different phases of development common to us all. It is like a *Pilgrim's Progress* with imagery from China." He did not, however, feel compelled to follow Geddes's interpretation of the postures directly, preferring his own intuitive understanding in this matter.

In Laoshi's view of that journey, the punch and withdraw and push sequence represents our awakening to the power that resides in all of us for confronting the challenges of life. Unlike some philosophies that encourage us to declaw and defang ourselves, solely relying on the beneficence of the universe, Laoshi believed the universe supplies us with the means to protect ourselves. For him, a philosophy that did not offer practical help in the common human struggles with conflict was inherently useless.

As Laoshi would say, "What good is our spiritual and philosophical development if the supermarket guy can succeed in imprisoning us at the checkout and force us to dance to the tune of the bar code?"

It was one of Laoshi's examples of how daily life hurries and harries us, leaving our nerves jangling as we struggle to complete the simplest tasks for survival in our modern, prepackaged, throwaway society.

While physical attack is, for most of us, a rare event, our everyday lives are often blighted by emotional conflict with wives, husbands, children, bosses, and colleagues—in fact just about everyone we encounter, including ourselves. In this respect, the punch and withdraw and push movements are metaphorical tools we can use with the goal of applying their lessons to dealing with life.

While the punch, with all its power, is to be understood, respected, and mastered, its use in daily conflict is limited. It is a "battlefield" response, which (and this was important to Laoshi) may be used occasionally. It is not practical for the vast majority of our interactions through the day.

Laoshi clarified, saying, "Using overwhelming force is not to be demonized. Remember what Zheng Manqing said: 'If you are attacked by a group of men, or men with weapons, and they are seeking your life, then you should get mean.' Getting *mean* means responding with as much ferocity and destructive energy as is necessary to protect your life and those you love. But how often do we find our lives in danger? Is it appropriate to respond with the same meanness to the old lady who skips in front of us in the post office?"

Of more practical use is the idea contained in withdraw and push. Laoshi explained: "The universe in its compassion has made us a promise: there can be no yang without yin. You do not need to accept this notion dogmatically. Just look around you. We live in a dualistic universe. There is no up without down, there is no high without low, and, more important for us, there is no strength without weakness. Therefore, when someone makes an attack on you, no matter what form or how powerful, there will be a corresponding weakness. Your mission, should you choose to accept it, is to avoid the force of the attack upon your body, mind, or emotions, and apply your response to the weak point. In other words, yield to the yang and push on the yin."

The more I thought about this idea, the more profound it became. In the martial application, the attacker pushes on your arm, seeking to trap it against your body. You turn, yielding to the direction of the push while moving back, allowing the attack to land on nothing. The momentum of the attacker, meanwhile, continues, and he overextends, exposing his yin side. You can then counter with your own push to the attacker's weak spot. Applying this in the real world, however, is very difficult, particularly because of our tendency to tighten up and resist any kind of push.

Laoshi further explained that the idea was far more sophisticated than a turn, grab, and shove: "To understand this correctly," he told us, "we cannot just grab our attacker's arm with our free hand. There is no 'grab' in tai chi. Grabbing only makes us rigid. The value of having 'gotten' someone is offset by the fact that he has also 'gotten' us.

"Metaphorically, most arguments are like this. They grab you and you grab them, and you dance around for a while, holding on tight, as if you were drowning and they were the life belt. In the martial application, a better idea is that of 'substitution.' The attacker pushes your arm, but your other hand makes contact from below; you substitute one hand for the other. The attacker is fooled into thinking he still 'has' you, and he persists in his folly for a while, slipping further and further out of position until he is out on a limb.

"In the martial application, this lasts only a short time—but in an argument, leading a person off balance can take longer."

It is also easier said than done. It is a commitment to a way of dealing with conflict, which we must first understand and then practice. The critical thing is that the "push"—physical, verbal, or emotional—does not trap us. In daily life, this means we do not let the negativity of the attack land on us, but instead lead it beyond its potency, and then make our reply. When this works, it is wondrous.

One day I was having a discussion with some officials in a youth organization where I worked. Over lunch one of the older managers attempted to persuade me against our boss.

"You are too influenced by Danny," he said. "You should be more your own man, instead of following what he wants so much. You shouldn't be so easily led."

In a rare moment of clarity, I replied, "So . . . you think I'm easily influenced?"

"Yes," he replied, "I do."

"Well in that case," I suggested, "it should be easy for you to influence me."

He could not reply and did not bring the topic of conversation up again.

In the perfect manifestation of this principle, the yin point cannot be defended and, we are assured, there is always such a point available, but usually, because of our own fears and doubts, we are not centered enough to see it. The "should've said" experience—*l'esprit de l'escalier*, as the French say—is a common one. The insightful response or action is somehow inhibited and only comes to us later, when we are on the stairs departing the building.

Laoshi often brought up the matter of appropriate response in push-hands class. "The withdraw-and-push technique is often used in push-hands to counter the yin attack, where the pusher does not try to push you squarely on your center but, instead, tries to push your arm to the side to trap you. We might say it is the physical manifestation of passive aggression, not dealing with the issue head on, but in an oblique or covert way. The 'push' only happens after you have been tied up by your own arm and deprived of your room to maneuver. In everyday life, this is the sort of attack we are most likely to encounter, even from family, friends, and colleagues. Hostility is dressed up as something else in order to have deniability when playing to the gallery. The object is to cause us to be complicit in our own wounding, because we cannot respond without looking petty or over-sensitive."

Ironically, many of us were guilty of utilizing the "passive-aggressive" push in class, especially with Laoshi. His push-hands was so polished that a direct push was totally ineffectual, so we all tried various tricks and tactics to get the better of him, despite his constant exhortation that we keep to the purity of the practice. It was a testament, both to our desperation in our attempts to "get" him, and also to his skill, that we all resorted to such methods. True to his philosophy, however, Laoshi did not demonize these methods, only saying, "These 'deviations' can only get you so far." We heard his words. Some of us even believed we understood his message. Yet most of us, for too long, remained "deviant."

It may be the curse of our time, or the nature of mankind, but our need to be reassured of our progress and level of ability compared with others seems inescapable, even in tai chi. The problem of measuring how far we are along the path is a constant preoccupation for many of us, even though progressing through levels of achievement is, to a great extent, arbitrary. If everybody lives by the same illusion, however, then it can be extremely difficult to remain free of it.

My aikido teacher, Billy Coyle, did not believe in grading during those years I studied with him, although some time later even he was obliged to make concessions to the *kyu* and *dan* system common in Japanese martial arts. We would practice without the limitation of grades, the most experienced students practicing with the least experienced, and everybody benefiting as a result. This was not the case at other schools, where there was often a tendency for the high grades to practice together, rather than "waste time" with their perceived inferiors—ignoring the timeless dictum of martial arts schools the world over: you can learn from everyone.

Coming to tai chi class, I was pleasantly surprised to find no belts or grading system. There was no gi or mandarin suit to buy, no badge or insignia to display. Even the idea of club T-shirts was positively shunned by Laoshi. We wore pretty much what we arrived in, the only concession being, for most of us, a change of footwear to help the feet connect more effectively with the ground.

And yet it would not be true to say there was no etiquette, only what is explicit in other martial arts is implicit in tai chi. In the seemingly haphazard and random, there is order. There is etiquette despite the lack of bowing, titles, and photographs of the founder, and there is a ranking system, subtler, perhaps, but no less real.

Laoshi followed something akin to the Chinese system of familial ties, where he as the teacher inhabited an almost fatherly role, while we the students were the children. As with families, there are older and younger brothers and sisters, senior and junior students—only in tai chi class this is usually determined by length of time in the school, rather than age.

As students of the Zheng Manqing approach to tai chi, we were also loosely connected to the Zheng Manqing family throughout the world. Within this sphere, lineage is tremendously important. When meeting another teacher, for example, the first question usually is, "Who is your teacher?" If the name you mention is not someone he knows, he will ask, "Who was his teacher?" If that name is also unfamiliar, this line of interrogation will continue until a name is recognized. It is a subtle way of determining how close you are to the source— Zheng Manqing—and discerning the approach you may favor.

In Laoshi's school, the older "brothers and sisters" were further classified as senior students, class assistants, assistant teachers, and teachers—but to an outsider, it might have taken some time to work out who was who. Without visible signals of rank, a new student, if it occurred to him to do so, would require to observe how students interacted in order to discern seniority.

It seems inevitable that some kind of hierarchy is necessary when more than one of us is gathered together. Indeed, people seem to clamor for such a system when there is none in place. Even Zheng Manqing had this problem when he taught in New York. According to Wang Lang, Zheng Manqing was frequently approached by his students wanting him to acknowledge their progress with a grade of some kind. He eventually conceded to these requests and held a grading of sorts within the school.

Zheng Manqing's grading system was based on his understanding of the levels of development of a tai chi player, described in the first instance as "human," "earth," and "heaven." Each of these three levels contained three further sublevels, for a total of nine.

The first level, the human level, is concerned with opening the gates of the qi in the arms, legs, and torso. The second level, the earth level, centers on developing and moving the qi to the *dantian* (丹田), arms, and legs. The final level, the heaven level, addresses the subtleties of the internal power of tai chi.

On the appointed day, Zheng Manqing gave his students their position according to the nine levels. A few, the most senior, were told they had reached the level of the elbow. Others had merely attained the level of the wrist, while the vast majority of students had yet to register a grade at all. Hearing of this incident, it struck me that, in fact, opening the gates of the wrist, elbow, and shoulder was all part of the first sublevel. In effect, Zheng Manqing had told his students they were all the same.

I began to wonder if Zheng Manqing had hoodwinked his students in much the same way a parent might distract children from crying for sweets—for in considering his levels of development, it seemed he had succeeded in giving the appearance of grading his students without actually doing so: the relaxation of the ligaments of wrist, elbow, and shoulder are, after all, part of the same level —the first sublevel of the human level.

As this thought entered my mind, I resolved to ask Laoshi if Zheng Manqing had played a trick on his students. Another story concerning Zheng Manqing's explanation as to why the Americans had reached the moon before the Chinese showed he was entirely capable of a little humorous distraction to change the energy in a room.

The story goes that in response to the hubris generated by TV presenters when Neil Armstrong took his momentous first steps, Zheng Manqing took the opportunity to explain to his New York students why the Americans had achieved the feat ahead of the Chinese. "It is obvious," he explained, holding a ball and indicating with his finger that the moon was directly above the United States. "The moon is closer to America."

The next time I had a moment with Laoshi, I asked, "Laoshi, do you think Zheng Manqing was playing a trick on his students when he 'graded' them? After all, he effectively told them they were all the same."

Laoshi shrugged a little before replying, "It is possible, I suppose. We will never know for sure, but I can tell you about a trick that was recently played on some jujutsu students. Would you like to hear?"

"Of course," I responded, wondering if Laoshi were distracting me from my question.

"Well," he continued, "it seems an accomplished Brazilian jujutsu teacher and tournament winner by the name of Alex Vamos was invited to visit a BJJ school in the south by the local teacher. Despite the fact that he was a distinguished black belt, the plan was that he would wear a white belt and masquerade as a beginner. The story was spread that he had been doing gongfu for some months in a school where grappling was part of the curriculum. For good measure, he acted the part of the annoying beginner, putting on his belt the wrong way and asking about his chances in the elite Pan Am competition.

"Since he played the part well, the high grades in the school assumed Vamos was nothing, until one by one they were choked out or had to submit to his superior skills. They asked themselves how this could be happening; how could a beginner do this to them?

"It was a good lesson. They made the mistake of judging a man by a piece of cloth around his waist and were quickly shown how foolish this can be. Whether Zheng Manqing was playing a trick or not, it would have been wise of his students to consider the value, or otherwise, of thinking in terms of grades.

"As tai chi students, we learn to be sensitive to, as Wang Lang would say, 'the total energy statement' from the other person, whether in class or in the outside world. We should not be unduly influenced by his wardrobe, his status, or, for that matter, how much money he has. In class, grades and colored belts encourage us to see the belt, not the man. In life, symbols of status blind us to the man completely."

Pondering Laoshi's words, I realized how lazy we all are when it comes to really looking at people, seeing them as they are. We make judgments about those we meet using the merest and most obvious evidence. How often have I decided the worth of another person on only a few seconds' superficial observation?

Laoshi added, "Zheng Manqing told us we should practice push-hands as if standing on the edge of a cliff. This is not to encourage us to fear a push, but to really pay attention. The same is true when dealing with people. When you look at someone, really look."

Chapter 14: The Pillar of Heaven Collapses

進
步
搬
攔
捶

As with many students, prior to finding a teacher, I bought a book on tai chi. It was Zheng Manqing and Robert Smith's introduction to the thirty-seven-posture form, the form that bears Zheng Manqing's name. It was written for Western students and was a very good reference book and aide-mémoire for the aspiring student of the time—before YouTube and the subsequent explosion of film available at the click of a mouse.

As a method of learning the form, however, it left a lot to be desired. I still remember standing, book in my left hand, trying to decipher the terse instructions while stepping blindly around the room. It was close to impossible to teach myself satisfactorily, I concluded, and began looking for a teacher.

The book still proved valuable, however. Of more immediate benefit at the time were the general chapters on tai chi, focusing on the history, principles, and thoughts of Zheng Manqing. These thoughts included a list of the benefits accrued from practice: namely the flexibility of an infant, the health of a lumberjack, and the wisdom of a sage. "Wow!" I thought, and all for just seven to ten minutes of practice a day? Who would not want that?

Another well-known teacher cites the benefits of practice as good health, psychological well-being, and a truly functional system of self-defense.

As sales pitches go, this was pretty hard to beat: the promise of health, happiness, and personal safety—all the major fear groups addressed. And indeed, there is much truth contained therein, although all these years later I am, myself, wary of overselling, as there are plenty of examples of tai chi players who become ill or depressed or fall victim to assault.

Fortunately or unfortunately for the tai chi equivalent of the dodgy market trader, there is a simple, if dubious, get-out clause in the implicit contract: "What? Your condition hasn't improved. You can't have been doing it right." The failure of the art to live up to the hype can easily be blamed on the customer. After all, who actually practices twice a day, every day? Miss a day's practice and the guarantee is void.

I had a similar experience with a couple of evangelizing religionists who turned up at my house one day and asked me to read a chapter of their holy book so my heart would be opened. I felt some pity for their situation, as they were constantly faced with rejection on the doorstep, and occasionally outright hostility, so I agreed to their request. They returned a week later to check on my progress. When I reported that the chapter in question had not resulted in any noticeable opening of my heart to the spirit, they chastised me venomously, warning me of the dangers that would befall me for not reading the chapter properly. It was a case of damned if you read it and damned if you don't—literally. My pity evaporated and I threw them out.

At least I was on safer ground with tai chi, right? My eternal soul was not in jeopardy—only my health, sanity, and personal safety.

In truth, the vague sense of despair I carried around for many years began to lift shortly after I embarked on my tai chi studies. My health improved, as did my stress levels, measured, in the first instance, by the health of my teeth, which needed less attention from the butcher masquerading as a dentist, in whom I had mistakenly placed my trust. (Perhaps even my judgment of character improved, as I later found a very competent dentist.)

My confidence in the world was growing and my devotion to tai chi and the Dao felt so true that I reduced my working hours so I might study with Laoshi more closely. I felt I was being protected by the Dao and, provided I did not break any of the unwritten rules, I would continue to develop my qi, which would protect me in my new shiny, happy, healthy, and safe life. Since the Daoist approach to life is not one of rules and regulations, I felt confident I would not be breaking any, and I relied on my conscience to be my guide.

There were, of course, a few challenges along the way, like the minor car accident I suffered some years after starting class. The resulting debilitating backache was merely a challenge to be overcome and learned from. In everything else, my life seemed blessed.

Then it happened. Jumping out of bed one morning to answer the phone, my back "exploded." It was unlike anything I had ever encountered before. I could hardly move. I was terrified, but not as terrified as when I began to experience numbness in my right leg. Worse was to come in the following hours, as the numbness spread across my pelvis and into my left leg as well. I had known fear before, but not like this. Those few hours were among the worst of my life. I feared I was going to be paralyzed.

After a long day and a dark night of the soul, I called for an ambulance in the early hours of the morning to take me to the hospital, where I had an emergency operation that same evening. To have left it another few hours, I was told, would have resulted in irreversible damage. I was in shock. Tai chi for health? Really?

I was utterly disheartened. Lying in a hospital bed in great pain, unable to do anything and, essentially, paralyzed from the waist down was a major shock to my worldview. A disc in my spine had prolapsed and was pressing on my sciatic nerve. This was not supposed to happen to me. I was on my path, after all. Tai chi was supposed to protect me from just this sort of thing. What had gone wrong? My faith in the Dao and tai chi was shattered.

Worse still, the words of Zheng Manqing came mind: "When the Pillar of Heaven collapses, what hope can there be?" The Pillar of Heaven for Zheng Manqing was the spine, and mine had definitely collapsed.

As I waited for the operation, I feared worse to come, as they advised me the longer the delay, the greater the possibility of permanent loss of function—if not paralysis, then potential double incontinence. My will to live was leaving me. How could I live like that? I entreated the doctor, "If you make a mistake on the operating table and cut my sciatic nerve, just finish me off." The doctor looked at me with a blank expression. "I'll give you something for your depression," he said. I grasped hold of his sleeve and fixed his gaze to mine. "I'm not depressed," I said weakly. "I just don't want to live in a wheelchair."

The operation went as well as could be expected. I woke up on the lift back to the ward, in no pain and able to move my legs. I relaxed and slept until morning.

I began my physical rehabilitation, but mentally I was more fragile than at any time in my life. I felt truly lost; the faith I had in tai chi was severely, if not permanently, dented. I did not know whether my back would recover fully, and fear became my companion when the visiting bell sounded and friends returned home.

After a few days Laoshi came to see me. At first I did not want to see him. I felt ashamed. I had let myself down and I had let him down. I was at a loss to know which was worse.

"How are you feeling?" he asked quietly as he took a seat by my bed.

"Terrible," I replied, not even looking up. "Look at this. They have me connected to a catheter and bag, as I cannot even piss on my own."

My mind had been plagued with the lyrics to a Billy Connolly song "Sergeant, Where's Mine?" about a soldier lying paralyzed in a hospital bed:

> I'm lyin' in bed, I'm in room 26
> Thinkin' on things that I've done
> Like drinkin' wi' squaddies and bullin' my boots
> And countin' the medals I've won
>> These hospital wards, they're drab-lookin' joints
> But the ceiling's as much as I see
> It could do with a wee touch of paper or paint
> But then again, maybe that's me
>> Oh sergeant, is this the adventure you meant
> When I put my name down on the line?
> All that talk of computers and sunshine and skis
> Oh, I'm askin' you, sergeant, where's mine?

As I was telling Laoshi, a rush of anger came over me. "Laoshi, where's mine?"

His gaze did not waver. He paused for a moment, then took a breath and said, "You feel betrayed by the Way. This I understand. You made a commitment to the Dao and you feel it has deserted you. What is worse, you feel it has deserted you just when you needed it most."

My anger abated slightly. He seemed to know what I was feeling and did not appear to judge me.

"It happens to us all," he continued quietly. "We find the one thing in life we can believe in, that we can trust in, that we can live our lives by—and then it shits on us."

I was a little surprised. Laoshi never talked like this. He was always sincere, but he did not use coarse language very often.

There was a moment of quietness, amplified by the sterile hospital surroundings; then he continued, "All I can say to you is this: what has happened to you is also part of the Way and we all go through something like this. Even the great ones like grandmaster Ueshiba had to endure bitter periods. His words are a testament to this: 'In extreme situations, the entire universe becomes our foe.' That he was a sincere and noble man who followed the Way with every fiber of his being did not spare him these trials. They await all of us. We cannot escape them."

"Then what is the point of studying tai chi?" I asked, mildly irritated by the we-have-to-endure mantra that is a common theme of the quasi–martial arts master on TV and in fiction.

"The study of tai chi," Laoshi said, "is a series of abandonings. You abandon hard, stiff force and look for the soft power consistent with the qi. You abandon your own resistance and insistence, and blend with the energy of the universe. You abandon the desperate need to achieve. You abandon the impulse to protect what you have gained. And finally, you abandon the Way itself.

"We are human and we recognize our vulnerability in this world, so we cling to whatever makes us feel less afraid. We cling to distractions like alcohol, drugs, or television when the pain of reality becomes too much to bear. We cling to ideas of morality in order to bargain with our fellow man so we can preserve the illusion that we are civilized. We cling to religion, hoping our prayers will soften God's heart and stay his hand. We cling to the law to control the excesses that lurk in our hearts, and we cling to family as a final refuge when all goes astray. All the while, the Way is gradually stripping away what we cling to, dumbfounding our expectations and attachments.

"Some of us understand this intuitively, but mistakenly seek refuge in martial arts or philosophies of liberation, thinking we are safer because we have some insight into our own plight. The rational mind fools itself into thinking it has found a solution, but it is still the same clinging, only clouded in illusion. The Dao uses strong medicine to deal with this particular illness."

I was utterly deflated. Laoshi had come along to cheer me up and I felt even worse. I rounded on him, "Are you telling me this is my own fault because I was deluded enough to think studying tai chi would help me in my life and make me feel less afraid?"

"No, no," he replied with a shake of his head. "Studying the Way helps you by not adding to the burden life offers you. In time, you will come to see life is a series of ups and downs. This cannot be avoided, and indeed, should not be avoided. It gives flavor to life. However, we are eminently capable of causing ourselves phenomenal suffering by our own actions. Study of the Way trains us to avoid what can be avoided and endure what cannot.

"You remember the Daoist story of the farmer and the horse?" Laoshi asked.

"Uh-huh, I know, Laoshi," I responded. I had been given this lesson before many times. "Good and bad are relative and they change, and things are only as good or bad as our opinions make them. But what has that to do with what can be avoided and what cannot?"

He nodded, acknowledging my point. "I don't think you have missed the fact that I tell these stories over and over." A small smile. "The reason I do so is because the stories are multilayered. On a superficial level, the story of the farmer and the horse gives comfort to people by suggesting good luck will follow bad. On a more sophisticated level, as you have just mentioned, it suggests good luck and bad luck are defined as much by what we think as what actually happens. But on a deeper level still—and this is important for you—how you react emotionally to events is the key. When bad things happen, we tend to catastrophize and become self-destructive."

I held up my hands as if to ward off the point. "OK, OK, but isn't it better to have the horse?"

"Maybe," he replied, "maybe not. But that is not the issue. The point is to live in the moment with what happens, not to project failure into the future. We have to live without clinging to fantasies, to live without clinging even to the Dao. The Way cannot be grasped by the rational mind, but we need something to give us a clue and get us started. The point is not to create false expectations about the Way. Then, when the time comes, we find the courage to abandon the Way and to bond more intuitively with life."

The concept was not new to me, but it was just that—a concept. I knew the finger could be mistaken for the moon, as the Buddhists might say, but this time the significance seemed more immediate for me.

I remembered Laoshi once talking about how Master Huang Xingxian (黃性賢) only began to get "it" when he gave up tai chi in frustration at his lack of progress. The implication was that the method itself had become the hindrance to further progress, and when he stopped trying to make it happen, it did. But how do we know when to give up? I pressed Laoshi to tell more, saying, "But surely there is a chance we abandon the Way too soon and fool ourselves into thinking we have arrived when we have not."

"Ah, you see the problem," Laoshi said, lifting his finger to indicate the significance of the point. "The rational mind wants to know when to give up. If you 'know' when to give up, it is just a tactic of the mind. You cannot decide to give up. You just say, 'Fuck it,' and you have given up. In a real sense, it gives you up, not the other way around. It cannot be faked. It must be total. Then there is a chance of a breakthrough. This is where you go past technique. You cling to nothing, not even the boxing method. You reach the point of practice that is, as the Japanese say, *mushotoku*."

"What does that mean?" I interrupted.

"It means to act without wanting to achieve a result. It means you are spontaneous. It means you practice because it is an expression of who you are. Everything gets dropped and you are just what you are."

I was beginning to see what he was talking about. The Dao was not a crutch, even though most of us sought some comfort in the idea of a benign Dao enveloping us. At some point we have to give up that notion. I also saw that until we reach the point where we are ready to abandon even the Dao to arrive at complete spontaneity, there is a benefit to using the Dao as if it were an intermediary with cruel destiny. By allying ourselves with an energy greater than ourselves, we derive comfort in an insecure world and, by following a path of wisdom and power, we limit our own self-destructive inclinations. Like a child who has limitations to prevent him from hurting himself, so the Way limits us to keep us safe, while at the same time preparing us for the time when we no longer need it.

"Have you given up the Way, Laoshi?" I asked after a pause.

"Very nearly a few times," he said, picking up his jacket to leave, "but I am stubborn. I think I need very strong medicine to cure me of the Way, as, I think, do you. See you soon."

Chapter 15: Is That So?

It is always interesting when a student from another school pays us a visit. Some come only to watch, others to assess if there is any merit in pursuing the art as we do. In their presence, I often detect in myself and others an undercurrent of tension as we lay ourselves open to evaluation by an outsider. The honor of the school is at stake after all, and some of us feel the need to present Laoshi's approach in the best possible light, although Laoshi himself seems singularly unaffected.

Not all teachers allow visitors to observe. Billy, my aikido teacher, allowed no one to watch, though all were welcome to take part. I harbor the suspicion that Laoshi permitted visitors precisely because it made some of us feel uncomfortable. He once said, "Zheng Manqing has told us when practicing alone, we should do the form as if someone is watching, and when doing the form in public, as if no one is watching." He continued, "We can use the visits of others to help us understand what this means. It is all right to feel a little intimidated when people are watching; it tells us something of where we are. Of course, it is much better if we are not affected by their presence, and even better if we forget they are there."

I suspected Laoshi was talking more about our "spiritual" progress than our technique. Most of us, in our daily lives, are so sensitive to the opinions of others that we mentally and emotionally contort and misshape ourselves to the point where balance is no longer possible. The seeds sown in the mind soon come to fruition in the body. Part of our practice is to develop a stronger center so as to be gradually less affected by the opinions of others.

I have firsthand experience of how even the benign presence of other people can virtually derail confidence years in the making. It happened while I was holidaying in Canada one summer, about three years after I began studying tai chi. I had not yet met Laoshi and was studying with another teacher. I had learned the Zheng Manqing form, as well as the original Yang long form and a sword form. I felt I was making progress in push-hands and other partner exercises. All this, combined with my experience in other martial arts, wrought in me confidence that bordered on arrogance.

Not long after my arrival in Welland, Ontario, I discovered a tai chi class not far from where I was staying with relatives of a friend. I decided to pay them a visit in the role of assessor. Such was my superior state of mind at the time.

There were about forty people in the hall, a mix of senior citizens and students from the local college. The teachers were a couple who appeared to be in their sixties. My confidence was undaunted. My initial assessment, arrived at even before they had started their form, placed their standard as clearly below mine.

One of the teachers approached me, asking if I wanted to join in. She was very friendly and warm. I brusquely informed her I would just watch. I took a seat at the back and waited for them to begin.

They did a few warm-up exercises and then proceeded to do the Zheng Manqing form, albeit with no shoulder width in the step and with a forward tilt in their postures. I was not overly impressed but, like the respectful martial artist I thought myself to be, I was not going to embarrass them by pointing out their faults. I was not an insensitive brute after all.

About halfway through there was a break, and the warm, friendly lady came over to speak to me again.

"Do you do tai chi?" she asked, leaning toward me, as I had not bothered to stand up.

"Oh, yes," I answered. "I've been doing it for about three years."

"Three years," she echoed politely. "And where do you come from?"

"Scotland," I said. "I'm just over here for a few weeks and I saw your class advertised."

"What style do you do?" the lady inquired.

"The same as you," I replied, "but we have a shoulder-width stance and we do not lean forward."

The conversation carried on courteously in that vein for a few moments more before she returned to lead the class.

As they were about to finish, she again approached me to ask if I would mind showing the class how the art was practiced in Scotland. I agreed with undue alacrity borne of brimming self-confidence, thinking, I am ashamed to admit, "About time."

I stood up and walked onto the floor as she introduced me as a fellow tai chi student from Scotland who was going to show them our form. Now, it was not that I was unused to speaking in public, having filled in for my teacher at one or two aikido classes and having worked as an instructor in a youth organization, but, as I approached the center of the room, I began to feel extremely nervous. I experienced a cold sweat for the first time in years and, as I stood there before forty pairs of eyes, I felt my knees start trembling. This very definite physical reaction fuelled my anxiety and I commenced to spiral downward in confidence.

I began the form, shaking enough to be concerned that I might not be able to maintain my balance as I took my steps. I felt like a newborn foal as I struggled toward the first single-whip posture. Then, somewhere before I reached cross-hands posture, less than one-third of the way into the form, I experienced a complete mental blank. I simply could not recall what posture followed. I found myself improvising a form, doing whatever movement came to my body, all the while panicking. "How do I get out of this form?" Nothing seemed familiar, and I could not think clearly enough to get to cross hands and finish.

I do not know how long I was imprisoned in this "form," but finally I found myself in the withdraw-and-push posture and saw a way to escape. I was able to conclude the form and stood there in completion posture, feeling totally humiliated. But my audience was very kind—kinder than I had been to them— and gave me a round of applause.

With no hint of irony, the other teacher asked me, "How long have you been doing tai chi?"

"Three years," I muttered.

"Three years, everybody," he repeated enthusiastically for all to hear.

I left as soon as I could.

I learned a lot from that incident. Never again would I watch another class with such a haughty attitude. Never again would I underestimate the effect an audience could have on me. And never again would I be so eager to show off my form.

However, I also learned to use the opportunity to feel how my center was developing each time I was being watched by a stranger. I have not yet reached the place where I might do a form completely oblivious to the presence of others, but I am getting closer. Sometimes I forget about them for long periods of the form, my awareness immersed in breath, or root, or flow—whatever I happen to be focusing on at the time.

As is often the case, this lesson from the tai chi studio translates readily from practice hall to everyday life, with more than a few parallels concerning how we have been educated into needing the good opinion of others. The psychotherapist Anthony de Mello likens our need for approval to a drug administered in childhood. He comments on our addiction to the "positive strokes" that made us feel loved and wanted as infants and the incredible lengths to which we will go in order that praise and approval will continue. It is a mark of spiritual maturity to be unaffected by other people's opinions and to absent ourselves from the foolishness that follows as we clamor for the approval of others.

When I mentioned my Canadian experience to Laoshi one cold morning after practice, he told me the story of the Zen master Hakuin, who endured the hostility of his village due to a false allegation that he had fathered a young girl's child.

His experience among the villagers went from veneration at the outset to castigation and antagonism in the wake of the accusation, to isolation as he tended without complaint to the needs of the baby, and finally to reverence once again when the truth emerged. All he would say in response to the accusation and abuse was, "Is that so?"

"Of course," Laoshi continued, "the story is just a story. Life is sometimes a little more complicated. I was once invited to teach a workshop in Spain by a prominent wealthy businessman. He had become fascinated by tai chi and pursued the art by inviting teachers to his native shores to hold seminars for the entertainment of him and his friends.

"I liked the man and his friends well enough, and I was impressed by their desire to learn. The workshop I was teaching took place over a weekend and was going well when, near the end of the first day, a wealthy Dutch woman and her traveling companion, both visiting friends of the businessman, came to watch. We did not speak, but later that evening my host invited me to a dinner party at his well-appointed house, along with the Dutch-ess, her companion, and others.

"Her companion bored us for a while with a lecture on matters of popular psychology, a field in which he claimed expertise. The Dutch-ess nodded, interrupting from time to time to remind us all of our great good fortune to be in the presence of such brilliance. She even had time to correct me on my table manners, at one point reaching across me to put my fork and knife in the right place after I had left them scandalously adrift on the plate.

"Like Hakuin, I did not react, but unlike Hakuin, I was very angry. Exactly who did she think she was?

"After some time, the companion paused, no doubt feeling the effects of the impressive quantity of wine he had managed to drain between morsels of food in and mouthfuls of dreariness out. The conversation turned to tai chi. At last, something to salvage the party. But my relief proved short lived when the Dutch-ess felt it appropriate to inform me she did not think too much of my form, and that some of the students in the course were better. This was in spite of the fact that she had never practiced any tai chi herself.

"I was a lot younger and far more inexperienced than now and simply did not know what to say. I was almost glad when the companion, suitably refreshed, resumed his monologue on the vagaries of psychodynamic theory.

"There were a number of irritations that weekend, including travel delays and a three-hour wait at the airport for the businessman to collect me, his mobile phone switched off. There was also his attempt to short change me on the fee for my services. Nevertheless, in hindsight, it was a valuable experience. As with your experience in Canada, I was forced to reflect upon my centeredness, or lack of centeredness, in unexpectedly trying circumstances.

"I asked myself, what should I have done? But then I realized that was to miss the point. There was no 'should have done' this or that. My gongfu was simply not deep enough to deal with the situation. No course of action would have been appropriate from a place of resentment and anger. Appropriate behavior comes from a deepening of gongfu, to the point where the ill-mannered behavior of others is more a matter of mild amusement than biting critique.

"Many of us who feel angered at rude or insensitive treatment look to arm ourselves with witty or withering ripostes for defense against similar attack in the future. But we would be wiser to develop our centeredness and let our actions emerge from clarity of perception and spontaneity of mind. Such development is not about techniques found in self-help books, but rather in the practice of a method. Tai chi is a method for deepening our gongfu, which in this case can be applied to the caustic comments of insecure, status-obsessed hungry ghosts of modern times."

As I considered Laoshi's experience in Spain and my own in Canada, I understood he was drawing my attention to the question of knowing versus being. Knowing the art is not enough; we have to be the art. Our modern expectation is that there will be a technique or a formula for dealing with each and every one of our problems. We ask ourselves, "What should I do?" when it might be wiser to ask, "How should I be?"

Chapter 16: Chasing the Sparrow's Tail

十
字
手

The Zheng Manqing form starts off with a series of four postures collectively known as grasp the sparrow's tail. These four postures form the basis of the Professor's approach to push-hands, the part of the *quan* (拳 boxing method) I find most interesting. If what Laoshi's former teacher Wang Lang says is true—that we all have a lead discipline in our tai chi that informs the rest—then push-hands fulfills that role for me, exhilarating and frustrating by turns, but always stimulating my interest and exercising my intuition. It is the vanguard of my study and the place where my insights, such as they are, spring from.

Push-hands is an elusive skill to pin down, even for the experienced student. It is a subtle game where the rules are not clear and the goals keep changing. I wonder, occasionally, if it is deliberately designed this way in order to discourage us from the mistaken view that we may have at last mastered it. No sooner has a little progress occurred than we make discovery of a deeper level, just at the very limits of our ability and understanding.

Professor Zheng describes push-hands as follows in his book *Master Cheng's New Method of Taichi Ch'uan Self-Cultivation*:

> Grasp the Sparrow's Tail is an ancient dance similar to "Grasp the Ox's Tail." But here it is employed as a generic term applied to the four movements Ward-Off, Roll-Back, Press, and Push—the basic postures of push-hands. Push-hands is a two-man form that emphasizes sticking and adhering to an opponent. Both partners alternately perform these four basic moves, circling back and forth, trying not to disconnect or resist. A player's arms are compared to a sparrow's tail, which each opponent tries to grasp. Push-hands develops a sensitivity for interpreting energy and is indicative of this exercise's potential for high levels of awareness.

As if the method itself were not difficult enough, there seems to be a limitless variety in the way teachers within the tradition understand and teach push-hands.

Laoshi often told us of his frustration at the outset of his training with one of his early teachers, who, as a virtual novice in push-hands himself, would preside over such a variety of approaches that learning seemed all but impossible.

"I remember my first push-hands class," Laoshi recalled one day. "I paired up with a senior student as we engaged in fixed-step pushing. As one of the seniors, he took it upon himself to advise me that I must keep going back as I was pushed. He could go so far back as to be almost sitting on the heel of his back foot, but was bent in the middle like a half-closed penknife. The next student did not go back at all when I pushed him. He said I was going back too much and that it was all about turning. The next student added to my confusion with another strategy: he held his arm out rigidly before him and just rooted against my push before, with seemingly indecent haste, grabbing my arm and heaving me off balance. There was a considerable degree of argument among the students as to which method was correct, with Lenny, the teacher, in the role of ineffectual referee. As a result, he oversaw something of a free-for-all, giving freedom to his students to pursue any crackpot idea they dreamed up. Had the students not been fairly decent human beings, things could have turned nasty, as debate about superior technique could have escalated into something more physical. It was a classic example of how too much freedom may be detrimental, but it reflected my teacher's avowed philosophical position of not using his power over people.

"The confusion was compounded by the supposed solution," Laoshi continued. "In an attempt to educate both himself and his students in the finer points of push-hands, he invited a whole procession of teachers to Glasgow to conduct workshops. Although this was a noble attempt to remedy the problem, it was wasted by the fact that these teachers too were all doing something different, and usually not that well—a sad reflection on the immaturity of the art in the UK at that time.

"I was terribly frustrated by this," Laoshi said, "and I asked my teacher Lenny once why everybody was doing something different.

"He answered, 'They're not. They're all doing the same thing. You just can't see it.'

"I might have been convinced my perception was lacking," Laoshi said, "but my confidence in Lenny later went through the floor when he told me of a conversation he had with another student. This student was having a crisis of confidence in regard to his practice. His sincere attempts to learn had yielded nothing. In particular, he was dismayed because, after six months of faithful study, he had yet to feel the warm tingling in his hands, as described by other students. Lenny assured him progress would come and it was only a matter of time. Later, however, Lenny told me, 'I didn't have the heart to tell him I've been doing this shit for twenty years and I've not felt a fucking thing.'

"As one class wag remarked to me, 'It's not that Lenny has twenty years' experience in tai chi; it's that he has had two years' experience, ten times.' While some students did not seem unduly bothered by the level of push-hands on offer, I was more ambitious and was looking for progressive training rather than the pass-the-time variety he was offering. I made a mental note to myself: time to change teachers."

Laoshi's frustration spurred him on in his efforts to find teachers who could deliver deeper levels of understanding in push-hands. Most of us, his students, were grateful to find ourselves inheritors of the knowledge he gained in those early years. Although the adventurer in me understands the draw of traveling to far-off lands to become immersed in the exotic before finding the master our hearts have been seeking, I realize that is no easy task. Some years earlier, I had even tried it myself, heading off to India in an ill-conceived and poorly executed search for my guru, secure in the knowledge that it would all work out in the end. What actually happened was that I was detained at Delhi airport and deported by the authorities before my search could actually begin. As a result of my experiences, I realized the search for a real teacher would require something more concrete than an airline ticket and a romantic notion.

Having been blessed by finding a gifted aikido teacher in Billy Coyle in my home city, I presumed, incorrectly, that good teachers were ten a penny and that even better teaching was to be found in fabled lands to the East. There is a certain romanticism to this notion, but it could also be regarded as a sort of inverse racism, as an acquaintance of mine once demonstrated by telling me he was specifically looking for a Chinese tai chi teacher. When I asked him why, he replied, "No Westerner has the real oil. The Chinese would not teach a Westerner the real secrets of the art." His delusion, as with any really good delusion, did not limit itself with even a miniscule helping of elementary logic. He seemed oblivious to the fact that, by his own logic, as a Westerner himself, he would be served the mediocre fare he wished to have no part of.

Laoshi also found his search for the authentic to be time consuming and expensive. He told us once how many teachers, even those within the Zheng Manqing lineage, did not teach push-hands at all, and those who did often avoided using the peng-lu-ji-an method.

"On a trip to New York," Laoshi explained, "I made contact with a teacher who had studied extensively with Zheng Manqing during the sixties and seventies. This teacher took me to a push-hands session with Stanley Israel, one of Zheng Manqing's most senior students. From my observation, I could find no evidence of peng-lu-ji-an, rather a lot of sumo-type pushing and shoving up and down the floor. I joined the session in progress but found my push-hands skills did not measure up in such forceful company. It was Sunday evening and the room was full of strong young men bracing against each other—calling to mind Zheng Manqing's image of bulls butting heads. In this class, however, forcefulness was virtue, not fault. There were even a couple of young men drilling some wrestling moves, and another pair wearing judo gis, pulling each other so as to collide chest to chest.

"I was astonished. It was so entirely different from anything I had experienced previously. I noticed the teacher who had taken me to Stanley's class—and who had pushed hands with me, very skillfully, earlier that day using the peng-lu-ji-an method—did not take part. 'Why do you come here?' I asked him. 'Well, sometimes there is someone to fence with,' he replied.

"It was my baptism into what has been described as the 'religious wars' of tai chi," Laoshi continued. "On one side are the devotees of softness and co-operative communion who worship at the altar of 'no more than four ounces.' On the other side, the 'sacrilegious' promulgators of a more pragmatic and competitive liturgy. I was faced with a choice between a faith-based, arcane approach to push-hands and a no-nonsense 'intelligent use of strength' path. I chose the former and returned to my study of peng-lu-ji-an in order to discover its secrets.

"From my interaction with Stanley Israel's students that day I gained the impression that, to them, the peng-lu-ji-an approach was a basic exercise to be used prior to the real stuff. In practicing with them, however, I learned some of the students who attended the class did not even know of its existence. I was pushing with a young man from upstate New York who regularly made the Sunday evening trek down to Manhattan to attend class. He traveled with his teacher, a former student of the Professor. After we had been pushing hands freestyle for a while, he asked me, 'So, is this how you push hands where you come from?' When I replied it was not, he asked me to show him our style. He was intrigued and called to his teacher to come and observe. 'Look at what this guy is doing,' he said.

"His teacher replied, 'Yeah, that's the real push-hands,'" Laoshi said.

"I could tell this came as a surprise," he added. "The young man then asked his teacher, 'Then why have you never taught me this?' His teacher made no reply."

As Laoshi wound up this story, a fellow student asked why he had chosen to concentrate on the peng-lu-ji-an approach. "I did not choose it; it chose me," Laoshi replied. "You can only study what your heart allows. To do otherwise is to do violence to your soul."

As a result, Laoshi's push-hands classes concentrated on a deep study of the peng-lu-ji-an method, with the less-structured free pushing relegated to a supporting exercise practiced occasionally. Class consisted of pairs of students lined up against a wall, one partner with his back to the wall, the other facing him.

Practiced this way, the distance between one and the other is close, probably as close as possible without entering the realms of grappling, with both students in front stances with their lead feet parallel, as if they were the sides of a rectangle. It is important to note that the students are not standing face to face, but slightly to the side of each other. This off-center setup may appear slight, but it is of major importance in push-hands.

Most people coming to push-hands, myself included, initially, do not question why the set-up position should be so close. Neither do they ask why their partner might be standing slightly to the side of them rather than directly face to face. If they do, they are likely to be told the position is more effective in deflecting a falling opponent to the side rather than have him fall right on top of you, if, in desperation, he resorts to launching himself forward as he falls.

Laoshi's explanation, however, reflected years of exploration in push-hands and an understanding of minor details and their significance: "You practice at this distance to become familiar with the fighting distance preferred in tai chi," he told us. "You become comfortable at this distance when face to face with another human being. Over time, and with practice, your instinct will be to close to this distance and contest matters from there. You understand fighting distance is a critical concept in martial arts: kicking arts prefer a greater distance, while punching arts prefer a shorter distance—but tai chi prefers an even shorter distance still. There is, as you are aware, a certain safety in being close to an attacker. The power generated from punching and kicking usually requires space to be most effective.

"Similarly, we practice standing slightly to the side of the partner to get an instinctive feel for and affinity with the position. Standing directly in front of an attacker is dangerous. We are underneath his heavy weapons, so to speak. As karate sensei Gichin Funakoshi reminds us in his Twenty Precepts, 'The fight depends on how you maneuver guarded and unguarded positions.' A slight angle can be enough for us to avoid an attack and be in position to counter to the undefended side of the attacker."

Laoshi's observations afforded me a sudden insight as to one of the practical training methods favored by Billy Coyle in aikido class. He would demonstrate a particular technique while we sat Japanese style and observed. We would then find a partner and practice the technique shown until he clapped his hands. This would be the signal for us to sit once more and receive the next piece of instruction. It became part of our training, however, to first look at Billy in order to see how he was armed—with bokken, jo, tanto, or empty handed. We would then arm ourselves accordingly before sitting down.

I had always assumed this was merely an efficient way to conduct a class, without a teacher requiring to tell students to pick up the appropriate weapon.

After listening to Laoshi, however, it became clear this was a subtle form of training. I suddenly realized my habit when sensing danger from someone I encountered on the street is to immediately look at his hands. It had become a reflex of which I had remained unaware for a long time. To this day I am convinced that these countless glances toward Billy's hands upon his signal clap have resulted in an automatic assessment of any weapons that might be deployed in the hands of an attacker.

It occurred to me that many of the lessons of push-hands were similar. We thought we were learning one thing when, in fact, we were learning something else—something subtler, less explicit. When I put this to Laoshi, he nodded, saying, "This is a good insight. Sometimes we cannot see the point of the practice, and so we make up our own rationale. If we start forcing the techniques we are learning to fit into our own expectation of what they should be, we risk losing the whole point of studying them in the first place."

Laoshi added, "This brings us to peng-lu-ji-an. Many people lose faith in so deceptively simple an exercise and either abandon it or gloss over its teachings. By doing so, they throw away a wonderful gift, that, if understood, can help keep us on the right track. When we have doubts concerning push-hands, we can return to the method and ask ourselves, 'Are we keeping to the purity of the method? Are we maintaining the principles?' As Zheng Manqing said when talking about the teachings of Confucius, 'How do I daily rekindle the teaching that has been passed down to me? Not just think about the teaching, but that it's alive. Even more, that it burns.' The lessons of peng-lu-ji-an should be treated the same way. Do you keep to the spirit of the practice, not just as lip service, but till it burns?

"This is the way it must be," Laoshi continued, "with peng-lu-ji-an. You must study it till it burns. You must study to squeeze every last drop of insight from the method. Only in this way will you develop real ability in push-hands. There is so much hidden in grasp the sparrow's tail, but many people are too impatient and lose faith in what it has to offer. It is all contained in grasp the sparrow's tail."

Laoshi asked us—indeed, demanded—that we make a serious commitment to a way of practice that might seem limiting but was, for him, the key to progress in the pathless land that is push-hands. Sometime later I came across a story that made a similar impression on me. One of Morihei Ueshiba's early students, Gozo Shioda, quoted him regarding *shihonage* (four direction throw): "Shihonage is the foundation of aikido. . . . All you ever need to master is shihonage." Shioda Sensei then tells of a time when a famous judoka, whom he calls "K," came to the Ueshiba dojo to test his skill. One of the senior students, who himself had been a Kodokan third dan, put himself forward to meet the challenge. Perhaps as a result of falling into the pattern of the challenger, he was defeated. The next student to step forward was Zenzaburo Akazawa, who had such faith in Ueshiba that, as Shioda tell us, "He devoted himself solely to the practice of shihonage. Since his daily training only consisted of squeezing as much as he could out of shihonage, outside of this one technique he had almost no other moves. Practically speaking, you would expect it to be difficult for him to put up a good fight against a fourth dan in judo."

Shioda then relates what happened as the judoka came to attack. "Mr. Akazawa took hold of K's wrist, spun around, and shifted his body, and executed a beautiful shihonage. A dull snap came from K's elbow, which had been locked against itself. His elbow was completely destroyed and he couldn't even execute a break-fall."

Shihonage is the most fundamental technique in aikido, but it contains the very essence of the art. In the same way, grasp the sparrow's tail is tai chi in its most basic form, yet it too contains the very essence of the art. As Zheng Manqing might say, "It has meaning." The question is whether or not we can be bothered to look for it.

Chapter 17: Study the Form, It Has Meaning

抱
虎
歸
山

As a teacher Laoshi did not always follow precisely the approach of his own teachers. This was evident in progressing students from form to push-hands. His teacher Wang Lang, for instance, preferred that a student complete Zheng Manqing's thirty-seven-posture form to ensure a solid foundation prior to commencing push-hands. Laoshi, on the other hand, encouraged students to begin push-hands as soon as they wished.

Imagining there must be a reason, I asked Laoshi about the discrepancy between the two approaches.

He explained: "It is a result of my early teaching experience and the dilemma I faced in trying to advance my own training. My first group of senior students was uncommonly receptive to the task we had set ourselves. They embraced the principles of push-hands conscientiously and became soft and sensitive. They became good tai chi players surprisingly quickly, neither resisting nor insisting. They used to joke about being the softest guys in town. Therein lay the problem. The mean streets of any town are not populated by soft, refined, well-schooled tai chi players. We may have been the softest guys around, but I feared we were in danger of refining ourselves into absurdity. I felt I needed to mix it up with more robust, gritty opponents not hampered by our conventions. I felt I needed to say to a push-hands partner, 'Do as you wish,' and be able to deal with those wishes. I wanted to face hard, strong men to learn how to deal with the aggressive and uncooperative.

"As you know," Laoshi continued, "a beginner who is physically big, strong, and shoves with hard force can be a source of limitless frustration, even for a very experienced student. The ability to deal with such force is so difficult to acquire that, as you have seen, a relative novice can have a great deal of success against the best students in the school, using only brute force and speed. As the teacher, I felt in need of more practice with such people, even if they broke the rules of the form and adopted all kinds of strategies, tricks, and deviations. To this end, I even enlisted the help of a friend who weighed more than three hundred and fifty pounds and had an arsenal of dirty tricks at his command. I lost more than I won with this monster, but I always hoped with practice I would be able to match Zheng Manqing, who once said, 'One of my students is seven feet one inch and weighs four hundred and thirty pounds, but I handled him like a child playing with a ball.'

"It was for that reason I admitted those without a solid foundation in the principles of the form to push-hands class. Of course, not all of them became less resistant and insistent over time. Some responded by deviating further and further from the form into erratic, idiosyncratic awkwardness. While this was good practice for me, it was not so for them and I began to lose students who were tiring of being my training tools at the expense of their own progress. It also meant some students, after several years with me, were not much more sophisticated than raw beginners.

"I came to realize that a student who does not pay strict attention to the lessons of the peng-lu-ji-an form denies himself a good foundation on which to build. For these students there is a danger of frustration fuelling a descent into resentment and self-destructiveness. It is another hidden lesson of push-hands: faced with the feeling that they will never 'get it,' many people become unreceptive and begin to react against other people, or themselves. There is a similar pattern in society at large, where those who feel marginalized find their energy diverted into antisocial and self-destructive behaviors. In push-hands, the sparrow's-tail approach provides a framework from which to study what is challenging and comforting in equal measure. There is a reason why we use it.

"Without the refuge of the peng-lu-ji-an method, we would have to practice bad sumo. Not only would we get bored with this fairly quickly, but as our strength diminishes, we would reach a point of permanent irreversible decline in our skill. It is one of the reasons, I believe, why some long-established teachers no longer teach push-hands. After all, there is a huge loss of face to be endured when a raw beginner comes to class and throws the teacher with twenty or thirty years of experience all about the hall.

"On the other hand, if we do not expose ourselves to difficult, unpredictable, and forceful people, we will not learn how to deal with them and, even worse, will demonize them as being at fault. Unconventional and awkward people are a gift to the serious push-hands player—as are raw, pushy beginners who invest heavily in winning.

"I think there is a balance to be found that treads a path between the twin dangers of wild, mindless force and the self-hypnosis of a stilted, lifeless ritual. I feel my job as teacher is to allow enough challenge to the senior students while at the same time schooling the insensitivity out of the gawky greenhorn. Each may benefit: the senior students gradually refine and polish the coarseness of the beginner, while at the same time tempering their own ability in a furnace hot enough to forge them. As long as the polish does not wear away the beauty of the grain and the furnace doesn't melt the steel, both will benefit. It is for this reason I continue to allow less-experienced students to begin push-hands. It is their very inexperience that is helpful to the seniors, who, in turn, are an example for the beginner. It is as Laozi reminds us: 'What is a good man but a bad man's teacher? What is a bad man but a good man's job?'"

Laoshi then took the opportunity to give me an impromptu lecture on the finer points of push-hands, quoting Zheng Manqing's dictum, "Study the form, it has meaning." It was not that he had hitherto failed to mention these points, but I felt readier to receive them and began to realize the extent to which I only paid them lip service in the midst of heated pushing with both "good men" who were my teachers and "bad men" who were my work.

"Remember," he said, "keep the spine straight. Not just straight, but with the tailbone dropped. You study this in the hand form, so why do you discard it in push-hands?" This had been the most important concept drilled into him by Master Lin during Laoshi's trip to Taiwan. "While doing the hand form," Laoshi added, "many of us incorrectly tilt the body forward a little without realizing it, but when it comes to push-hands, the temptation to lean forward into the pusher often proves irresistible. Looked at from the side, you and your partner should resemble the letter H, your spines connecting heaven and earth in a straight line; instead, you often look more like the letter A—heads leaning forward and backsides sticking out."

The lesson of keeping the spine straight was one Laoshi stressed regularly. He told us how the straightness of the spine is not simply aesthetically pleasing; it also aids efficiency in turning at the waist. If the spine is not straight, it is like a bent axle. Following this analogy, the hips and shoulders can be likened to the wheels. If the axle is straight, then turning the hips will result in an equal turn of the shoulders. If the axle is bent, not only will one of the shoulders dip, putting you off balance, but the spine is likely to twist as a result. In push-hands, this in-evitably means more strength will be required to deflect the push of the attacker.

Laoshi also taught if the lower spine is not dropped, then the contact the foot makes with the floor will be less rooted. Ever since Master Lin in Taiwan had told him he had a false root, Laoshi had pondered the old master's observation. After some time, Laoshi came to realize what Master Lin meant: unless the lower spine is dropped, there is no connection between the upper and lower body; there is a break at the hip, and the weight of the body is not efficiently channeled through the leg into the foot. It is akin to stacking building blocks on their edges rather than their sides, leading to instability. In the human body, such instability is compensated by tension in the muscles. Naturally, this is not good for tai chi.

The ability to connect upper and lower body is vital for accessing the soft *jin* (勁) energy sought by tai chi players in preference to the harder *li* (力) energy. Laoshi reminded me of the point: "If you have the arms, the soft connection from shoulder to wrist that expresses the jin energy, then you have nothing; if you have the legs, the dynamic connection that generates the jin, you have nothing. And, if you have both the softness in the arms and the dynamism of the legs, you *still* have nothing. It is only when you connect the softness in the arms with the dynamism of the legs, through the spine, that you are in a position to have it. So, you must study the nothingness in the arms and legs until they become something."

I had heard Laoshi say this many times, and each time I noticed the little smile that came to his lips as he said it. For a long time, I thought he was pleased with himself because it was a good line: study nothingness until it becomes something. It reminded me of the famous line from the Heart Sutra: "Form is emptiness; emptiness is form."

When I mentioned my assumption to one of the senior students, he corrected me. Laoshi was not congratulating himself on a natty line; rather, the phrase contained a double meaning that amused Laoshi.

The first meaning relates to the fact that we must practice a concept that yields no discernible result until, as if by magic, something clicks and the energy of the ground, which is the foundation of the jin energy, becomes available. The second idea is that the actual process of accessing the jin energy requires, as a prerequisite, the elimination of tension in the arms to allow the more dynamic jin energy to make itself known. Until that feeling becomes a reality, taking the hard force out of the arms leaves us with apparently nothing. We have to become comfortable dealing with this nothingness to find progress.

Laoshi moved on to another key principle: "When receiving the push of your opponent, do not resist with tension in the arms. Use the principle of folding. It is one of the most important ideas in push-hands."

As I understood it, folding meant letting the ward-off arm recede toward the body in response to the push. The idea is to entice the pusher in and control him by bringing him close instead of holding him out at a distance.

"Like a planet circling the sun," Laoshi said, "we allow the pusher into orbit around us, under our control until we cut the ties and send him hurtling out into the universe." The first time I ever heard Laoshi mention this principle, I could not help thinking this might be the real meaning of the saying, "Keep your friends close, but your enemies closer."

This aspect of Laoshi's teaching was not without controversy. A number of other teachers advised students to keep the ward-off arm away from the body, as if holding an inflated beach ball, keeping the pusher at arm's length. Since this was a significant point of variance between Laoshi and other teachers, Laoshi was asked about it often. I particularly recall the response he made to a questioner in regard to this principle.

Laoshi said, "One of the Professor's senior students, Dr. Qin, once told me, 'Your fencing is getting good, but your push-hands is rubbish.' I had been studying sword with Qin in London, as I felt there were considerable weaknesses in my understanding of fencing. After he had tutored me in the finer points of his method, he took me to a regular Sunday gathering of Zheng Manqing–inspired students in order that I could test myself against some seasoned fencers. He watched in approval as I held my own fencing in this company, but he was clearly less impressed by my push-hands.

"The next day, Dr. Qin and I went to a small park near his apartment," Laoshi continued. "He told me, 'The mistake you are making is to let your arm collapse into your body when getting pushed.'

"What a disappointment: that same old chestnut. As if I had never heard that before. I tried to counter diplomatically by saying, 'But Wang Lang taught me to let the arm fold, and Master Lin sometimes didn't even present an arm for you to push against. You'd just push directly on his chest.'

"'Hmm . . . well, let's have a go,' Qin suggested.

"We took up position and he pushed," Laoshi said. "I neutralized him easily and pushed him back about ten feet. He tried again and, once more, I yielded to his push, letting him in close before neutralizing a second time and launching him a considerable distance.

"Qin conceded. 'Well,' he said, 'maybe what Wang Lang is doing is OK.'"

Laoshi elaborated: "The argument for practicing fullness in the arm is to develop ability in letting the push connect into the root, immediately bouncing it back as if it were a tennis ball hitting a racquet. This is called receiving energy. However, for the most part those who advocate this approach are using force against force. Zheng Manqing talked of receiving energy as 'a complete negation of the notion of countering force with force. The interpreting, adhering, withdrawing, and attacking energies are all involved in an instant.'

"It is also worth noting that according to Wang Lang, the Professor, in his earlier writings, spoke of receiving energy as the pinnacle of the art; however, in his later work, he seemed to suggest it was really only a starting point. This suggests that while understanding receiving energy is important, the skill of allowing an attacker in—and then neutralizing him so he lands on nothing—is the real pinnacle of the art. By folding and encouraging him to advance beyond his base, you are, as Zheng Manqing would say, setting a trap. Even the strongest man becomes weak when off balance. So, rather than overpower another's root, you allow him to push into nothingness until he falls, before adding your own push. In effect, he is complicit in his own downfall. Now, does this not feel in keeping with a Daoist approach to dealing with conflict?"

Laoshi turned his attention to another often overlooked principle. "Remember," he said, looking directly at me to stress the importance of the point, "keep the three points of contact with the arms as clear and clean as possible."

It was another idea I had heard often but, equally, had often lost sight of when I found myself confronting an opponent who prized winning above purity of technique. In the peng-lu-ji-an style of push-hands, the hands and arms connect in a very particular way. Face to face with someone about to push, the receiver uses his own forearm and hand as a barrier, albeit a soft one, to prevent the pusher from putting hands directly onto the receiver's body. The pusher starts out with two hands on one of the receiver's arms, connecting at the wrist and elbow. This leaves the receiver with a spare hand, which he connects to the outside of one of the pusher's arms, elbow to elbow.

This is far more difficult to describe in words than in practice, and people generally line up this way fairly easily. However, when the circling nature of the form gets going, it can be very difficult to keep the elbows in contact as they whirl around each other. Without this contact, however, the leverage required to deflect the push can be lost.

Still eyeing me directly for emphasis, Laoshi added, "You may question why the elbows should be connected—after all, it is easier to push without thinking of where the elbows should be. If you are just interested in shoving, as you would push a stalled car, then you would keep the elbows out of it, but the car is not going to slip out to the side and neutralize you. It is predictable. Your push-hands partner is not. On the contrary, he is deliberately attempting to deflect you and catch your energy. By pushing as if you were pushing a car, you are making it easy for him by only being able to push in one direction. If you wish to change direction, you have to stop, readjust, and begin pushing again. In martial arts terms, you create a gap your opponent can exploit with a counterattack or simply escape. That is why fighters are seldom successful when throwing one punch. They are taught to throw combinations."

Laoshi continued, "It is similar for us in tai chi, but also different. We do not attempt to combine pushes but, instead, we push with the idea of an expanding hoop, or the ripple created by a stone thrown into a pond. Each and every point on that hoop can issue energy. We are like a wheel that is strong all the way around its circumference. If you push with elbows down, it is like making a wheel with only two spokes."

Laoshi was also keen to stress that practicing push-hands is a means to lead us to an appreciation of a principle that can be useful in our everyday lives. He was also keen to relate the seemingly ritualistic practice of the peng-lu-ji-an method to the fighting arts proper.

"We have to understand the deeper reasons for our method and the value in performing it as we do. As pusher, we learn how to link the body, using the ligaments instead of muscle to channel force from the ground to the hands. With a slight modification, this linking can become a very powerful strike without the need for a windup to generate power. It is the perfect counter-attacking weapon for the short-range fighter. It has the additional benefit of making any part of the arm or body the issuing point of this power—not just the fist or elbow.

"In the role of neutralizer, meanwhile, we are actually trying to develop what Wang Lang called impendence: the ability to 'hear' what the other person is going to do before he does it. Robert Smith relates that Zheng Manqing could hear and distinguish four stages of an attack: planning to attack, getting ready to attack, attack imminent, and finally attacking. This is the real lesson we gain from practicing neutralization. If you know what your opponent is going to do just before he does it, you will have an amazing advantage in a fight. But you cannot gain such sensitivity with arms like sticks. They must be soft. They must be more like antennae.

"Sadly, very few of us want to study this way," Laoshi added. "The reason is as Zheng Manqing has said: 'Nobody believes this is possible.'"

I left Laoshi that day determined to improve my push-hands in the areas he had mentioned. For a long time after, of course, my good intentions quickly evaporated in the heat of pushing, concerned as I was with winning against my fellow students. Over the years, however, Laoshi's words have gradually begun to penetrate my resistance. I am aware that I have slowly changed as a result of following Laoshi's method. The lessons inherent in the peng-lu-ji-an form have developed in me a greater sensitivity to the movement of an opponent and fostered an ability to link the joints of my body effectively for an instant to deliver a push, before immediately softening once more. The method is slow, but then, as Zheng Manqing would say, "Gradually, gradually."

On pleasant summer days, I am in the habit of walking down to the River Kelvin near where I live to practice my form close to nature. It is a lovely little spot, slightly elevated above the river with two trees for shade when it's sunny, or for cover when it rains. There is a path winding along behind, but not many people pass and those who do are neither troubled nor troublesome.

I suppose over time I have become quite possessive of the place, and so I was dismayed to find people close to my spot as I arrived one morning. As I approached, I noticed two men carrying bokken. Moving closer still, I could see one of them was teaching the other some sword movements with which I was unfamiliar.

"What style is this?" I thought, irritated but curious as well.

"Hello," I said as I arrived at my spot. "I guess you guys won't mind if I do a little exercise over there?"

The taller of the two, who appeared to be teaching, was friendly enough, assuring me they would not be disturbed.

On completing my form, I watched for a while as they performed their sword routines. After a few minutes, the teacher came over to chat. He was about forty years old, six feet tall, and lean. He would have been unremarkable save for an almost completely shaved head, highlighted by a long ponytail, which, oddly, seemed to be slightly offset to the side of his skull. The question in my mind was whether this was the result of a school tradition or a dodgy barber. Still his energy was friendly and positive.

"Was that tai chi you were doing?" he asked.

"Yes, that's right," I replied. "What are you doing?"

He mentioned the name of an art that failed to register with me. After asking him twice to repeat it, I thought it rude to ask a third time, and so the precise name of the art has remained a mystery. The only word I could make out was *ryu*, which I knew means "school" or "style" in Japanese.

He told me it is an Oriental sword art and that he was teaching it here in his native Scotland after spending most of his adult life in the East, studying martial arts. He spoke amiably enough—but as we talked, I could not help feeling something was amiss. He said all the right things, but something seemed off-key. I could not quite put my finger on it.

Over the next weeks and months, I would see him from time to time near "my" spot at the river. He did not wear a specific martial arts uniform, but I always spotted the ponytail from afar. He would have one or two students with him and I would sometimes linger to watch awhile. Occasionally we said hello, but mostly we watched each other at practice.

A few months later, I was early for class one evening. Laoshi was there and told me he was expecting a few visitors to class.

"Who are they?" I inquired.

"The man who contacted me is a sword master of some *koryu*, one of the 'old school' styles. It seems he is coming with a high-ranking taekwondo master and one of his own students who, he assures me, is a highly experienced martial artist with extensive knowledge of tai chi."

"Such exalted company at class tonight!" I exclaimed, intrigued and a little excited at the thought of high-grade martial arts masters coming to watch our class.

Shortly after, an unremarkable-looking bearded man in his late forties entered the hall. He was of average height and build, but he carried a harried look, as if constantly expecting the worst. He looked around and approached Laoshi.

"Is this where the sword master is teaching tonight?" he inquired in a slightly edgy tone. He seemed rather high-strung. Could this be the experienced martial artist and tai chi aficionado? It seemed he was. Laoshi advised him that we were, indeed, expecting a visit from some martial artists, but that they would not be teaching. Our visitor nodded, then revealed to Laoshi that he had been studying tai chi for years, but had never had the opportunity to try push-hands and so was keen to give it a go.

As the room filled with Laoshi's regular students, our visitor could not stand still. After changing into a T-shirt sporting the logo of his tai chi school, he paced about and fidgeted and would occasionally start whistling to himself. Laoshi glanced his way from time to time but said nothing.

The look on Laoshi's face was a little strange. It seemed to me Laoshi was quietly ignoring our jumpy visitor, avoiding eye contact, and when he did look our visitor's way, he was not impressed by what he saw.

Shortly afterward, our additional expected visitors made an appearance. I immediately recognized the sword teacher from my practice spot near the river. He was accompanied by a slightly overweight, not-very-athletic-looking young man in his late twenties. He was wearing thick-framed spectacles, which may have been too heavy, as he regularly used his forefinger to slide them back up his nose. His manner was easygoing, but he was clearly the sidekick and subordinate of the sword master. They made their introductions and I realized the other fellow was the anticipated taekwondo master.

Class was a little different that evening, with less form and more push-hands in order that our visitors could get some idea of the content and style of our practice. After the form period of class had ended and we transitioned into push-hands, our visiting duo seemed to be actively avoiding contact with any of Laoshi's students, preferring, instead, to pair with each other. Laoshi, meanwhile, spent some time with the "experienced" tai chi student to introduce him to push-hands. I had no doubt Laoshi would be curious to discover the skill level of an experienced tai chi player from another school. As they connected hands, Laoshi said, "Push." The fellow obliged. Laoshi turned his body very slightly in response to the push, and Mr. Experienced fell to the floor. Laoshi sighed and then helped him up, and spent a few more minutes with him in instruction before letting him practice with some of the other students.

At the end of class, all three visitors approached Laoshi to say thank you and goodbye. I never saw them again. The sword master never returned to practice beside the river.

After allowing some time to pass, I asked Laoshi if he had heard from our visitors in the intervening period.

"No, but then I did not expect to," he replied.

"Really? Why not," I asked, curious at Laoshi's complete lack of concern.

Laoshi explained: "Martial arts are a playground for all sorts of people. While many are sincere, there are also lots of . . . what could we call them?" He paused, searching for a word. "Eccentrics? If you were less kind, you might call them 'fantasists.' They have created in their minds a persona such as 'warrior sage' or 'budo master.'

"You must have met them in your aikido days," Laoshi said, smiling. "The white British teachers, for instance, who affect Japanese accents when teaching, to better fit their heroic images of themselves?"

I had, indeed. I recalled an experienced teacher from central Scotland who would teach in a Japanese accent, making hissing sounds and repeatedly intoning "Hoh" and "Ah so." Such wannabes amused my old teacher, Billy, who observed that some wanted to be samurais so much that "They would have an operation to narrow their eyes if they could."

Billy had a unique way of bringing some of the young bucks, who tended toward fantasy, down to earth.

"I ask them," he told me, smiling, "if they are aware that most samurais had sex with young boys. There is even a name for it: *wakashudo*—the way of the youth. They don't like hearing that!" he said, laughing.

I could well imagine. Working-class Glasgow in the 1960s was a pretty macho place. The youth of the day craved the reputation of "hard men." In a city where being "pure fucking mental" in regard to violence was a compliment, the implied effeminacy of being "a poof" was the ultimate slander. Some years later, however, the sensibilities of the "mean city" seem to have changed. Glasgow has become wealthier and no longer deserves the unsolicited accolade of "stabbing capital of Europe." It would appear the persona of "hard man" is giving way to a new veneer: *les hommes débonnaires*.

"What is wrong with these people?" I asked Laoshi, referring to our guests in particular, but the type in general.

"You must not be too scathing of them," Laoshi responded. "They are just like the rest of us, only a little more idiosyncratic. We all have a view of ourselves based on some ideas that have taken root in our psyche. These ideas have grown to create a screen between ourselves and reality."

Laoshi continued, "We all tell ourselves stories about who we are and the world around us. Much of our behavior stems from these narratives and, incomplete as they are, we could not do without them. Our world feels too complicated to live in without mental models that help us to understand what is going on and to predict what will happen. One of the most important of these narratives surrounds our notion as to whether the world is essentially benign or hostile. Much of how we react to events depends on the answer to that question.

"The important thing to understand is, necessary as they are, these stories are simply stories. Our stories can change, and as they change, we change. This is what is meant by 'As a man thinketh, so he is.'"

"But how can we make our stories, and ourselves, change?" I asked.

Laoshi smiled. "There is no need," he said. "Just becoming aware will generate change within you. This too is part of the Way. When you really begin to see something is a delusion, you will drop it—just as when you feel tension in the body, it gradually dissolves."

"Are these stories a kind of tension in the mind, then?" I asked.

"You could say that," he said, nodding. "The tension comes from a deep-seated fear and the biggest delusion of them all: that we are separate from the universe."

Chapter 19: Cross Swords

倒
撵
猴
右

Laoshi's teacher Wang Lang once told him of an incident concerning Stanley Israel, one of Zheng Manqing's "big six," the most senior students in the school. According to Wang Lang, Stanley did not spend much time fencing with the rest of the students at Shr Jung, Zheng Manqing's school in New York. As a result, his fencing was not as accomplished as the rest of his study. Perhaps with that in mind, he approached Wang Lang and asked him if they could do some fencing together to further his understanding.

Wang Lang was delighted and, indeed, honored that Stanley should seek him out and, in effect, ask for his help. They arranged to meet and began fencing. At the time, Wang Lang was seriously studying fencing and had put in a good many hours developing this part of the system. As a consequence, he was able to cut Stanley at will.

By the time they finished, Wang Lang, who was thoroughly delighted with his own performance, asked Stanley what he thought. Stanley's reply was as unexpected as it was troubling. "What you do is quite interesting," he said, "but I noticed it is not what really good fencers do."

To his credit Wang Lang did not simply dismiss the comment but pondered the matter. After a while he came to realize all his skill in fencing up to that point had little to do with tai chi, and more to do with reflexes and speed. He began to reconsider what he was doing, as he realized those reflexes would diminish with age and his understanding would start going backward.

Laoshi related this tale to the fencing class at regular intervals to remind us progress is not to be defined simply by who can cut whom, but how a person does it. For Laoshi, just as good push-hands relied on a deep understanding of yin and yang, so fencing had to incorporate the same ideas to develop beyond slashing and hacking with speed and strength.

Naturally, we first had to acquire some understanding of the basic principles of fencing, but then he would set us to work, looking for how yin and yang manifests within fencing. At this point we were, effectively, moving on to the intermediate level of fencing.

"The first thing to understand at this level," Laoshi said, "is the yin point and the yang point are very close to each other on the sword. The point where your sword connects with your opponent's sword is where all the action takes place. The pressure you feel from your opponent's sword through yours is his yang point. In sword, the yin is just to the side of, or behind, this yang point. Think of a shuttlecock: the heavy bulbous end is the yang point; the cone, created by the feathers, is the yin part. If you can slide the point of contact off the bulbous end and make contact anywhere on the cone behind it, then you can control the opponent's sword."

This is a tricky idea. It has to be understood that the style of fencing we practice begins with both players' swords connected. The goal is to keep the swords touching and avoid disconnecting, if possible, while maneuvering the sword to gain a dominant position. The superior fencer will, once the swords touch, keep contact until the opponent has been maneuvered to a bad position and can then be cut safely. This leads to a commanding position from which to end the fight, and is a safe way to engage another swordsman without leaving openings when attacking.

A feature of real sword fighting is that it is more likely that both fencers will be cut, rather than one win without injury. The old adage is particularly apt here: "When two tigers fight, the outcome is certain. One will be dead and the other seriously injured."

Bearing this in mind, Laoshi counseled against any attempts to cut an opponent without first reaching a position of dominance. He constantly exhorted us to maintain control of the opponent's sword and follow his energy until he became "stuck." The final cut was then not only safe, but also a formality. The tendency of some martial philosophies toward taking a hit in order to land one was to be avoided in favor of a more measured approach.

It might be argued that the more aggressive approach is the influence of the spectator in martial arts competitions. Gifted fighters who are almost impossible to hit but do not "stand and bang" will have relatively short, poorly paid careers. People do not pay to watch the noble art of self-defense, but to see knockouts and brawls. It is just too boring otherwise. Indeed, Olympic wrestling, one of the original Olympic sports, is in a precarious position due to its lack of appeal in this regard.

As one of Laoshi's students I have frequently noticed, however, that when a beginner has completed learning the sword form and is finally allowed to fence, he gives little regard to defending himself and rushes headlong into the fray, attempting to "cut" someone. The temptation to have at it seems overwhelming, even in the most unlikely of persons. I have witnessed a few genteel ladies of a certain age unleash themselves at their opponents with, if not a look of frenzy in their eyes, certainly an intention of purpose quite at odds with their usual deportment.

Laoshi had an innovative way of demonstrating this point when asked to give introductory workshops to fencing novices. He would give instructions for each student to find a partner and commence fencing as best he could, until one partner managed to touch the other with a wooden sword. Once tagged, the loser had to leave the floor, while the victor, having dispatched his first partner, would look for another victor and repeat the exercise. The field would narrow from, say, thirty to fifteen, then down to eight, eventually arriving at the last two, before the ultimate winner would emerge.

For the entire exercise, Laoshi was not the slightest bit interested in who was winning; rather, he was timing the whole thing. Once the exercise was completed, he would point out to the students that they had all managed to get themselves "killed" in less than two or three minutes. Such was their desire to attack, rather than to defend. Often, two students would cut each other simultaneously, and then both would have to sit down. A smarter strategy might be to pretend to fence and wait till nearly everyone else was "killed," only risking an attempt to win at the very end. No new fencer ever employs this strategy, but all experienced fencers perhaps should consider it. Of course, the result would be a lot of not much happening, with everybody waiting to take advantage of the aggression of others. Sounds like tai chi to me.

Attempting to gain control of the yin point of an opponent's sword is frustrating business. Becoming frustrated by the difficulties of the task, students would readily complain: "As soon as I get on his yin point, he changes and I lose control of his sword! What happens then?"

"Ah, that is where it becomes interesting," Laoshi would reply. "As your opponent changes the pressure on his sword, or changes the angle, you must also change and remain on his yin point. It is like those airplane dogfight movies: you must keep him in your crosshairs, so to speak, as he twists and turns to throw you off. This teaches you sensitivity through your sword. In time, you will be able to keep on his yin point no matter what he does, until he gets stuck or runs out of room."

Laoshi often then introduced another principle that added to the intrigue surrounding the yin and yang of fencing. He referred to it as the "figure ten" principle.

He would explain as follows: "As you may know, the character for 'ten' in Chinese is in the shape of a cross. This is roughly the shape your swords should make when you are practicing control of the yin point. Now, of course, you must realize you could just as easily hold the point of your sword toward your opponent and finish it, but what would you learn? Using the 'figure ten' idea, you can remain in contact for longer with his sword, listening all the time. Herein lies progress. You develop more sensitivity when the 'jaws' are not always trying to bite. You are like a cat playing with a mouse. You let the opponent run about but, always, you have control."

Such instruction likely accounted for the fact that some of Laoshi's more senior students had the appearance of contrivance as they fenced. They would circle each other, often rapidly, seeming to do anything but try to cut each other. The whole exercise looked more like a dance than a sword fight, but it did develop a greater feel for what was going on. Critically, the person in control could, at any time, use the "jaws" to bite.

As I continued to study fencing, I began to see both how angles worked and how to find the yin on my partner's sword. However, I also grew irritated: Laoshi, along with one or two of the senior students, sometimes clearly in an inferior position, still ended up in control of me. I expressed my frustration on this point to Laoshi one day. He simply smiled. "So now . . . here is a further principle for you to wrestle with," he said. "Having good basics, including angles, is vital to fencing, but knowledge of yin and yang trumps angles. It is a bit like a change of technology, progressing from bow and arrow to rifle. So knowing yin and yang trumps angles. But, *sente* trumps yin and yang, like progressing from rifle to machine gun."

Laoshi borrowed the word sente from the game of Go (Weiqi in Chinese) and translated it as "initiative."

He explained further: "If both fencers have reached the level of studying yin and yang, then they will both be trying to control each other's yin point; only one can achieve this—the one who has sente. The other is trying to escape. Having sente means remaining in the driving seat, even though we are responding to the evasive action of the opponent. Once a dominant position is reached, keeping the initiative is the most important thing. We adjust to every movement the opponent makes and keep the pressure on, never letting up, even for an instant, to let him recover. With sente we may continue as long as we wish, until we decide to end it."

Here was a clear parallel with Laoshi's ideas on all other martial arts. Once you get an opening, you pounce on it and do not let your opponent recover.

So now the game became even subtler. In theory, pressure on your opponent's sword is yang, and if he can "hear" this, he will slip around it and move onto your yin spot. In reality, however, both combatants have a yang point if the swords are connected; therefore, the fencer who is most sensitive will feel the yang of his partner first and be able to take advantage of the corresponding yin point. Understanding this begins to make sense of the saying "the fight is over as soon as the swords touch."

It took most of us years to gain an idea of how to find the yin point and then exert some kind of control over it. The wonderful and annoying thing was there always seemed to be another level of subtlety lying in wait. No doubt sensing this, a student asked Laoshi if sente was the ultimate principle. Laoshi replied with a smile, further upping of the ante: "Sente, along with some idea of timing, which we will go into later, lies at the upper end of an intermediate level of fencing. However, the secret to mastery in fencing is in the 'point of illumination.' If you understand the point of illumination, you will become unbeatable. This is the realm of the advanced fencer."

The point of illumination is what most people call the point of rotation. It is not necessarily the point of balance—though it can be—where the weight is equally distributed on either side of a spot on the blade; rather, it is the point on the sword that appears to remain still during the changes of direction, executed both in fencing and sword form.

For Laoshi, just as, ultimately, the power of the body derives from the dantian—the center of rotation for the body—true ability with the sword comes from an understanding of the point of rotation of the sword, the dantian of the sword. This was the focus for his personal study and experimentation for much of the time I studied with him. It occurred to me in a sobering but exciting moment that, if we were up to the level of rifles and machine guns, then Laoshi was already developing lasers.

Wang Lang often told his students that Yang Chengfu, Zheng Manqing's teacher, said the word "relax" a thousand times a day. He usually added that Professor Zheng used the word "gradually" almost as much.

倒
撵
猴
左

From talking to Laoshi, it seems Wang Lang himself had a liking for the phrase "the greatness of the qi."

As I got to know Laoshi, I noticed he often said "relax" to his students and was comfortable using the word "gradually," but he rarely referred to the greatness of the qi, and only when quoting Wang Lang. I thought this behavior rather curious, since Wang Lang was Laoshi's teacher for longer than any other, and Laoshi himself said about 80 percent of what he taught came directly from Wang Lang. It seemed peculiar to me that Laoshi should avoid using one of the key phrases of his main teacher and even avoid talking about qi in general.

Although I occasionally wondered why this should be, I was not inclined to broach the subject. However, as it happened, another student one day asked a blunt question that shed some light on the matter. Laoshi had just quoted Zheng Manqing's assertion that the secret of tai chi is that the qi and the heart-mind mutually guard each other in the dantian. The student then asked, "What happens if you don't believe in the qi?"

It was a very interesting question, and I wondered how Laoshi would reply. Laoshi was quiet for a moment, no doubt considering both the question and the questioner. "I once asked Wang Lang a similar question," he began. "I had been reading an article suggesting, in direct contrast to the accepted notion of how qi moves in the body, that meridians do not exist. Instead, the article argued, the body should be regarded as a qi sponge—or, said another way, qi seeps into the body the way tea seeps into a sugar cube."

Laoshi continued, "This placed some doubt in my mind, and so I resolved to ask Wang Lang, 'Do you think meridians are real?' Wang Lang answered, 'Well, it's like my old pappy used to say: it wasn't William Shakespeare who wrote all those plays; it was somebody else with the same name.' That is a direct quote," Laoshi said, smiling.

We all laughed but, as the room quieted down, one of the other students, Raymond, said, "But Laoshi, you didn't answer Tommy's question."

Laoshi nodded in acknowledgement. "People accused Zheng Manqing of the same thing and, when pressed on the matter, Professor Zheng used to say, 'I answered the energy of the question.' Can you imagine a politician using that line?"

There was a ripple of laughter once again, but I could see Raymond remained perplexed. I have to confess I had some sympathy for Raymond, as I had often been on the receiving end of Laoshi's habit of answering the energy of a question. Laoshi had not finished, however.

"The question of what qi is and what its use might be is not something you can describe simply. It is like trying to describe snow to desert people, or the color green to a man blind from birth. How can this be done? The best you can say is, it is like this, or it is not like that. That is why we have a boxing method, a *quanfa* [拳法]. Our method does not ask you to believe in anything you cannot see or feel. You practice, and you notice what happens."

Raymond looked doubtful.

Laoshi continued: "OK, Raymond. Raise your hand into the air. You can all do this too," he said, nodding to the rest of us. We all duly complied.

"Now," Laoshi continued, "what do you feel happening inside your hand?"

"Er . . . nothing," Raymond said, slightly embarrassed. A few other people concurred.

"OK then," Laoshi said, nodding. "Now, imagine on the ends of each of your fingers you have an eye looking outward. Now what do you feel?"

"Ah . . . it feels like something moving in my hand," Raymond said with growing interest, "like some kind of flow." A few other students reported similar feelings.

"OK," Laoshi said. "Now imagine the eyes on your fingertips can swivel around and are looking down through your fingers to your wrist. What do you feel in your hand when you do that?"

"Hey, that's impressive!" Raymond said, smiling. "It's like the flow is going the other way—like it's flowing back into my hand."

"Like what is flowing back into your hand?" Laoshi asked.

"I don't know," Raymond replied, shaking his head, "but it's like something is moving inside. Is that the qi, Laoshi?"

"It is as good a word as any, don't you think?" Laoshi asked. "But you have not told me what it is. You have just made up a name for a feeling. It may be the qi that people talk about, or it may be something else by the same name."

Raymond nodded, acknowledging Laoshi's point. Had he just experienced the flow of qi, or had he just labeled an experience with a word other people might use for something else? The exchange between Laoshi and Raymond led me to understand why Laoshi was reluctant to talk about something that could not be demonstrated. Laoshi was by no means alone in his reluctance, as a number of Zheng Manqing's American students, who later became teachers themselves, said very little about qi to their students. Like Laoshi, they found difficulty in expressing ideas that were not a concrete reality for them personally, despite having no doubts that experiencing qi was a reality for Zheng Manqing.

As class came to an end, I sauntered over and asked, "Laoshi, do you think Raymond was satisfied by what you said? About the qi, I mean."

"For me," Laoshi said, "the more important question is am I satisfied with what I said?"

"And are you?" I inquired.

"No, I never am when I talk about qi," he admitted. "My understanding of it is not deep enough. Qi is the cornerstone of what we study, yet it remains elusive. The feeling of movement in the hands and feet, the sensation of a ball of energy contained by the hands, the tingling in the *laogong* [勞宮], *yongquan*, [涌泉], and *niwan* [泥丸] points—all these exist in my experience but, like all sensations, are entirely individual, subjective, and therefore difficult to talk about. Until we can make some objective use of them, it is maybe better not to say too much about them. People may get funny ideas."

I took Laoshi's advice and did not ask him about qi for a while, but my curiosity got the better of me one long, hot summer. It had been uncommonly hot for August, and in class we sweltered, as air conditioning was not a feature of the old church halls in which we practiced. As I was holding a posture for what seemed like an age, I began to notice the strangest feeling in my forearms. A sensation of growing heat seemed to be generating from the marrow of my bones. This sensation increased in intensity, becoming like a furnace—and yet, not unpleasant. After class the feeling subsided, but my curiosity was aroused.

A few days later, again while holding a posture in an uncomfortably warm class, I began to experience a rushing sensation from the sole of my left foot all the way up to my knee. It was as if I were standing on a jet of water, gushing up from the ground. I became tremendously excited. "I've got it!" I thought. Now the descriptions I had heard of a "rushing spring" made complete sense to me. I was convinced I was on the cusp of something mystical; the qi was going to be a reality for me!

I went home from class that day with a grin that said, "I know something you don't know!" At class the following day, I continued to experience the rushing sensation as we held postures—although it did not feel as intense as it had the previous day. Nevertheless, it was there.

The next day I returned to class with a feeling of expectation. Disappointment! The feeling did not return and, in the intervening years, it has been absent even at a reduced wattage. The burning sensation in my forearms is also now with me only in memory.

I mentioned my experiences to Laoshi, hoping he might somehow confirm or applaud these extraordinary feelings. But Laoshi only looked at me for a moment and smiled. "That's very good," he said. "Keep practicing."

Since that summer, I have secretly hoped for a return of similar feelings. But I also realize there is much more to gain from tai chi than the exotica of those few memorable days. There is even a school of thought that argues unusual feelings like the ones I experienced are, at best, an irrelevance, and at worst, a hindrance to progress, in the same way that visions experienced in meditation can lead away from the true path.

Perhaps it is best to leave the last word to Laoshi, who, when questioned by a student as to how to encourage the kundalini to rise, replied, "Don't be too keen to set fire to your spine. You might not be able to put the fire out."

Chapter 21: Mutually Guarding

斜
飛
勢

So keen was I to learn from Laoshi that I attended every class I could, even the beginners' classes. Although I had learned the form, it seemed as if every class added a new twist to my understanding. Laoshi seemed able to find new ways to explain the concepts and principles underpinning the art. He once said, "There are only a small number of principles, but they can be expressed in an infinite number of ways." It was his way of keeping the ancient principles alive and fresh.

Much as I appreciated a class that went smoothly, I enjoyed even more witnessing those occasions when something out of the ordinary happened and, in particular, I enjoyed watching Laoshi acting spontaneously to deal with awkward people. Such episodes were often informative and amusing.

One evening a young Chinese woman came to class with her older Scottish husband. I was standing nearby as they introduced themselves, the husband informing Laoshi of his desire to learn tai chi, having heard so much about it from his wife. Laoshi turned to the wife to ask if she would also be taking class, but she answered, saying, "Oh, no. I already know tai chi."

Laoshi merely nodded, but I had a pretty shrewd idea of his thoughts based on a story he once told me about the mother of a friend of his. On learning that Laoshi was a tai chi teacher, his friend's mother told him she knew all about tai chi, having learned from her grandmother in China when she was young. She no longer practiced and appeared, from her tone, to hold the art in low esteem. She was busy with far more important matters.

With the passing of time, the friend's mother became seriously ill and one day mentioned to Laoshi that perhaps tai chi might help her. When Laoshi suggested she come to class, she declined, citing the traveling distance as the impediment. So Laoshi offered her one of his own teaching videos in order that she could practice at home, try to get back into the swing of things, and hopefully regain her health. After a few months had gone by, Laoshi asked his friend how his mother was getting along with the tai chi video.

"Oh, she only looked at it once," his friend said. "She said your tai chi is far too involved and she couldn't understand it."

Laoshi commented to me later, "It is the same with many people. They nibble at the rind but think they have eaten the fruit."

Back in class that evening, Laoshi gave no indication that his thoughts ran in this direction, but I had an inkling the woman of the story and the woman standing in front of him were of a kind. There was about her an arrogant disdain that irked me from the moment she and her husband arrived. Her subsequent conduct did little to moderate my view, since, in spite of her avowed expertise in tai chi, she sat at the back of the class, rather obviously trying her best to learn everything she could. She swayed about, copying Laoshi's hand positions, craning her neck, and even shifting seats from time to time, as her view was impeded by students in motion. I could not decide if she was too tight to pay for the class, felt too superior to join in, or felt she might lose face participating. What I do know, however, is my initial dislike of her shortly afterward extended to her husband, who, finding the movements challenging, sought to blame Laoshi's teaching style for his own insufficiencies.

There was a positive side to their attendance at class, however. After one of the classes they attended, as students were leaving, I happened to be standing close to Laoshi when the Chinese lady and her husband approached.

She asked, "Could you explain to my husband what qi is? Of course, I know but my English isn't good enough to explain properly."

I suppressed a smile, as it seemed to me her English had not failed her so far in class, and my dislike of her increased a notch.

Still, Laoshi replied graciously. "No one can explain qi adequately, and often people are not even speaking about the same thing when they attempt to discuss qi. As you know, the Chinese language uses the word 'qi' in various ways. *Tianqi* [天氣], for instance, is literally the qi of the heavens, which means the weather. *Keqi* [客氣] translates literally as 'the air of a guest,' but more prosaically means 'politeness' or 'manners.' Tai chi teachers disagree on the nature, function, and expression of qi. Indeed, some even doubt its existence."

"But," she interrupted, "what about being able to use qi when someone hits you? Like the Shaolin monks."

Laoshi answered, "That has more to do with body conditioning—and not a lot to do with qi."

"Yes," she continued, unabashed, "but they break steel bars and sticks on their bodies without being hurt."

I could see Laoshi was getting a little irritated and I was not surprised when he said, "That has more to do with the weakness of the steel bars and sticks than it has to do with the strength of the qi. They are strong men, I do not doubt, but why can they not buy proper steel bars that don't break? Or are they obliged to use the junk steel that was left over from Mao's Great Leap Forward? Take care in believing every story about qi masters knocking people down without touching them and being impervious to blows. There may be some truth in them, but most of those who claim such powers are scoundrels."

The couple left, never to return—and they were not missed.

Once the dust had settled a little, I asked Laoshi about his remarks.

"When people don't hear what they wish to hear, they try to put words in your mouth," he said. "They were tiresome and I was glad to see the back of them. I may have been a little ungracious to them, but what I said is essentially true."

"So can I ask you, Laoshi, what is qi?" I was sure he was going to fob me off, but to my surprise, he did not.

Laoshi paused, glancing upward as if for inspiration: "Asking what qi is may be asking the wrong question. Ultimately, we have to say we do not know. You may think this answer is a revelation of ignorance, but actually it is not."

"I'm not sure what you mean, Laoshi," I interrupted.

"Well, for example, if I ask you, 'What is coal?' you might say, 'It is a collection of carbon molecules assembled in a particular way.' I might then ask, 'But what is a carbon molecule?' You might proceed to describe atoms as comprised of neutrons and electrons, and I might continue asking, 'And what is that? And what is that?' Fairly quickly, you would reach the limit of your knowledge and have to say, 'I don't know.' It is a bit like a child asking why to every answer his mother gives. Eventually, she has to say, 'Enough.'

"The things we see in front of us," Laoshi continued, "and even the things we cannot see, are all defined by something else, as components of, or by comparison with, something else. If you look up a word in a dictionary, it is defined by other words, which you can then look up in turn, in the same dictionary. If you continue to look up each word in the definitions, it would only be a matter of time before you returned, full circle, to the word with which you started. Unless you can answer the question 'What is this?' by directly pointing at something, you will have to reply by saying it is like this or unlike that. Alan Watts relates the story of the teacher who, holding up a matchbox, asked the students, 'What is this?' When someone inevitably said, 'It's a matchbox,' he would throw it at him, saying, 'Matchbox is a sound. Does that feel like a sound?'

"If we have such trouble defining the things we can see, how much more trouble will we have defining the things we cannot see, like qi? It is precisely because it is impossible for us to say what qi is that we have the method of tai chi ch'uan. The form is a device to lead us to a feeling we might say is connected with qi. Even then, I cannot be sure the feeling you have is the same feeling I experience. Such feelings are subjective and unique to the individual, not only in their strength but in characteristics."

"So what is the right question?" I pursued, unsure of where exactly Laoshi was going, but enjoying the process nevertheless.

"Well, let's see," Laoshi said. "Bear in mind you can define things not only by their component parts, but also by their function. For instance, if I use a microscope to pound a nail into wood, is it a scientific instrument or a hammer? Similarly, at some point a car becomes scrap metal; a pen that runs out of ink is a plastic tube; a chair can function as a table—or it can be used by a lion tamer. In other words, the object has not changed, but its use has."

"So, we should be asking in what way might the qi be useful?" I offered.

"It is a better question," Laoshi conceded, "if you have to ask a question at all, but it might be better still to consider qi as a tendency and, more important, whether it may be possible to influence or make use of that tendency."

"You've lost me again, Laoshi," I said, shaking my head.

"Think of it this way," he continued. "As the planets have a tendency to spin, so the body has a tendency to heal and to age. The question would then be this: is it possible to influence the body to heal more quickly and age more slowly?"

"Well . . . of course," I said. "You can smoke and drink yourself into an early grave or stress yourself to the point of nervous collapse, but that is nothing new, Laoshi. Everybody knows that. That is completely natural."

"Have you not heard that qi is completely natural as well?" he replied with a smile. "It still follows that there are actions that aid the tendency and those that hinder. If we can practice those things that assist the tendency and refrain from those that hinder, then that is enough for most of us to be going along with."

"But what about Zheng Manqing and O Sensei Ueshiba?" I protested, growing seriously disappointed the discussion of the "greatness of the qi" was becoming so banal. "Weren't they able to do miraculous things?"

"It is miraculous enough," Laoshi replied, "to be able to live healthily and happily in this world. It is enough, but it is also supremely challenging. The rest will reveal itself when the time is right. Being able to perform tricks with qi will not make you any healthier or happier. Indeed, you could end up worse off.

"We must be careful not to blind ourselves with dreams of mystical powers," he added. "At the same time, though, we should understand our practice is about positively overcoming ill health, stress, fear, and the actions of those who would do us harm. This is a kind of power. It is one of those strange contradictions we face in following our Way. The path is a balance between accepting the flow of life and bending life to our will."

"So, how do we balance the two?" I asked, my interest quickening once more.

"By remembering Zheng Manqing's secret of tai chi," Laoshi said. "The qi and the heart-mind mutually guard each other in the dantian. This is the most challenging concept to grasp in tai chi because it requires you to understand three things. First, the working of the qi—this is the power of tai chi. Second, the nature of our relationship with the heart-mind—this concerns wisdom and harmony with the Dao. Finally, how the qi and the heart-mind relate to each other."

Laoshi paused to gauge whether I was still paying attention before he continued. "It is also strange, is it not, that the qi and the heart-mind guard each other?"

I had to agree. I had always thought this was a peculiar choice of word. What did "mutually guard" mean precisely? Laoshi had previously stated it was an expression to remind us to "maintain constant vigilance." He explained that soldiers in guards regiments in the British Army stand motionless in front of the places they guard, like Buckingham Palace, for a very good combat reason. "They stand," Laoshi had informed us, "without being distracted from their task precisely because they are guardsmen. If you instruct them in battle to watch a road or a gap in a hedge, that is exactly what they will do, not start talking or smoking cigarettes. It is a kind of mental discipline they are training. It is the same for us."

Now, however, Laoshi was introducing a deeper level of meaning to the phrase "mutually guarding."

"Zheng Manqing's tai chi is all to do with balance," he said quietly. "So important was it to Zheng Manqing's view of tai chi that it is one of the few words he took the trouble to learn in English. We might think of the word 'guard' here as being related to this view of balance."

"I don't get that, Laoshi." I shook my head. "How is the word 'guard' like the word 'balance'?"

Laoshi nodded. "Well, think of a fire guard. It prevents bits of burning coal from shooting out and burning the house down; it also stops children from getting too close and burning themselves. It limits the spread of elements from two worlds, keeping them from completely dominating each other. By doing so, it keeps the balance between them."

This was indeed an interesting way of looking at Professor Zheng's seminal advice. Laoshi continued. "The heart-mind guards us against using the qi only to seek powers, or *siddhis*, as the yogis say. The qi guards the heart-mind from becoming dominated by the rational mind—for if this happens, the heart-mind turns upon itself and becomes a destructive force in our lives. Thus power and wisdom watch over each other, minimizing the possibility of one gaining too much sway over our lives.

"You will find there are times when our energy becomes so full within us that we can hardly contain it. At times like these, we are more likely to do something foolish. Talking of guards, do you remember the story of the young Scots Guards officer who led an assault in the Falklands near the end of the war? He was so exhilarated after fighting his way to the top of a mountain that he celebrated victory standing atop the summit. Unfortunately, in so doing he silhouetted himself against the moonlit sky and made himself a target for a sniper. He spent the rest of his life partially paralyzed. We might say his qi was so full that every fiber of his being was brimming with energy. He would never have felt so alive. However, he would have done well to have heeded Gichin Funakoshi's advice on guarding against impetuous courage. It is as Wang Lang used to say, 'There is only one thing worse than feeling bad and that is feeling great—as this is when we are most likely to do something stupid.' Therefore, when the qi is running rampant through our bodies, we must temper our actions with the wisdom of the heart-mind."

I chewed over Laoshi's words. "And what about the heart-mind?" I asked. "Should we temper it too?"

"It is similar, but also slightly different," Laoshi replied. "Problems with the heart-mind can occur when our energy becomes so weak that those fears and terrors that usually lie dormant within us may come to the surface. Then the naturally joyful creativity, which is the province of the heart-mind, turns sinister and destructive. I knew a young woman, for instance, who began practicing visualizations for success, money, and fame. Her qi was weak and unable to support her creativity. Her mind became so unbalanced by the constant repetition of affirmations and endless envisioning that it began to create its own unsolicited visions of devils and monsters. The mind can then fragment, making it impossible to distinguish our own intense imaginings from reality. Our qi must be strong enough to hold our minds together and prevent fragmentation."

As I pondered Laoshi's interpretation of Zheng Manqing's teaching, I wondered if this were related to what Zheng Manqing once said about wanting to be a human being, not a Buddha. I had always assumed it was a statement of humility, of consciously not overreaching in terms of goals set. And yet, it had always seemed to me Zheng Manqing was an ambitious man. Why else would he work twenty hours a day? Furthermore, Zheng Manqing was a man who wanted to display his undoubted knowledge. Ben Lo relates how Zheng Manqing preferred to let the majority of an audience struggle with his meaning rather than let the one or two experts in the room think he had a low level of understanding.

As I considered all this, I thought I began to glimpse where Laoshi was guiding me. He was suggesting that I not forsake the near for the far, as the saying goes. The miraculous stories of qi remained out of my reach, but the way to progress is not to fantasize about miraculous powers and instead to work on what is immediate. Whatever happens then, happens. I still had one more question though:

"Laoshi, do you believe, as Zheng Manqing believed, it is possible for a man to be shot at and for him to use qi so the bullet bounces off him?"

Laoshi smiled. "You refer to Zheng Manqing's tale of how the martial artists gained the faith of the people during the Boxer Rebellion?"

These martial artists, so the story goes, had displayed invulnerability in the face of bullets fired directly at them, using their qi as a protective shield.

I nodded.

"Who knows?" Laoshi said, shrugging. "There have been magicians in China over the centuries, men like Zhang Daoling [張道陵] and Zuo Ci [左慈]. It is possible that unscrupulous martial artists developed tricks that fooled the peasants into thinking of them as invincible. Superstitious and ill educated, they would have been easy prey to skilled illusionists. We also have to recognize that the weapons available in those days were not the high-velocity firearms available today, which can send rounds through three men, never mind one. The world of Asian martial arts is riddled with tales of supernatural abilities, which are pure fantasy. The abilities you mention, to my knowledge, have never been demonstrated under rigorous conditions. Even Zheng Manqing did not attempt such things, though it would seem he thought them possible."

I nodded again, a little crestfallen. I had long since dismissed the notion that the Loch Ness Monster exists, or that we would one day find a family of yetis living on some Tibetan plateau, but I was still disappointed. After all, what sort of world is it where mystery is denied us? Where imagination has been wholly replaced by diamond-sharp logic, and creativity has been reduced to providing greater memory for our computers? Is this not an imbalance in itself?

Perhaps noticing my disappointment, Laoshi spoke again. "Mind you, have you ever heard of Joseph L. Greenstein, nicknamed the Mighty Atom, the circus showman and world-famous strongman of the early twentieth century? He attributed his feats of great strength to his mental and spiritual power. A coordinated mind and body might be able to do remarkable things.

"Apparently, Greenstein was shot in the head at close range by a man who was obsessed with his wife. The bullet, from a .38 caliber pistol, hit Greenstein in the forehead with enough force to become flattened on impact. Greenstein was knocked out and taken to a hospital. Miraculously, he left that same day, none the worse for the incident."

With that Laoshi left while I pondered what he had just said. Was he saying he believed you could withstand a bullet fired at you, or not? I was confused. I went away to look up the Greenstein story and check the facts. I found this quote from Greenstein, referring to the incident:

I was on the ground. I knew I was shot . . . a burning pain between my eyes . . .
and then somehow I wasn't myself, but something much more. . . . And I knew
in that instant that I wouldn't die. Couldn't. Not even a bullet between the eyes
could kill me. It has all been for a reason. . . . All for a purpose.

I was struck by the similarity in the feeling contained within his words to
the sentiment of Ueshiba's description of his first great *satori*, his insight into the
way things really are. He had just concluded a sword duel with a naval officer
and was cooling off in his garden, pouring cold water from the well over himself,
when he had the following experience:

I felt the universe suddenly quake, and that a golden spirit sprang up from the
ground, veiled my body, and changed my body into a golden one. At the same
time my body became light. I was able to understand the whispering of the
birds, and was clearly aware of the mind of God, the creator of the universe. At
that moment I was enlightened: the source of budo is God's love—the spirit of
loving protection for all beings.

Not long after my chat with Laoshi, I had a dream in which I attended
a seminar with a famous martial artist from somewhere near Tibet. In the
dream, the martial artist demonstrated his ability to withstand the blows from
fists as well as a variety of weapons. I was not convinced, but stood watching
as everybody else was spellbound. Perhaps noticing my reluctance to share in the
veneration of his skills, he approached me and handed me a Chinese-style saber,
inviting me to hit him on the head. I asked him if I could perhaps submit him to
a less dangerous test, but he smiled and refused, offering his head once again as a
target. I declined and he walked away.

All through the following days, the memory of my dream not only
remained with me, but it increased in intensity. It held me captive and harassed
me mercilessly. I was afflicted by the knowledge that my motivation in refusing
to strike was not my fear of killing him, but in fact just the opposite: I was afraid
his ability would prove real. I had chosen not to know, rather than be confronted
by a true master. I was afraid because I knew if he were genuine, I would have to
make a choice between following him and settling for something second rate. I
would have to choose between abandoning everything to study deeply with this
man on one hand, and keeping my comfortable existence on the other. I knew I
lacked the courage to give up the superficial to seek the sublime.

The dream seemed to mirror the limited way in which I approached my
training at that time. I was quite happy to go to class, get pushed by Laoshi, and
revel in the glow of a great teacher, but I was not at all prepared to go all in and

make my practice a matter of life or death. I was disappointed to realize I was not only unwilling to pay a high price to reach the pinnacle of the art, but I was not even resolute enough to risk finding out what that price might be.

I remembered something Laoshi recalled Wang Lang saying: "If all it took to be really happy were for us to go down to Times Square and push a button, most of us would find an excuse not to go."

Perhaps it is as Zheng Manqing said: small loss, small gain; big loss, big gain. The predicament many of us find ourselves in is that while we want the big gain, we are not willing to endure even a small loss.

Chapter 22: Fair Lady

雲
手
右

When I studied with him, Laoshi was married and lived in a four-bedroom house just outside the city. He never had children, which I am sure was out of choice rather than fate. As a result, it left him and his wife free to take in tai chi lodgers—students from abroad and some of his regular students who wanted to live in with Laoshi to get the full flavor of what he was teaching. He did not think the live-in experience was absolutely necessary for regular students, but it was clearly essential for his foreign students, whose contact with him was limited because, by this time, Laoshi had stopped traveling abroad to give workshops.

I used to go and stay for a week or two, or for a long weekend when my work allowed. Rather than the practice, it was contact time with Laoshi that I wanted. Often after morning practice we would retire to the ample kitchen and talk tai chi and anything else, as the mood dictated. He would tell stories of his training and his teachers, and offer his Daoist perspective on life in general.

One afternoon when we were alone, I took the opportunity to solicit some advice. One of the students who had been coming to class had taken my eye. Her name was Kelly and I was, it's safe to say, more than just a little interested in her. She seemed to be single and gave off the right signals, or so I hoped, but I was uneasy about mixing my tai chi study and a possible relationship with a fellow student.

I asked Laoshi about the etiquette in such situations. I was not too keen on asking some of the class seniors, whose remit was to keep students right about the unwritten rules that exist, to greater or lesser extent, in all martial arts schools. I felt the issue to be too personal to blabber out and was unsure of the reception I would get from any one of them. They were not, after all, Laoshi.

"What you are talking about is indeed delicate," Laoshi began after a sip of tea. "It is true to say you have less responsibility in these matters as a student than a teacher, but it is not a trivial thing we are talking about."

He then went on to highlight the issues for me.

"Many of your fellow students who come to learn the art are looking for help in dealing with their lives. You cannot know what state they are in. There are some who experience great difficulty in dealing with the usual daily problems we all face. You do not want to add to their problems; neither do you want to harass a young woman, who will have many admirers, and chase her out of the class. I have seen it a few times. A young man pursues a girl in class and ends up becoming a nuisance. She is left with only one option—leaving the class. That is a matter of regret. She comes to class to learn to deal with problems, only to find additional burdens. As someone becoming ready to enter the senior class, you would not want that, I am sure.

"On the other hand, I have seen a number of times that relationships forged in following the Dao can and do become the basis of long-lasting and loving unions. You can only remain aware of yourself and your motives, and act with the sincerity of your heart. Tread lightly where you can and move patiently.

"There is a Daoist saying that will help you with this. 'Even when the right person does the wrong thing, it still turns out right. And even when the wrong person does the right thing, it still turns out wrong.'

"When you become a teacher, the matter is more serious, and you, like all of us, will make mistakes. The only thing is not to compound them with dishonesty."

"Have you made mistakes in these matters, Laoshi?" I asked, regretting the intrusion as soon as it was made.

"Of course," he replied with a sigh. "That is how I can tell you the problems that can arise. Furthermore, my teachers also made mistakes, but some of them compounded the error by deluding themselves.

"As a teacher, you have power. People think of you in ways you are not. You cannot help this, but you must guard against it. Women will have an unrealistic view of you and unrealistic expectations. It is easy to prey on such women. One of my early teachers used his female students this way. He was a man who lived off people, a kind of parasite. He spoke as one who cherished the rights of others and as a champion of the abused, but secretly was the biggest abuser himself.

"He had a certain charisma, I suppose. He managed to manipulate people very well. On one occasion, he invited me to a meeting at the home of the Vollmer family. Ingrid Vollmer, married with two young boys, was one of his students, as I was at the time. The reason for the meeting is irrelevant, but as we were concluding and people were leaving, I decided to wait for my teacher— we can call him Lenny—and walk part of the way home with him. He was sitting with Ingrid on the sofa and was massaging her feet, a little unusual, but not so crazy for him. Once while sharing a room with him at a course, I came in to find him wearing only a pair of red shorts, sitting astride a naked male student, massaging his body. That night at the Vollmers', it gradually became clear to me, when only three of us were left, that I was in the way. Ingrid's husband, Kriss, was at home, but in another room. I realized my teacher was going to spend the night. I later discovered they were sleeping together while Kriss spent the night in another room. Incredible, don't you agree?

"The affair only lasted a short while, but the damage was done. Ingrid left the class and I did not see her for a few years, and only when I too had left the class. We were both at a dinner party given by a mutual friend when she asked me if we could meet for a coffee, as she wanted to talk to me about something. It turned out she was finding life hard. Kriss had returned to his native Switzerland, leaving her to cope with the boys, who had no respect for her and were misbehaving constantly. She had no work and little money, as Kriss only gave her a modest allowance. There was very little joy in her life and she felt worn out. She had not seen Lenny for years and was counting the cost of meeting him.

"As life would have it, I wandered into a bar one evening a couple of years later. I was alone and killing time. As I looked around, I spotted a familiar face on a slightly fatter, but still very big, powerful body. It was Kriss, over for a visit—business or personal, I do not know. I bought him a beer and we sat down to talk. He was already pretty drunk, and when I asked about the family, he began to cry. A sad sight indeed. He and Ingrid were permanently separated and he only saw his boys occasionally. 'That fucking Lenny,' he said. 'He ruined everything.'

"He wanted to talk, and I let him. He was almost crying on my shoulder in the middle of a packed bar.

"'Why did you not take matters to the physical when you found out?' I asked him. 'You are a big man with a lot of strength.'

"'I wanted to,' he continued, 'but when I met him, he seemed like such a nice guy. I didn't know what to do. He besotted her, but I still loved her. He was fucking her while I was in the other room, trying not to hear. They were in my house because he and his wife were separating in a *planned way*. She, however, would not let him bring his new girlfriends into his family home. At that time I was so confused, I even lent him some money for a business venture that never got off the ground. He owes me thousands of pounds.'"

• • •

We took a break when Laoshi went to make more tea. He mentioned his teacher Lenny from time to time, usually as a cautionary tale. When he returned, I asked him, "Why did you study with this guy?"

"At that time there was so little tai chi here," he said. "This was twenty-five years ago. Now there are so many tai chi 'masters' to choose from. At that time there were only a few teachers, and the others were not much better. You have to put up with the—how should I put it?—peculiarities of your teachers, if you want to learn. After all, you must put up with mine.

"Now, where were we? Ah yes. It happened to me one time, when I had just started teaching, that one of my students, a married woman who was having problems in her marriage, offered herself to me. She was a good, kind, and gentle woman who wanted to betray her husband. You can, perhaps, imagine the turmoil she must have been in."

"What did you do?" I asked, eager to hear more. This level of revelation was unusual for Laoshi. He was usually a little more reticent. Later I realized he was not just indulging in gossip, but felt these episodes had instructional value: always the teacher.

He continued: "I told her I could not, but the episode was—how would you say?—beneficial. Remember, 'Even when the right person does the wrong thing . . .' She realized she had to make drastic changes or her marriage would not survive. She and her husband did make changes. He even became one of my students. Their marriage became stronger."

"That was impressive. You showed a lot of restraint," I commented, trying not to sound too ingratiating.

"Ach, no," he said with a look of mild annoyance, regarding me as if I were an idiot. "Not restraint. She was not my type. Had she been, who knows? Maybe you would be meeting her husband in a bar in a few years' time, talking about me. I was lucky.

"The point of this story is not I, but my teachers. After I stopped seeing Lenny, I began studying with another teacher called Don. He was different from Lenny. He wanted to be the wise guru who would guide us all to enlightenment. His drug was the power of being 'the master.' Were it not for this need in him, he would have been a good teacher. He was knowledgeable, articulate, and he had a big school spread all over the country, but unfortunately, he had an ego to match.

"One day I mentioned to him the approach I had from my student. He asked me what I did and, when I told him, he said sagely, 'That was good. In this work we do, energy starts to move and can be mistaken for many things, even sexual feelings. If you want to help your students, you cannot confuse them. Do not sleep with your students.'

"I thought it was good advice, but then after talking to other people in the school, I realized he did not follow his own counsel. He had married one of his students, divorced her when he had an affair with another student who was already married, and finally, married a third student, as much for her money as anything else. Perhaps he had seen the errors he had made and, wiser for it, gave me sincere advice, but my feeling at the time made me doubt his sincerity. My feelings have not changed with time.

"Finally," Laoshi said, "on this subject, I can tell you about Wang Lang, who you know was my main teacher for a long time. His wife, of many years now, was one of his students who he pursued shamelessly until she decided she did, in fact, love him. Their marriage was a great benefit to both of them even though, as she told me, he was not what she thought she was looking for.

"To have strict rules on matters such as these is futile. The Dao is contemptuous of our petty morality and concepts of right or wrong. Remember the *Dao De Jing* [道德經]:

> When the Dao is lost, there is goodness
> When goodness is lost, there is morality
> When morality is lost, there is ritual
> Ritual is the empty husk of true faith
> The beginning of chaos

"Do not be fooled by the rules of foolish men. Look sincerely into your deepest feelings and be guided by them. As one of my Zen teachers once said, 'Everything is allowed, provided you can accept the consequences.'"

I thought about Laoshi's words but proceeded to make my own mistakes. Kelly and I became an item before we realized we could not even deal with our own imbalances, let alone each other's. I just about handled the consequences, but she left the school, unable to be in the same room with me. It was one of numerous mistakes I made and lessons I learned. I do not believe the Dao is contemptuous of us, but I guard against its loss every day.

Chapter 23: The Alert Cat Catches a Cold

金
鷄
獨
立
左
式

Zheng Manqing said, "If you do push-hands with the idea of pushing or not being pushed, then it is not tai chi." Despite this statement, plenty of film exists, as do written accounts, of him pushing, usually much bigger people, with considerable power. There will always be debate about the existence and nature of qi, but an ability to launch people thirty feet across a yard into the hands of "catchers," who are needed to arrest the momentum, makes a convincing enough statement about the power of tai chi. Indeed, it was the promise of such ability, in part, that attracted me to study within the Zheng Manqing family of teachers.

It soon became clear to me, however, that the correct push was a difficult thing to master, even at its most basic level. It was not simply a shove. The push involved a quality of lifting. Hence it is usually known as "uprooting." Furthermore, as can be seen from both film and the testimony of Professor

Zheng's students, there was the perplexing phenomenon of the push gaining momentum: the person being pushed was obliged to scramble backward, sometimes frantically, in order to keep from falling on his rear end. Students found themselves continuing to accelerate as they were propelled backward, necessitating the use of the catchers, or a wall, to bring them to a halt.

Laoshi told me of the first time he was pushed correctly and his surprise at the unique quality of the feeling.

"The first real push I experienced was with Wang Lang," Laoshi told me. "Though I had been pushed by other people before, they could only manage rudimentary shoves, which were not only unedifying, but rather annoying—the result of hard force, and neither well placed nor skillfully executed. There was no mystery to how they achieved what they did, and I knew I could replicate it without much difficulty.

"Wang Lang's push, on the other hand, was infinitely subtler, even delicate. It lacked the forcefulness of a shove, and yet I was propelled backward as if being pulled to the rear by a rope tied around my chest. I could not feel his hands on my body, only my body moving backward, away from him, my feet frantically scurrying rearward to catch up with my center, which was falling backward.

"Unable to stop myself from backpedaling, I stuck out my right arm and my fingertips made contact with the corner of a wall. I experienced the amusement of running backward, around the corner, my feet describing an arc, while my fingertips remained in contact with the wall, acting as the center of the circle I was making with my movement.

"In all, I only traveled around fifteen feet, but it seemed much more. Had the edge of the wall not been within reach of my outstretched hand, I am sure my momentum would have carried me considerably farther. Normally, when pushing with Wang Lang, the recipient of the push would have his back to a wall, restricting the distance traveled. Hitting the wall was not unlike doing a breakfall in aikido but substituting the floor with the wall. I think I was fortunate that in my first push-hands class Wang Lang pushed me away from the wall and I felt the power a correct uprooting push can generate.

"I had a feeling of wonder because I did not understand how he could do what he did. The push seemed to have some special quality in it—it certainly did not generate any kind of negativity in me. On the contrary, I was eager to be pushed again, not only out of a desire to learn its secrets, but because it was a novel experience.

"As the months and years passed and I developed my root and acquired neutralizing skills, it became more and more difficult for Wang Lang to replicate that initial push; nevertheless, the memory stays with me."

As with much in tai chi, learning the uprooting push is a long and difficult process. It took Laoshi almost four years of dedicated practice to even begin to understand it—and he was considered something of a genius by Wang Lang, who took rather longer. Laoshi did not agree with Wang Lang's assessment of his genius. Instead, he concluded he was fortunate to glimpse the truth that uprooting was nothing out of the ordinary. Often teachers employ poetic language in their attempts to describe the subtleties of the process, but unfortunately lead their students to search for something otherworldly rather than something completely natural.

Like Laoshi, I assumed once I acquired the uprooting skill, I would be able to push anybody and everybody with the merest twitch of my body, and, as I progressed, I would be able to increase the power at will, sending other students across the room or crashing them into the wall with enough force to leave them groggy. I positively salivated at the prospect.

What I discovered, however, is just as skill in uprooting can be improved, so can the ability to thwart it by effective neutralizing, and by other less technically sound means. As we might expect with tai chi, pushing soon proved to be a lifelong pursuit that would never reach the point of perfection. Laoshi's students came to regard the skill of uprooting as the beginning of skill, not the end. The ability to uproot was merely the equivalent of throwing a six to get on the board. Only then did the game really begin.

The story of Laoshi's glimpse into the reality of the correct push has many clues as to how learning works in tai chi.

He referred to the incident, saying, "Wang Lang was an excellent communicator who had a poetic soul, and so, for him, the push took on an almost mystical air. 'Once we have our partner stuck in position, we should withdraw the weight backward slightly to break his root,' Wang Lang would instruct us. 'Then, come forward so the jin energy moves from the back foot, goes under the floor, up the front foot, and rises up to the middle of the spine and out of the hands, whereupon our partner is hurled back without our feeling as though we are doing anything.'

"From my current understanding," Laoshi said, "I can see how his description might be arrived at; taken literally, however, it gives the impression of some disembodied force becoming available to us at some point in our training—that the push is something removed from any normal use of the body. This, to me, feels misleading and, I think, may be the reason so few of Wang Lang's students were able to demonstrate uprooting skill, in spite of the fact that he himself was very proficient in its use."

Laoshi added, "Wang Lang 'got it' while watching a film of Zheng Manqing. Similarly, I 'got it' while watching Wang Lang push another student. The understanding happens in a flash—although the groundwork has to be there.

Many thousands of shoves have to be made before the first good push happens.

"Interestingly, in my case, I was very ill at the time," Laoshi said, "and perhaps that illness made me more receptive to what I was seeing. I was prone to looking with my analytical mind, but on that day I was depleted of energy due to a very nasty cold. As a result, I was gazing aimlessly, while Wang Lang was pushing a fellow student against a wall in his house. All of a sudden I thought, 'Ah, that's how you do it!' And when I stood up to have a go, I could indeed do it. Not perfectly, but it was definitely there.

"In a way, I have Wang Lang's dog to thank for my insight. A couple of days earlier, the dog was struck by a train near his house and died shortly afterward. As I was staying with Wang Lang at the time, I buried the dog in the garden for him. The ground was very stony and hard, and the rain began almost as soon as I started to dig. The following day I had a miserable cold and felt extremely weak. This I firmly believe was the catalyst that stilled my mind and allowed a moment of insight. I was just too exhausted to analyze what I was seeing and, ironically, my vision became clearer."

From listening to Laoshi's account of his insight into pushing, it is clear there was a substantial amount of necessary groundwork—literally, to bury the dog, but also, more important, in the thousands of incorrect pushes we have to make in order to get to the point where the discovery of uprooting is awakened within. This is "investing in loss" in regard to pushing: we must struggle with the concept for a while to ripen ourselves in preparation for that moment of understanding. Then we need to relax in order for a shift in consciousness to take place and for insight to occur.

The provoking of insight was a recurring theme with Laoshi. The balance between hard work and insight in learning is a tricky one.

"People often say, 'You must work hard in order to get results,'" Laoshi remarked. "There is some truth in this for sure, but to think it is the sole secret of success is nonsense. Hard work must be coupled with insight. There is no value in working hard just for the sake of it, or, worse still, if it is damaging to the body. O Sensei himself told one of his *uchi-deshi* that extreme practices, like sitting under waterfalls, were neither useful nor necessary.

"The problem is that insight comes, apparently, unbidden. It seems to arrive, if at all, according to its own timetable. It is in the gift of the heart-mind, an alien territory to most of us, dominated as we are by the rational mind. Since we apparently control through willpower the degree of effort we devote to our practice, we presume the more we do, the greater should be our reward. It soon becomes clear, however, that this formula does not always bear fruit. To misquote the Dalai Lama: 'Insight is an accident. All we can do is become more accident prone.'"

In the absence of insight, we look for clues in the words of our teachers and our own practice. In my own search for the elusive uprooting push, one of Laoshi's "clues" was especially useful.

Laoshi once said, "I came to understand a successful push has three parts. First, the arms must be aligned correctly so they are connected with the middle of the back, between the shoulder blades. Unless the arms have this structure, they will not conduct any power at all. They will rely exclusively on muscle power to transmit the energy generated from below. Be absolutely clear, though, that even if you have the arms, you still have nothing.

"Second, you need the legs. By this I mean you have to be able to draw the bow—that is, to generate power from the legs. If you have not practiced sufficient rooting exercises, your legs function as springs, rather than rods of iron. In daily life, the legs act like springs, like shock absorbers, which is useful for walking and running, but when we want to push from the ground, power is dissipated by flexing the legs. When pushing, we must use our legs to make use of gravity in a different way, as if driving down into the earth with steel rods, like the legs of an oil rig.

"Making the legs like rods of steel means no force is dampened down and lost when we connect the body and push. This feeling of rods of steel in the legs is what is usually meant when we say we root into the ground. Being able to root means we can, at will, make that connection all the way from the ground up to the hip.

"But, as with the arms, even if we can root, functionally, we have nothing. Furthermore, even if we can root and have the correct shape and feeling in the arms, functionally, we still have nothing. We need to connect the arms and legs. The power generated by the root has to pass up through the spine and into the arms for the beginning of an uprooting push to occur.

"The ability to push someone with considerable force is not about power, but about connection. It is about being able to connect the components of the body to make a solid structure for the instant the push is needed, then to immediately relax the joints so they can once more move independently when neutralizing an attack.

"In effect, we must be like a nine-section staff—that is, nine individual hollow sticks all connected with a string through the middle. When the string is pulled tight, the nine sections all link up to become one stick. The result is that when pushing, the sections all link together; when yielding, the sections all work independently."

Once I understood Laoshi's analogy in relation to pushing, my ability improved overnight, and the elusive uprooting push was mine to command. As always, however, my joy at the progress I had made was short lived. It was not long before Laoshi spoke to me at class one evening as I blasted people into the wall with a satisfying thud. "Very good," he said. "Your uprooting has become very strong. Now you need to push from the feet."

"What?" I replied, shocked. "I thought uprooting meant pushing from the feet."

"No," Laoshi replied. "It means you have the structure. But imagine you are going to pick up a chair: you can pick it up from the top at the backrest, from the seat, or from the leg. You have not changed the shape of the chair, but the method is different for all three. It is similar when pushing. It is a question of where the motivation for the push comes from. The lower the physical structure you can push from, the better. Pushing from the middle of the back is good for now, but pushing from the base of the spine would be better. Of course, a push that comes from the soles of the feet is the best of all. Once you have mastered this, we will talk about *ti fang* [提放]."

Ti fang is the slight pause and backward movement good pushers use to upset the balance of the person they are pushing. Once you feel the other person's resistance, he is ever so slightly leaning on you, and therefore you are supporting him. By withdrawing slightly, you take away this support, and he must arrest his forward movement so as not to fall forward. We make use of this slight recoiling by timing our push to coincide with it, thus increasing our power by effectively adding to the opponent's pulling back.

"But I thought I was using ti fang," I countered.

"No," Laoshi said once again, "you are overpowering them. Once they learn to root against you, you will not be able to push them.

"Bear in mind also the deeper ideas contained in these studies. What good is it to you if you push them but you undermine yourself as a result? The manner in which you push has great relevance for your interaction with people in general. Becoming desperate to win at all costs may rob you of something more important in your life."

I was only too aware of the feelings of annoyance and anger when other people pushed me, and so I presumed they felt the same way when I pushed them. Was this what Laoshi was referring to?

"The best push," Laoshi said, "even when the other resists, should have the feeling of a ripe fruit falling. It is true that the opponent is pushed, but he does not feel violated or cheated. This is a difficult thing to understand and is very seldom witnessed. It is perhaps best illustrated by a story an old teacher once told me of a meditation course he attended with a great spiritual master. According to my teacher Don, one of the attendees at the course, was a rather conceited sex therapist who, in the regular discussion groups, irritated everyone with his brand of bragging and his know-it-all attitude. All throughout the week this fellow raised hackles, but he appeared to be unaware or unconcerned with the reaction around him.

"At one of the final group sessions, the sex therapist made a great show of asking the master a question: 'What is the difference between making love and just fucking?' he inquired.

"The master merely smiled and quietly replied, 'You will never know.'"

I grinned. "Ouch. What a push."

"Indeed," Laoshi replied, "but the remarkable thing was that despite the cutting nature of the master's reply—or maybe because of it—the guy seemed to open up. According to Don, the guy changed instantly. The mask of his cool, indifferent bravado was shattered, and the real human being inside came out for the first time. He had no resistance to the master's words, and his veneer cracked.

"A good push has a similar quality. There can be great power behind it. You may hit the wall with so much force that you shake the foundations of the building, but you do not feel abused. This is the type of push to aim for, the kind that does not cause a negative reaction. You are not aiming to be either personal or superior; rather, you are like a force of nature. This is what I guess Zheng Manqing was referring to when he said, 'Push without the idea of pushing.' After all, you would not blame the fire for burning you when you put your hand in it, would you?"

Laoshi's last remark suddenly reminded me of a story Billy Coyle once told me. At the time, Billy—a third dan, I believe—attended many weekend courses all over the country with Chiba Sensei. Chiba's aikido was renowned for its spirit and power. The evening before one such course, Chiba Sensei phoned Billy to tell him he would be unable to teach and that Billy should take his place.

Feeling uneasy at the prospect, Billy pointed out to Chiba Sensei that the local instructor, who had organized the course, considered himself a third dan and would likely object to someone of equal grade turning up to teach the course on his patch. (The fact that the origin of the local man's grade was dubious was known to both Chiba Sensei and Billy. The suggestion had been made by a class wag that the fellow was third dan because he had read three books on aikido and would consider himself fourth dan when he finished reading his fourth book.) Billy feared his own arrival to teach in place of Chiba Sensei might cause the local instructor to feel the need to defend his authority.

Chiba Sensei's reply astounded Billy: "Well, if necessary, kill him, but it shouldn't come to that."

"I can't do that," Billy replied, shocked.

Chiba Sensei returned calmly: "If a man says he is a third dan tightrope walker—and he is not—then when he tries to walk across a rope in the air, he will fall. The rope does not wriggle around to knock him off. You are like the rope. You will go and he will ask himself who he is; if he stands on the rope and falls, you are not responsible."

Billy remained hesitant, so Chiba Sensei continued, "When a man walks out into the sea and drowns, is it the sea's fault?"

As it turned out, there was no problem. The local man accepted that Billy would be teaching in place of Chiba Sensei.

I noticed Laoshi was listening with interest as I related the story of Chiba's remarks. As I finished, Laoshi nodded in acknowledgement: "Chiba Sensei's language may seem a little extreme, but there is, nevertheless, a common idea here: Chiba Sensei was being authentically 'Chiba Sensei,' and he was asking Coyle Sensei to be authentically 'Coyle Sensei.' A real push demands that you be genuinely who you are. It is asking you to be sincere. People often talk about the 'egoless push,' as if that is possible or, indeed, desirable. As if it is only possible to push without eliciting resentment by somehow being virtuously 'egoless,' as in Zhuangzi's empty boat. But I am who I am—and I need to speak and act in accordance with who I am. Pushing is training in being able to sincerely accept who I am and not be afraid to let others know it too.

"In this sense, a push, whether physical or verbal, is a statement of who I am—no more, no less. This is how to deal with people in a meaningful way. We do not pretend to be nice, nor do we make ourselves feel superior by making others feel inferior. People feel our presence. They may or may not like it, but our presence is honest, just as our push should be. We do not try to trick people or manipulate them. Rather, when the conditions are there, we push. We push only to assert our right to be who we are and remain balanced."

It occurred to me later that Laoshi was asking a lot by encouraging us to be who we are and push when the conditions are there. Our society has encouraged us to become victims and claim discrimination and offense without a thought that there may be an alternative. No wonder so many of us become ill and depressed when we are badgered into behaving so weakly. The price we pay in a politically correct world is that we no longer behave with authenticity. It is the ultimate mistrust and betrayal of our heart-mind, in favor of rational-mind dogma. It is a chilling consequence that to lose trust in ourselves leads inevitably to a loss of trust in the Dao. Loss of trust in the Dao leads to ill health and misery.

Chapter 24: The White Ape Offers Respect

The word "respect" goes hand in hand with martial arts everywhere and, at times, lingers like the stale smells characteristic of rundown gyms and practice halls all over the world. Having studied karate, aikido, and iaido for years prior to starting tai chi, I had imbibed the notion of respect for teachers, seniors, and

雲
手
左

other students from my first steps onto the mat. We would bow before entering the dojo, bow before stepping onto the mat, bow before the photo of the founder, then bow, bow, and bow again to show our understanding of respect. We also had to scurry. When sensei said go here or go there, sauntering was not the order of the day. A sense of urgency was required in all we did.

All this ritual led me to unconsciously assimilate the notion of respect in martial arts without ever questioning the process or its rationale. I was convinced I understood, without the need for detailed explanation, that we should conduct ourselves with respect for others, since we were practicing potentially dangerous techniques. We were turning ourselves—at least in our own imaginations—into warriors. Some code of conduct was indispensable, lest we martial students, gorged on our own power, run rampant through the mere mortals surrounding us in our day jobs as toilet cleaner, bus driver, or hospital porter. Not only were we martially superior to our fat-cat bosses, who regarded us as mere wage slaves, but we were morally superior also, for we had the means to convey them to the River Styx, but chose not to, due to self-restraint borne out of commitment to respect. Were we not indeed gods? Perhaps the case is a little overstated in keeping with Zhuangzi's inclination, but the point remains.

Respect was necessary and we were trained to respect just about everything. It was a variation of the injunction to army recruits: If it moves, salute it; If it doesn't, paint it green. For us the motto might well have been, if it moves, respect it; if it's dead, respect it more. All very commendable, or so I thought, until I broached the subject inadvertently with Laoshi.

I was in his kitchen after a good morning session of push-hands. I felt I had discovered a new insight into the push and was feeling way too content with myself. I should have recognized the feeling and remembered Wang Lang's admonition: "There is only one thing worse than feeling bad and that is feeling great—as this is when we are most likely to do something stupid."

My stupid thing was simply to express my feelings to Laoshi: "You know, Laoshi, I just wanted to say I really respect you and all of your teachings."

It was an expression of a genuine feeling of admiration and gratitude for a man I felt made my life more livable and enjoyable. The sincerity of the statement, though possibly clumsy in its expression, made his reply all the more shocking.

He rolled his eyes, sighed, and said, "What am I going to do with your respect?"

I was astonished. All I thought I knew from years of study did not lead me to think I had said something so obviously irritating.

"Sorry, Laoshi," I blurted out, feeling stunned and, in truth, hurt. "I didn't mean to offend you."

He rolled his eyes again, only more so this time, sighed even more deeply, and said, "You didn't offend me. How could you offend me?"

Great, I had annoyed him again. What was going on?

"I don't understand, Laoshi," I offered, gulping a little and hoping my distress was not showing too much.

It must have been evident, however, for Laoshi's demeanor changed and he said more gently, "Of course, you don't understand. Maybe I am teaching a little harshly today. But ask yourself, why do you feel so bad right now? You were really happy a few minutes ago, and now you are upset. What has changed?"

I could not deny the truth of what he said—but had he manipulated me in some Machiavellian way into feeling upset?

"You have hurt my feelings, Laoshi," I said. "I only meant to tell you I respect you."

"Exactly," he replied. "You see how dangerous respect is? By refusing your respect, you feel I have hurt you far more than if I had punched you in the face."

Still at a loss, I struggled to regain my composure.

Laoshi continued: "Respect is not necessarily the beneficent thing people take it for—and offense is not the vitriolic thing so many seem to think. We must look at these things clearly; see them for what they are before they turn on us. Do not forget the principle of yin and yang: understand that within respect there is also a sliver of its opposite—resentment."

"What?" I interrupted, not fully convinced.

"Of course," he continued, not particularly surprised. "It is the way with people. We hide what we really feel about other people, sometimes because we feel it is unworthy, sometimes out of self-interest, but mostly because we blindly live our lives conforming to the patterns others have set down for us.

"Think about it," he added. "If you say you respect someone—a teacher, for instance—you automatically put him in a position of authority over you. You are now obliged to listen to what he says and to do as you are told. Part of you resents this, but your resentment remains hidden as long as you think you are getting what you want. At some point things change. You feel you are no longer receiving a full measure, and you begin to resist your teacher. Have you not felt that resistance?" Laoshi eyed me meaningfully.

"Where is your respect then?" he said. "You begin to question your teacher and his motives. You wonder if he has changed, or if he has sold out—or you even suspect your previous high opinion of him was a mistake. You may, in certain circumstances, conclude your teacher has been deceitful and he is using you for his own purposes.

"This is doubly so for a martial artist. There must be tension between student and teacher: you are being trained to have a courageous and powerful spirit, yet you are simultaneously expected to obey the sometimes erratic dictates of an old man whose skill is declining as yours is rising. You are being trained to impose your will on an opponent, yet you are expected to neuter yourself in dealings with your teacher.

"Even the great O Sensei Ueshiba had problems with Takeda Sokaku, his former teacher. If some of his students are to be believed, O Sensei had a very trying time pandering to the demands of Takeda, who had an uncomfortable habit of arriving unannounced at O Sensei's dojo and causing havoc.

"If all students truly respect their teachers and vice versa, then why are there so many bust-ups in martial arts schools, so many students leaving to find 'better' teachers, or to start their own schools? The only time when respect can be guaranteed is when the master is dead. What a relief! Now your master cannot tell you what to do. He cannot scold you. He cannot humiliate you in front of your classmates. He cannot correct you when you misrepresent his teachings. You are free to love and honor him, and gradually, by your words and deeds, he becomes elevated to the status of a god."

"That makes sense, Laoshi," I interrupted, "but what harm is there in it?"

Laoshi smiled. "You think elevating your teacher to the heavens comes from solely noble motives?" he said. "The greater the teacher, the greater the student, right? When you start teaching others, it will not take long before your own students begin to understand that since you were trained by a 'god,' the only way they can equal you is to be trained by a god themselves. Hence, you now become immortalized as well."

I had to admit he had a point. I recognized myself in Laoshi's assessment. Still, I found it hard to simply drop the habit of so many years of worshiping at the shrine of respect.

"But isn't respect the foundation of martial arts?" I said. "How can you talk about it as if it doesn't matter, Laoshi?"

"I did not say it doesn't matter," he insisted. "Respect has its place, and if it is sincere, it can be a beautiful thing, but often it is not. You would be wise to understand the origins of the need for respect in the old arts. Think back to the old days when you couldn't simply go forth and find a teacher on a whim. Life was not as it is now, with its labor-saving devices; life was hard and time and energy were precious. Few teachers were available, and those who were did not waste their time teaching an art, won through a lifetime of endeavor, to the merely curious. Their art was precious to them because it had been shaped through a lifetime of dedication and struggle. Everything costs, and in a world where resources were scarce, this cost was substantial."

Laoshi gazed upward, folded his arms across his chest, and began to paint a scene: "Put yourself in the place of one of the old masters. You would search relentlessly for students worthy to receive your teaching—a monumental task in itself, given the shortage of suitable candidates, the lack of advertising, and poor transport in a preindustrial culture. Then, once suitable students were found, another challenge would arise. Worthy as the prospective student might be in terms of health, talent, and desire to learn, would he have been schooled to know his place, and treat you as fastidiously as you once treated your own master?

"Since your teacher was hard on you, the same discipline would have to be meted out to future generations—each one softer and lazier than the one before—to resist the slide into mediocrity. Finally, after you have taken great care to pass on the precious jewel—your lifetime's work; the fruit of your time, energy, and money; the knowledge gleaned by generations of masters you have shed blood and sweat to keep alive—after all your efforts, you find your student, the worthy one, takes it all and says, 'Thank you and goodnight,' leaving you one evening, when you have nothing else to teach, like a dried out old prune.

"You are left with nothing. You have been robbed and you do not have the time to start again. If you did, you would be much smarter. You would not be so generous with your knowledge but, instead, reveal it slowly and hint at the ultimate perfection of the art, which you would only reveal to the most loyal student of a generation. If a student displeased you, then you would threaten to withhold the 'good oil' and leave him floundering in ignorance until he had made amends. You would introduce formal discipleship so that, in exchange for the real stuff, your students would have to make commitments to see your needs met through your weakening years, when your skills would be in decline and, as a vulnerable old man, you would be prey to the wolves."

Now in full flow, Laoshi added, "Then you would play your masterstroke. You would persuade your students this was the way heaven intended the world to be, and only ruffians and scoundrels without honor would not understand this. Indeed, did not Confucius say as much?"

Laoshi was smiling by now, eyes twinkling, enjoying his own exaggerated account of the "old days," but, nevertheless, I was getting his point.

"So the notion of respect is about controlling people?" I asked.

"Ah, insight at last!" Laoshi said, his amusement obvious. "Very often that is true. The reasons may even be understandable—but it is often about control nevertheless. If you have awareness of this truth, you can muzzle the tiger that is respect. If not, it will turn on you and maul you."

Laoshi's tone grew serious. "Take care before you buy into what some teachers say. One of my own teachers played the respect game with his students. He was highly traditional in many ways, mainly when it suited him—or so it seemed. This teacher used to say, 'You must respect me.' That was the traditional part. But the modern, politically savvy part added, 'or you don't really respect yourself.'

"This is the modern variation on an old theme. The shtick is if you come to study but don't look up to the teacher, then you are being untrue to yourself. Why, after all, would you be spending your money taking instruction from someone you do not fully respect? In the case of this teacher, the 'respect me to respect yourself' dodge worked very well. His students bought into the idea in droves, as did I for a while. However, there was an undercurrent of fear among his students, which reinforced his control as most people policed themselves strictly, lest they say or do anything out of step, which led to their ostracism.

"What this teacher was really insisting on was his own way, but since he also customarily styled himself as a champion of the oppressed and the underdog, he was subtle enough to suggest he was performing a service for his students.

"This beneficent, fatherly act worked well for the most part; however, every so often, a student would fall afoul of the teacher by some word or deed he considered challenging to his authority. Thereupon, the student would find himself cast out of the fold, cut off with the words 'You and I are finished.'"

"Is that what happened to you, Laoshi?" I inquired quietly.

"Yes," he replied with a rueful smile.

"It still bothers you, Laoshi?" I asked.

"I am not too bitter, if that is what you mean," he replied in thoughtful tones. "But my teacher told me I was family, so was I taken aback by his reaction? Yes. Did I feel the sting of his angry rejection? Certainly."

Given my own experience with controlling relatives, I felt a lot of sympathy for Laoshi. The rift between him and his teacher was clearly an old wound, but Laoshi steadfastly refrained from attacking his old teacher. He would only say he felt he had no choice but to break from his teacher, as he was put in an impossible position, asked to do something with which he could not honorably comply.

Not long after my discussion with Laoshi on the nature of respect, I witnessed firsthand an example of his meaning. I wandered into class one evening and overheard a woman who had been coming to class for a short while talking to some of the other women in the class. She was inviting them to a party at her house. I paid little attention at the time, other than to smile at the apparent camaraderie of the tai chi class.

The following week, however, I heard the same woman talk of the party again, only this time she was holding a catalog and pointing out the beneficial properties of aromatherapy oils. "Hmm . . . so it was that kind of party," I thought. I could sense the tension among the other women, who were now on the receiving end of a hard sell.

Laoshi must have noticed as well, for he called the woman over for a discreet word. Although I could not hear what was said, it was clear that when he was finished, she was not happy. All through class she radiated irritation and hostility. If Laoshi was aware of it, he made no comment.

The next week the woman arrived early and asked to speak to Laoshi. There were only a couple of us in the hall, but Laoshi motioned her to the side for a little more privacy. Even so, it was not difficult to overhear the conversation. Indeed, as it continued and the woman's voice grew louder, it would have been impossible to ignore the exchange.

"I didn't like what you said to me last week." Her tone was aggressive and her face betrayed anger that had been stewing for a whole week.

Laoshi's tone was neutral. "You cannot sell stuff in my class," he said. "This is my place of business, and my students come to study. They do not come to class to be put under pressure to buy things."

The woman could not argue the point but was still clearly annoyed.

"I understand that," she retorted dismissively, "but it was the way you spoke to me that I didn't like."

Laoshi inclined his head slightly and replied simply, "Get used to it."

The woman was taken aback, as was I. It is not the kind of response you expect.

"But you should be nice to me," she insisted. "I was nice to you. I brought you presents when I came back from holiday and made you some soup. You are a tai chi teacher—you should be nice to people!"

"I am nice to people," Laoshi said, unperturbed. "Don't you know how some teachers treat their students?"

She did not answer his question, but said, "If you want me to respect you, then you should treat me better."

Laoshi remained calm but leaned a little forward before saying, "Ah . . . so what you want is for me to behave the way you think I should? It is not up to you to decide how I should behave. I behave as I choose, and you decide what you want to do about it."

Now suddenly realizing the encounter was not going as she imagined, she changed tack a little. "I still want to be your student," she said, "but you have to treat me right."

Laoshi said simply, "What makes you think I want you as a student?"

There was stunned silence. A few more words were said, quietly this time, so I could not quite hear. She stayed for the class, but I never saw her again.

The incident all too clearly illustrated Laoshi's previous warnings concerning the notion of respect—how respect can be used as a weapon, and how teachers, like Laoshi, have to deal with the various manipulations in which some people specialize. I began to recognize my own vulnerability to manipulation of this kind and resolved to examine my own views on respect. I later remembered the wise words of an aging British Army sergeant who learned about life in the desert campaign against Rommel. He once told me between sips of his Glengoyne "medicine," "If you have to ask for someone's respect, you are not worthy of it. Respect is a coin that must be given freely to have value."

When I mentioned this recollection to Laoshi some days later, he nodded in approval. "Respect is a kind of drug," he said. "Be careful of it. When it is pure, it fills you with energy. Like true love, it never asks for anything in return. Its strength is in the giving, not the receiving. To feel a lack of respect and then demand it from others is to shackle yourself to their schemes and expectations. Give respect when you feel moved to do so—but never ask for it. Treat people fairly and, as best you can, have them treat you the same way. Do not fear losing peoples' respect. If this happens, you never truly had it in the first place."

Chapter 25: The Kicking Section

金
鷄
獨
立
右
式

I once mentioned to Laoshi that the kicking section is the part of the form I find most difficult. "Me too," he replied. Nevertheless, or perhaps precisely because Laoshi felt this section to be difficult, I thought his classes on the kicking section were some of the best he taught.

This part of the form is, as you might expect, referred to as the kicking section because it contains kicking postures: golden roosters, separate hands and feet, and turn and kick with heel. Two are performed on the right side and two on the left, while the final kick, the most challenging, is done only once. With a grand total of only five postures, it is a short little sequence, but a real test of balance, both physically and mentally.

It is widely held that our sense of balance deteriorates with age, but we can slow this decline so our actual age does not have to reflect our biological age too closely. Laoshi would have us test our biological age by standing with all our weight on our weak leg and closing our eyes in order to see how long it would take before we had to put the other foot down to prevent falling over. The longer we could stay balanced on one leg with our eyes closed, the better. Laoshi and many others believed one of the great benefits of tai chi is its ability to slow the aging process by maintaining healthy, strong bones and combating the increasing difficulty in balance. We might not be able to reverse the aging process, as Zheng Manqing claimed, but we can certainly influence it, in terms of increased bone density and enhanced balance.

In general, Laoshi's teaching was a blend of technical instruction, imagery to invoke the right feeling, and a philosophical foundation that gradually permeated our daily lives. The kicking section provided a particularly rich vein for all three components.

Laoshi would often introduce the kicking section as follows: "Now that we are close to the halfway point of the form, we are about to embark on the kicking section. To this point we have been studying *song* [松], the basic principle of tai chi. Song is often translated as 'relaxation'—but it means much more, for it includes the ideas of alignment and rootedness.

"These three ideas—relaxation, alignment, and rootedness—are all related. In tai chi, relaxation implies poise—that is, upright posture. The better your alignment, the less the muscles have to do to hold you up. However, we must not have the feeling of floating away from the ground. There must be a strong sense of letting the body's weight connect with the ground. This connection we call rootedness. Affect one of these three aspects of song and you affect all of them.

"The form is demanding. Not only does it ask you to perform the postures with precision, but it also asks that you gradually develop your song. Now that we have reached the kicking section, the form demands even more: it puts you to the test!"

Whether by accident or design, Laoshi would often talk about the form as if it were a living thing. It was not uncommon for him to say the form "asks you" or "likes" or "dislikes." At first I thought this a little strange. I had never conceived of exercises as having a personality. Over time, however, I found myself relating to the form as a friend, a relationship I found as challenging as it was comforting.

The obvious difficulty with the kicking section is the requirement for us to stand balanced on one leg while we lift the other. The difficulty increases as we move from the relatively straightforward golden rooster stands on one leg, through the more technically demanding separate hands and feet, to the testing turn and kick with heel.

As Laoshi would explain, "There will always be times when we are tested by our life's circumstances. It is easy to remain balanced physically and mentally when all is going well and we are happy. The true test of our gongfu, however, is when life is challenging, for it is only when we are being challenged and are struggling that we feel the loss of our equilibrium. The kicking section represents such times. We experience some form of duress but continue to rely on our internal strength to see us through. Through study of the form, we strengthen our contact with our own internal allies: relaxation, alignment, and rootedness. We remain straight—that is, true to our principles. We utilize gravity to help us remain centered, and we have faith in these forces to prevent us from becoming imbalanced, literally and metaphorically."

This was a simple idea for coping with adversity and it bore the hallmark of Laoshi's belief that we must all accept our fair share of difficulties. Hard times are inevitable, and it is not the function of spiritual disciplines to help us dodge our fate—only to deal with our difficulties gracefully.

Until I met Laoshi, I had always thought the point of a spiritual practice like tai chi was to teach us to avoid life's nastier events and so live a happier existence. Laoshi himself, however, did not endorse such a philosophy, believing instead that running away from life's challenges was not only impossible, but counterproductive.

For Laoshi, the danger lay not in "problems" per se, but in the loss of internal balance, with the potential consequence of a downward spiral into self-destruction. Thus the desire to escape negative feelings often leads to addictions and behaviors that are self-sabotaging. For Laoshi danger lay less in the problems we face and more in our reaction to these problems. "Do not attempt to rid yourself of your problems too quickly," he would often say. "You may not like the ones that come to replace them as much!" The implication for Laoshi was that a continual stream of problems in life, each replacing the previous one, is inescapable; struggling to be problem-free is, therefore, a fruitless exercise.

Another theme that emerged from the kicking section seemed to resonate strongly with Laoshi: the need for mental stamina in middle age. Learning the form, posture by posture, week by week, is a considerable commitment for most of us. At some point, usually near the middle sections of the form, we can feel inertia building. The once-liberating exercise can begin to feel like a slog.

Experiencing "air like water" as we move may be good for the qi, but when striving to learn the movements begins to resemble wading through treacle, many give up. Gone is the initial enthusiasm of learning the first postures—in its place, a never-ending stream of movements and principles to assimilate with no end in sight. We need to keep going through this part of the form just as we do in middle age, the time when our youthful enthusiasm has burned out and we find ourselves bogged down with more responsibilities and less energy to deal with them. (This brings to mind a sentiment echoed by Al Pacino's character in *Carlito's Way*, when he points out, "We are not reformed; we just run out of energy.") Our life difficulties may not necessarily be more severe at this specific period, but they certainly seem to last longer. Stamina at this time is vital.

Returning to the form, there may also be a parallel in a spiritual sense: the challenge of the kicking postures, coming immediately after the physical difficulties of squatting single whip, may highlight the emptiness we can feel in the midst of our spiritual regeneration. Having accepted the challenge of following the Way—with the subsequent explosion of energy, creativity, and optimism this brings—we might expect life would continue to reward us with spiritual and material boons. Instead, we are faced with a period where life, sometimes through trauma, seems intent on stripping away all the securities we have hitherto built around us in order to feel safe.

So much of spiritual rebirth consists in accepting the trials of a life lived in dynamic balance with the Dao. Instead of accepting the wisdom of insecurity, as Alan Watts might say, we have built our lives on the false gods of money, status, power, relationships, and family. At some point, we may well find our faith in such ideas being ripped away from us, as we come to recognize the limits of money; the draining effects of continually fighting for status; the realization that power never seems to satisfy; the disappointment in people who never live up to our expectations; and the loss of our families, who may disappear through death, physical distance, or emotional estrangement.

This is the time when life robs us of our certainty. In an allegorical sense, the kicking section is much the same: up to this point in the form, we have practiced becoming more rooted and more connected. We have located stability in ourselves and have connected with the ground of our being. Now the form takes away the security of standing with both feet on the ground and asks us to remain balanced—not only balanced, but free from tension and anxiety. You might say the form is asking us to tolerate the instability, appreciate it, and perhaps even enjoy it.

The specific imagery Laoshi used when teaching the postures in the kicking section interested me.

"From the end of squatting single whip, move all your weight onto the front foot and allow the right side of the body to rise."

I noted that Laoshi did not say, "Lift the right knee and right hand." For him, the idea of lifting took us away from the ground. Instead, Laoshi emphasized connecting with the earth, even when we might want to lift up.

"After the squatting single whip, as your weight moves forward, imagine a small post or stool beside your front left foot and place your left hand on it to balance yourself. Then, as you arrive completely on your left foot, think downward while allowing the other knee and arm to rise. The image is one of an elevator, where the car containing the people is connected to a counter-weight by a cable: as the car moves upward, the counterweight moves downward. It is better tai chi to think of your weight going down into the front foot, making the other leg seem lighter. You then allow this leg to rise."

The idea of an imaginary post placed in the ground to help us maintain balance while standing on one leg seemed, at first, ludicrous to me, but I found it does help. As Laoshi put it, "The imagery is merely a device to help us connect downward into the ground. Imagery is very powerful, as I discovered when I started teaching. In separate hands and feet, I used to encourage students to imagine holding on to the straps found on buses and subway carriages. I quickly dropped this image, as I found it encouraged the mind to rise upward, making the posture less stable."

In a similar sense, Laoshi would advise us: "Do not think about how high to lift the knee in golden rooster stands on one leg. Instead, focus on how rooted you feel in your supporting foot, because to think about lifting the knee to a particular height only encourages a raising of your energy—with the corresponding wavering in balance."

Laoshi sometimes added, "Of course, when I started, we were encouraged to lift the knee high enough to touch the elbow. Our teacher said we should do this, even though Zheng Manqing did not. By way of explanation, our teacher told us Zheng Manqing had learned from an obese Yang Chengfu, who could not get his knee high enough because his belly got in the way." Laoshi chuckled.

"Ask yourself: what is good tai chi? To raise the knee to the point where it creates tension in the body is counterproductive."

For Laoshi, the real skill in this part of the form was not measured by how high you could kick, but in how balanced and devoid of tension you could be through the entire section.

"Notice during this part of the form how the upper body tightens in response to our fear of losing balance," Laoshi added. "We have learned to deal with insecurity by tensing our bodies. This does not help our balance; it only makes things worse. This is especially true in turn and kick with heel. When we perform the kick as slowly as the form requires, our arms often tense up as if seeking some kind of help from outside as a prop. The metaphor is plain to see: we lose faith in ourselves and reach for something outside ourselves to hold on to. Gradually, we lose faith in ourselves and become prisoner to whatever that prop is: alcohol, drugs, shopping, gambling. Feeling discomfort, we seek to blot it out with distraction but find we have replaced discomfort with addiction."

In talking about addiction, Laoshi did not just mean drugs or alcohol. He was talking about the many distractions mankind has invented to avoid the emotional discomfort we all feel when left alone with our thoughts. He was fond of quoting Pascal: "All men's miseries derive from not being able to sit in a quiet room alone."

Laoshi had one key piece of advice that helped me most in my daily battle with the kicking section: "Do not rush."

When faced with trying circumstances or when stressed, we attempt to get through the difficulties as quickly as possible, often acting rashly just to escape the tension of the decision-making process. Laoshi advised us to take the opposite approach—to slow down and even savor the difficulty. "Winston Churchill is reputed to have said, 'When going through hell, keep going,'" Laoshi told us. "He was almost right," he added, smiling. "He should have said, 'Keep going, but keep going slowly.'"

Not so long ago I stumbled across a Zen saying: "Sit in meditation for twenty minutes a day, unless you are too busy; then you should sit for an hour." Laoshi would have approved.

Chapter 26: The Dao of Man

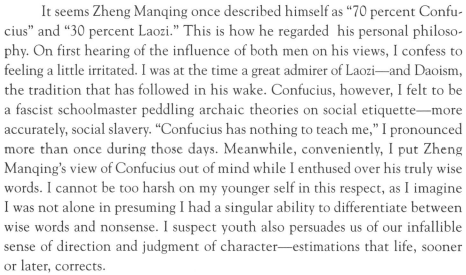

It seems Zheng Manqing once described himself as "70 percent Confucius" and "30 percent Laozi." This is how he regarded his personal philosophy. On first hearing of the influence of both men on his views, I confess to feeling a little irritated. I was at the time a great admirer of Laozi—and Daoism, the tradition that has followed in his wake. Confucius, however, I felt to be a fascist schoolmaster peddling archaic theories on social etiquette—more accurately, social slavery. "Confucius has nothing to teach me," I pronounced more than once during those days. Meanwhile, conveniently, I put Zheng Manqing's view of Confucius out of mind while I enthused over his truly wise words. I cannot be too harsh on my younger self in this respect, as I imagine I was not alone in presuming I had a singular ability to differentiate between wise words and nonsense. I suspect youth also persuades us of our infallible sense of direction and judgment of character—estimations that life, sooner or later, corrects.

This was certainly the case when it came to my regard for Confucius. One morning, Laoshi happened to mention Zheng Manqing's view that Confucius was "the most perfect man who ever lived."

"I don't get that, Laoshi," I said. I shook my head, slightly irritated. "Confucius was just a bully who wanted to imprison people in a social straightjacket. How can he be so highly regarded by a man as sophisticated as Zheng Manqing?"

"Do you have a problem with all schools of Confucian thought," Laoshi inquired neutrally, "or do any of them have something useful to say?"

"I didn't know there are schools of Confucian thought," I admitted. "I thought Confucius wrote some books and had students who just repeated what he said and added bits here and there."

Laoshi looked at me quizzically. "Would it surprise you to learn Zheng Manqing thought most interpreters of Confucius's thought were mistaken? As Douglas Wile tells us of Zheng Manqing, 'He swept away more than two thousand years of Confucian hermeneutics and took an obscure late-Ming thinker as his master.' This Ming thinker," Laoshi continued, "was a man called Lai Zhide [來知德], who introduced an early version of the yin-yang symbol."

"Er . . . what does 'hermeneutics' mean, Laoshi?" I interrupted.

Laoshi barely skipped a beat: "It means 'interpretation.' Would it also surprise you to learn Confucius said, 'What you do not wish for yourself, do not do to others'? This was five hundred years or so before Jesus said, 'Do unto others as you would have them do unto you.'"

I remained unconvinced. "Yes, but didn't Confucius go in for all those rules and rituals you were supposed to perform? And weren't you supposed to know your place and respect your betters?"

Laoshi smiled. "Perhaps you might consider that Confucius may be necessary if you have Laozi. They balance each other in philosophical terms. They are yin and yang. Daoist philosophy leads us to embrace freedom from convention, express our individualism, follow natural rhythms, and govern ourselves and others with minimal interference. These ideas no doubt appeal to you?"

"Yes, Laoshi," I replied, "very much so."

"They are indeed attractive ideas and appeal equally strongly to me, but consider, when we are in class, do we not do a form that is imposed on us? Are we not discouraged from inventing new movements? Isn't individuality only tolerated within limited parameters?

"Consider also," Laoshi added, "we are required to follow the rhythm of the person leading the group and not proceed through the form at the speed that pleases us. We are instructed to line up, almost in military order, with the teacher at the front, clearly the person in charge. The teacher tells you what to do and you comply. The class is neither democratic nor is it run by a committee. Rather, it is autocratic with a hierarchy, albeit a subtle one. So tell me, would these attitudes not be considered more like Confucian virtues?"

It was true. Here was a paradox. I was learning an art of liberation in the most confining of ways. Most tai chi and other martial arts classes, for that matter, are run as benign dictatorships, although some are less benign than others.

Laoshi continued: "Can you envisage the alternative? Chaos! It would be like my first teacher Lenny's push-hands class, although the word 'class' may be misleading. Everyone did his own thing; the only similarities among us lay in our sheer incompetence and lack of understanding. Lenny had not studied push-hands in much depth. As a result, he was not confident in what he was showing us. He accorded too much deference to any lame-brained theory devised by some of his more creative students. We all had a go at it, and our ideas were equally worthless. The class had no real structure beyond a beginning and end time. The freedom was positively stifling. Within this free-for-all, we could not focus on any one thing to begin to understand it. As happens in these environments, the greatest conviction came from the most deluded, who were inevitably the least skilled. Beware the push-hands class taught by committee!

"I was completely frustrated by the whole thing," Laoshi continued, "but I stayed around because Lenny, realizing his own limitations, decided to join the Still Lotus School, which seemed to promise more structured and competent instruction.

"He also invited a few good teachers from England to give us much-needed instruction at weekend courses. However, I soon discovered this only added to our difficulties. One weekend Lenny arranged a visit from Alec Jameson to teach da lü [大履 large roll-back]. Alec was a good man and a clear, precise teacher. More than twenty of us spent the weekend imbibing some of the most technically competent teaching I had ever experienced. The weekend was a great success. It was with high hopes that we convened at the next Wednesday class—only to find them dashed. We had all 'remembered' something different from Alec's teaching, and the arguments began. Lenny was not able to intervene with any authority, as he had been learning alongside the rest of us.

"The problem with freedom, like choice, is that too much of it leads to paralysis. A Daoist would not care and leave it all up to heaven and wander off, sniggering at the foolishness of men. I cannot live that way," Laoshi said, "nor, I suspect, can you. We need to have a counterbalance to unrestrained freedom. We need a little Confucius."

"I see what you are saying, Laoshi," I conceded. "It's just that I think of 'restraint' as stifling."

"Of course you do," Laoshi agreed. "That is why you need Daoism to show you there is freedom even in the most constraining situations. Yin is always evident in yang and vice versa. They are not mutually exclusive; they are mutually nurturing."

I continued to look doubtful.

Laoshi merely smiled and said nothing for a few moments. He then resumed: "Years ago I used to study *zazen* formally. Our group used to meet a couple of times a week and, now and then, a fully ordained monk came to Glasgow to lead all-day *sesshins*.

"I remember my first attendance at one of these day-long sittings. We used a room in a house, laid out as correctly as possible like a *zendo*, complete with a small table at the entrance to the 'hall.' On the table lay a pristine white tablecloth; a picture of the founder, Taisen Deshimaru; and incense, flowers, and the *kyosaku* stick, used for hitting us on the shoulders.

"The monk, Verner, a sixty-year-old Frenchman with many years of teaching experience, entered the room looking very dignified in his robes. He observed the required rituals and approached the little table. I was bemused to hear him tutting audibly. What terrible faux pas had we committed? He sighed, shook his head, and tutted some more before adjusting the apparently crooked kyosaku stick a few millimeters. He stepped back and nodded to himself with satisfaction.

"'What the fuck is this guy's problem?' someone muttered under his breath. This was Glasgow after all.

"Meticulous attention to detail is part of the deal with Zen, but all the tutting began to annoy me—particularly as it did not stop with moving the kyosaku. One of our number, Malcolm, a pleasant and gentle fellow, proved entirely beyond discipline due to his inability to read the energy of his surroundings. He would fidget; we heard tut, tut, tut. He got up in the middle of a session to go to the toilet—tut, tut, tut. He walked the wrong way out of the room. Tut, tut, tut. He then committed the major sin of passing in front of the picture of Deshimaru. TUT, TUT, TUT.

"At some point, the absurdity of it all took over from the pain in my knees, and I couldn't help but laugh. Naturally—tut, tut, tut. I tried to suppress the laugh and so began shaking: I heard tut, tut, tut, and then tut, tut, tut some more. Then satori! Sudden enlightenment! Or at least as close as I ever came. It all made not the slightest difference. All the rules in the world cannot take away your freedom, and all the freedom in the world cannot keep you from imprisonment."

Laoshi was grinning broadly as he recalled the incident. "Freedom has to be balanced by restriction. But there is more to Confucius's teaching than this, something that resonated strongly with Zheng Manqing. His writing includes the following paragraph: 'The Dao of heaven is yin and yang; the Dao of earth is hardness and softness; the Dao of man is benevolence and righteousness. Yin and yang and hardness and softness have already been fully revealed by Laozi, but only Confucius can speak of benevolence and righteousness.'

"Zheng Manqing is pointing out something very important to us here. He is saying it is not enough to live a life in harmony with the Dao; we must also learn how to live in the society of men in order to create the best circumstances for our happiness. We study Laozi's principles in order to maintain health and longevity, but we also study Confucius's core ideas, ren [仁] and yi [義], usually translated as 'benevolence' and 'righteousness,' so as not to become lost in the maze of our social responsibilities."

"So you are saying we should be nice to each other?" I interrupted. I could not help thinking this was pretty lame stuff.

"You are missing the point," Laoshi replied patiently, ignoring the note of scorn in my voice. "Benevolence and righteousness balance each other. You have heard Zheng Manqing speak of the zhong yong [中庸], haven't you? Zhong yong can be expressed in push-hands using the ideas of center of balance and correct timing. But zhong yong also applies to the balanced application of benevolence and righteousness."

"I don't understand, Laoshi," I admitted, shaking my head. Was this truly important, or was it simply archaic nonsense to which we are all required to pay lip service?

Laoshi did not waver. I felt his steady gaze upon me. "The question is this: do you want to live in the world of dust, or only on a mountaintop?"

I understood this reference. One of Laoshi's teachers had spoken of how our practice should be of use in the "world of dust"—in the marketplace, or the world of men, and not solely in the rarefied atmosphere of the temple or retreat center. Unconcerned with the difficulties of day-to-day existence, it might be relatively easy to find peace in such places—only for it to recede the moment we return to the confusion of life in the real world.

"If you are content to live only on the mountaintop, you can get by with Laozi alone. But if you want to live in the world of men, you must get to grips with ren and yi, or you will be ineffective."

"How do you mean, ineffective?" I could feel my interest growing.

"To be effective in dealing with people—to be someone taken seriously— people must feel you have some concept of justice and you can be trusted. But, they want to feel you are human-hearted too. Terrible things have been done in the name of righteousness, but terrible things have also been allowed to happen by those who only understand benevolence. Each must act as a brake on the other, not allowing situations to become out of balance. Being judgmental and without compassion may lead to bitter cynicism. However, being compassionate with little regard for rectitude may lead, ironically, to your own or other people's exploitation.

"Real effectiveness in the world requires the right blend of ren and yi, to be applied in each situation you find yourself. This is why it is so difficult to find the zhong yong—and this is why it is so difficult to maintain it. This takes a lot of reflection and study."

A few days later, I was reading *Sensei*, one of John Donohue's martial arts novels. There is a passage where Yamashita, the master, talks about his sword. Yamashita tells Burke, his student, why he has had the Japanese character for benevolence etched in the surface of the tsuba, the hand guard. The etched character is on one side only, the side visible to the owner when the sword is held in the ready position. It is not visible to the opponent; he only sees the blade. Yamashita says of the etched character, "This is to remind me of my duty . . . . The warrior's way includes an awareness of when to be merciful." I asked Laoshi if this is like the balance of ren and yi—the blade representing righteousness and the etched reminder for benevolence limiting the destructiveness the blade can unleash.

Laoshi nodded and smiled. "Indeed! He knows a thing or two, this Yamashita."

I corrected him: "No, Laoshi, he doesn't exist. He is only a character in a novel."

"He exists somewhere," Laoshi replied with a broad smile, "maybe only in imagination, but we would do well to take him, and men like Zheng Manqing, as our teachers, helping us to reconcile the teachings of Laozi and Confucius to understand wholeness."

Chapter 27: But It's Not Martial Arts

右
分
腳

Laoshi's teacher Wang Lang, who had practiced karate before meeting Zheng Manqing, once said in order to get the looseness back into his arms for push-hands, he had to undo every push-up he had ever done. On the other hand, Wang Lang also said Zheng Manqing had a soft spot for those students skilled in other martial arts. Furthermore, Zheng Manqing suggested that the martial spirit developed by sincere practice of traditional martial arts could go a long way in making up for weaknesses in technique.

To me these statements seemed to give a mixed message about the relationship of tai chi to other martial arts. To add to the confusion, Wang Lang also often mentioned the Professor's comment: "Tai chi helps with everything else you do, but nothing else you do helps your tai chi." I began to question whether the attitudinal benefits of studying other martial arts were worth the potential unlearning that was necessary to learn tai chi. And, if martial spirit were so prized, why did Laoshi not encourage his students to develop it?

My questioning coincided with one of those periods where I felt my progress had stalled and I grew pessimistic about my potential. I began to feel angry with Laoshi. Unable to make much headway, I began to question his methods and, subsequently, his character, as my disillusionment threatened to boil over.

I was losing faith in one of the three conditions necessary for success in learning tai chi: correct teaching. It was Zheng Manqing's assertion that progress in tai chi requires correct teaching, perseverance, and natural ability. Although I knew it was impossible to change the degree of natural ability bestowed upon me, I was willing to live up to my side of the bargain—to persevere—but I began to wonder if Laoshi were responding in kind. I believed the bond between teacher and student required that each give of himself to the best of his ability. I found myself beginning to doubt Laoshi—not his knowledge, but worse, his willingness to share it. He was, I felt, holding back, in my eyes, being dishonest.

These feelings were beginning to consume me but, ashamed of them, I did not reveal them to Laoshi, who would ask me from time to time if I was all right. I began to feel duplicitous myself.

Then one evening we had a visit from a young man who, having heard of tai chi, was wondering if his MMA skills could benefit from some cross-training. He preferred to watch the form class but asked if he could take part in the push-hands class that followed. Laoshi agreed and asked me to show him some of the basic ideas. His demeanor had been very respectful toward Laoshi, but as I attempted to verse him in the peng-lu-ji-an approach to push-hands, he continually interrupted me, asserting, "Yes, but if you do that, I would do this." He would then improvise a counter to whatever I was showing him. I tried a few times to persuade him of the value of learning the correct form, but he continued to sabotage my attempts until we descended into free pushing and, from there, into wrestling.

We became increasingly mutually resistant with the result that we tumbled to the floor. At that point Laoshi came over. He patiently explained the value of "listening" in push-hands, and our guest assumed a respectful manner toward him, but when we resumed, it became evident that our visitor just wanted to test the worth of his MMA skills. At the end of a most dispiriting night, I asked him what he thought of our approach. His reply could not have annoyed me more: "It's OK, I suppose, but it's not martial arts." And with that, he was gone into the night, never to return, while I was left quietly raging inside.

Then Laoshi came over and compounded my misery by asking, "So, what did you learn from our friend?"

"He's an arsehole!" I spat through gritted teeth. And then it all came out: my frustration with tai chi, my frustration with Laoshi, and my frustration with arseholes who could not tell their backside from their elbow.

"Hmm . . . looks like a cup of tea is in order," Laoshi said. "Let's go to the café."

The trip around the corner to the café seemed to take forever. Fortunately, a table was available and, after we ordered some tea, Laoshi merely waited patiently while I sulked like a spoiled teenager. I had managed to calm down a little when he asked, "So, what do you believe a martial art to be?"

It was one of those questions to which you always assume you know the answer. Until, that is, someone asks you. Then, as I was discovering in that very moment, a combination of who asks and how he asks can cause doubt to emerge.

"Well . . . it is a form of self-defense, isn't it?" I replied, with an air of assurance I by no means felt.

"There are many who would give you an argument about that," Laoshi replied quietly. "The two words, 'martial' and 'art,' seem odd bedfellows, don't you think?"

"Er . . . you mean because 'martial' is about violence, and 'art' is about, well, artistry?" I mused.

"Exactly," he added. "It is the marriage of two seemingly diverse ideas and, like a marriage, there is tension between them. So, perhaps we should start with another question." Laoshi paused, caught my eye. "Why do people study martial arts, or self-defense, or combatives or—whatever you want to call these practices?"

I decided to play it safe here. I did not want to risk showing Laoshi I was beginning to doubt myself.

"Well, I guess there are lots of reasons: some for health, some for meditation, some for self-defense—lots of reasons."

"Did I ever tell you why I began studying martial arts?" Laoshi inquired. I shook my head. Laoshi nodded and continued. "As you know, I came to live in Glasgow when I was nine years old. Both my parents were foreigners and, having been born in England but then moving to Scotland, I felt doubly estranged from my environment. My family was not like other people here, and I felt it keenly. Furthermore, my family's finances had taken a turn for the worse and the move up north was accompanied by a drop in social class. We moved from a more prosperous life in London to working-class Maryhill.

"It was a far tougher environment then, and people were poor. Some lived in squalid conditions that had more in common with Dickensian times than the twentieth century. I still remember the sign in the barber shop window: HAIRCUTS REPAIRED. For some, a trip to the barber was a luxury, and I saw many an unfortunate classmate with all the signs of a do-it-yourself haircut gone drastically wrong. I felt impoverished in more ways than one. My parents were going through a volatile period in their relationship and the world they deposited me into was grittier and more violent than I was used to. I felt threatened at home, in school, and on the street.

"Then one afternoon as I was leaving school, Davie, a boy in the year above, grabbed me from behind and put me in a headlock. It was a random attack and I was unprepared but, having played at wrestling as young boys do, I knew enough to turn his advantage against him, and reversed the position by getting him into a shoulder lock of some kind. I applied more pressure and he began to cry. I let him go and walked home.

"The next day, as I was approaching the school, I caught sight of Davie, but he was not alone. He was accompanied by a boy named Squirrel. I cannot remember his real name, but Squirrel was, by reputation, the best fighter in the school, and now, it would seem, Davie's bosom buddy. "It was him," Davie declared, pointing at me accusingly. Squirrel, bigger again, and better built than either Davie or I, strode over to me and said fiercely, 'Did you give him a doin' yesterday?'

"I was scared and I possessed limited street savvy, due to my earlier sheltered life—but I managed to explain. 'No! He grabbed me yesterday and I just bent his arm to get away.'

"'All right,' Squirrel said. Then, as if dispensing the wisdom of Solomon, he pronounced his judgment: 'Fight him now.'

"What could I do? I was going to get hit whatever I did. I moved toward Davie and punched him as hard as I could on the nose, mimicking what little boxing I had seen on TV.

"Davie's nose took the full brunt of my punch. He started crying again, holding his bleeding nose. I felt I was about to be beaten to a pulp by Squirrel, but then something odd happened. Rather than Squirrel taking my punch to Davie's nose as a cue to attend to matters himself and punish me for my efforts, he made it his responsibility to offer Davie some coaching. 'No, no, Davie,' he said. 'Put your fist up, like this.' Squirrel demonstrated by putting his fists up to protect his face.

"After a couple of minutes of cornering and advice from Squirrel, Davie was together enough for round 2. There was, it has to be said, something of an improvement in Davie's defense, but I still managed to get through, delivering a few blows while receiving very little in return. We seemed to follow bare-knuckle rules. It was a 'square go,' as they used to say in those days—that is, a fair fight. No chibs, as blades were known back then, were drawn, and Squirrel remained content to be coach and corner man. After a few minutes of sparring, Squirrel stopped us, saying, 'Hey, you're no' bad, wee man. Let's you and me have a go.' And with that I became Squirrel's *uke*. Whenever he was bored at morning break or lunchtime, he would seek me out for some sparring in the schoolyard, watched by the rest of the boys.

"Squirrel was—and I even recognized this at the time—an honorable kid. I know he took it easy on me, as I was a couple of years younger and a good bit smaller. When he hit me, as he did at will, he pulled some power; I, on the other hand, feeling outmatched, would hit him as hard as I could whenever I found an opening. I learned a few things from these encounters, apart from how to box a little. First, getting hit in the face is not that bad; it is the fear of getting hit that is the problem. Second, during that period I never had any trouble with the other kids at school.

"Looking back, I acknowledge my debt to Squirrel. He was my first sensei. Although it took me years to really understand what had happened, I came to appreciate that my real enemy was my own fear. Gradually, I have come to accept the truth that, of all the challenges we face, the only real problem is fear.

"Some years later, another incident cemented the lesson Squirrel had given me with his bare knuckles. I joined the Army Cadet Force as a first step to becoming a soldier. At the time, I hoped the Army might help me come to terms with my isolation and insecurity. This particular incident took place when we were away at one of our weekend camps. There was some bad blood involving the two senior boys, Reid and Wright, and another boy called Feaney, who at sixteen was two years younger than his ironically named antagonists. I say 'ironically' because Reid and Wright seemed to be strangers to pen and paper. They were, however, well acquainted with swagger and disdain. This low-level tension had been simmering for some time, but now, at the end of camp, there was going to be a reckoning. Being two years younger still, at fourteen, and none too popular with Reid and Wright, I was too scared to refuse when I, along with the other boys, was ordered to participate in an assault on Feaney.

"At a given signal, while Feaney was packing his suitcase in an old, rundown billet in an old, rundown Army camp, we moved in. There were about fifteen of us in total as we converged on Feaney's bed space. The only one not joining in was a guy called Alan, who was lying on his bed, reading a comic. He was another of the senior boys, and he had no interest in the operation. When I later asked why he had not joined in, Alan simply said, 'Feaney might be an arsehole, but he's never done anything to me.' At the time, I envied his moral courage and berated myself as we moved in to surround Feaney. What made matters worse was that, in truth, Feaney had been kind and encouraging to me during my first faltering steps into what I thought was going to be my profession. The stories of initiation rites that go on at first camps had terrified me, but with lads the caliber of Feaney around, I felt a little safer. He had a decency about him, something you could trust.

"Though outnumbered and standing alone, Feaney carried on, nonchalantly packing his case. We knew Feaney was hard. He boxed for the county, but even he could not take on Reid, Wright, and another dozen of us. Could he? Together with Reid and Wright, a couple of the lads were eighteen-year-olds, and more like men than boys. Still, Feaney gave no indication of fear.

"Getting no reaction to our menacing approach, Reid growled viciously, 'You're getting your head kicked in, Feaney.' Without looking up, Feaney replied casually, to no one in particular, 'I know that. But the first one or two of you at me are getting a broken jaw.'

"There was silence as those of us assembled there considered Feaney's offer. Who had the courage to be the first one or two? Reid and Wright did not fancy it. Neither did their swamp-snake henchmen. The rest of us, only there under duress, certainly did not fancy it either. Eventually, a few of us summoned up the courage to walk away. The power of Reid and Wright was broken. Now with only six of them left facing Feaney, they backed down and the 'reckoning' simply fizzled out."

I was growing used to Laoshi's stories, so I knew a question was coming my way, but he surprised me by answering it himself. "If I were to ask you," he said, looking directly at me, "which technique Feaney employed in his defense, you would have to say none at all, but his boxing saved him on that occasion."

"You mean they were too scared to attack him because he was a boxer?" I asked.

"Yes, and more besides," Laoshi said thoughtfully. "Feaney was in control of his fear. This was the vital factor that gave him a kind of spiritual power they knew they could not defeat."

"What, you mean like a mystical force around him?" I interjected but immediately regretted interrupting, as Laoshi gave me one of his looks.

"No," he said scathingly, "not like that. You are watching too much *Crouching Tiger* and not enough *Yojimbo*. It is more like an air of confidence, a presence that suggests strength. People can sense this sort of presence; they also realize it will take a lot to subdue someone with this kind of courage. Usually, under such circumstances, they find their own willingness to risk injury diminishes in direct proportion to the strength they feel emanating from their intended victim.

"Whether they realize it or not, people study martial arts, meditation, spiritual growth, and 101 other things because they are looking for something to help them deal with their fear—something that will give them the spiritual strength, not only to deal with the Reids and Wrights of this world, but all of life's difficulties."

"I see your point, Laoshi—really I do. But what happens when you encounter someone like that MMA guy? Why can't he see that martial arts are about more than techniques?" I was still smarting from my earlier encounter.

Laoshi smiled a little. "Well," he said, "we could take the view of Zheng Manqing when Robert Smith introduced him to an American second-degree black-belt rank in Okinawan karate. After a friendly 'test of conclusions' with a senior student, the American went away, scoffing at tai chi. When Robert Smith apologized for the fellow's ill manners, Zheng Manqing commented only that the American was a blind man, and we must be kind to blind men."

"Easy for Zheng Manqing to say!" I protested.

Laoshi laughed. "I didn't think that would satisfy you," he said. He always seemed to be one step ahead of me. "Let us return to our first question about the marriage of the words 'martial' and 'art,'" he continued.

"OK," I agreed readily. I had not forgotten the question and felt I had an insight into the direction Laoshi was leading me.

"Is it a bit like the Japanese distinction between *do* and *jutsu*?" I asked, eager to show Laoshi I had some knowledge relevant to the discussion. I had long been aware that martial arts were evolving as the ability to kill a man on the battlefield became less of a concern. The old arts were modified to become tools of personal refinement and were referred to as kendo, aikido, and judo respectively, rather than kenjutsu, aikijutsu, and jujutsu.

"Good, good," Laoshi said, nodding. "And as a result, a tension of sorts has developed among martial artists concerning the effectiveness of their various arts. Some believe that others study a diluted, ritualized practice that may have lost its martial component. This is what your MMA friend was getting at."

"He's not my friend, Laoshi," I corrected.

"Pardon me," he said. "I forgot," but I sensed he was simply playing with me. "But you can still learn from him. He has given you a push of sorts, and you must understand both the strength and the weakness in what he says in order not to be pushed. Only then can you neutralize and effectively 'push' him. I am speaking metaphorically here, you understand."

Laoshi waited for me to add something, but I thought it better to keep my mouth shut and listen.

"There are some peculiar paradoxes surrounding this issue," he continued. "Some people train so they can be better fighters; others train so they do not have to fight.

"Other people insist on full-contact sparring in the search for realism, but have to eliminate the most brutal and lethal techniques. Meanwhile, those who practice the most damaging and lethal techniques cannot apply them unrestrained, or else they would kill each other.

"Even MMA, which styles itself as virtual street fighting, is also keen to market itself as a sport. The unified rules make many lethal and vicious techniques illegal. In the end, the sport becomes what it is in response to the rules. Change the rules, and you change the sport.

"So what can we conclude from all this?" Laoshi asked. It was a rhetorical question. I was beginning to wonder myself. He paused, perhaps waiting for me to contribute before adding, "It seems to me that, while we are all looking for roughly the same thing, some of us find our gaze turning inward to look at our own reactions to challenging events; others look outward to deal with those same challenges in an external, physical sense.

"Laozi reminds us that just as the mountain does not laugh at the river because it is so low, so the river does not berate the mountain because it cannot move. It is not a question of which approach is better; it is an acknowledgement that there are different ways to deal with the problem of fear.

"Furthermore, as you know from your own experience, we can find ourselves changing approach throughout our lifetime, sometimes looking inward, sometimes looking outward, depending on what challenges are presented to us.

Isn't it true that your own aikido teacher changed his emphasis from aikido in his earlier years to something more like aikijutsu in later life?"

This was true. Over the years Billy had modified his approach from a more flowing, harmonious style to a more combat-effective style. I observed this gradual evolution myself during the time I studied with him, and had my feelings confirmed by some of Billy's writing. There were many who did not welcome this change in their teacher and left to find a style more in keeping with their own needs.

"Remember,'" Laoshi added, "people can go the other way too. Both Zheng Manqing and O Sensei Ueshiba were said to have taken a more martial approach in earlier years—only to lend more emphasis to the Way in later times."

"So . . . why does this happen?" I asked. I felt peculiarly sad about the whole thing. Rather than being a unifying force, collective martial arts seemed merely destined to splinter into ever smaller groups.

"I understand your vexation," Laoshi said quietly. "You would prefer that all martial artists were brothers in arms."

I nodded.

"Tomiki Sensei, one of Ueshiba's early students, was once asked about his teacher's spiritual approach. He said something to the effect that martial arts concern themselves with life and death. A number of notable people had explored this question and found the more they entered the world of danger and violence, the more they ended up moving in a direction that contradicted it all. By delving deeply into the problem of death, they found themselves on a spiritual path.

"This is understandable, don't you think?" Laoshi said. "Death is the ultimate representation of the separation between ourselves and the universe. As we delve deeply into the problem of death, we can go one of two ways: either we turn toward the universe and identify more fully with it, gradually feeling ourselves to be part of the totality, or we turn outward and identify more fully with ourselves as individual, separate, self-reliant beings.

"Zheng Manqing and Ueshiba, both of whom looked more closely into the face of death than most of us, turned their gaze inward in answer to the question of death. Musashi, on the other hand, cultivated the opposite approach and developed an attitude of supreme self-reliance. When plagued by a wound on his foot that would not heal, he went barefoot up into the snow-covered mountains to summon his own energies to either be healed or die. He challenged his own resources to mobilize and cure him. His attitude to the spiritual world and the gods of the time could be summed up by the phrase, 'They don't bother me; I don't bother them.'

"Like Musashi, those who practice the jutsu ways are strengthening themselves as individuals. They explore and develop this strength in reference to others. Conflict is an interesting experience, for it magnifies our fears, doubts, and isolation, and makes us unmistakably aware of our own 'individuality' in the world. Those who practice the *do* ways are seeking to dissolve the barriers between themselves and the universe, to become no longer just themselves but the universe itself."

I had been paying close attention to Laoshi's words—and the penny dropped: I realized that, as with everything else in life, there is a yin way to do something, as well as a yang way. It is a matter of our inclination and, as such, the direction that pulls most strongly within us is not really under our conscious control.

My thoughts returned to the MMA fighter, and I realized my difficulty with him was as a result of my own fears and inadequacies. The question was, in what direction does my inclination pull?

"For those following the individual path, like your friend, the arsehole," Laoshi said, grinning, "it is a bit more straightforward, though not easy. They accentuate the separation by cutting through fear, pain, anger, and doubt. You might say they use their metaphorical sword, cutting down fear in the same way they would cut down an enemy."

Laoshi was right. I remembered Billy's words when we were near exhaustion in our periodic *mysogi*, euphemistically known as "cleansing sessions." He would urge us: "Cut through. Cut through." By cutting through our tiredness, fears, and concerns, we would raise our energy again and keep going. For Billy, this was spiritual—reaching down into the depths of our being to access the strength we only know is there when we have reached our limit. Spirit to Billy meant fighting spirit, and his training brought us ever greater familiarity with its existence.

For Laoshi the way was different. I was now beginning to see this more clearly.

"Some of us," Laoshi said, "seek to integrate ourselves with the universe so our fear does not delude us into thinking we are at its mercy. Fear will always be there, on our shoulders, convincing us we are separate, but by becoming more and more relaxed, we remember that while we are individuals, we are also one with all of life. The more we relax, the less influence the voice on our shoulder has over us. As Zheng Manqing said, 'What we seek to relax is our fear.' He also said, 'The more you relax, the less you fear. The less you fear, the more you relax.' This is life's un-vicious circle—life's benevolent circle. Our path is one of learning to relax physically, mentally, emotionally, and spiritually."

Reflecting on Laoshi's words sometime later, I began to recognize that, over the years, the Way had gradually changed for me from jutsu to do. I also came to realize the only real difference was whether I was directing the energy of my awareness outward or inward. In earlier days I had tended to model myself on Daidoji Yuzan's advice: "When you leave your gate, act as though an enemy is in sight," or Funakoshi's admonition: "When you leave home, think you have one million enemies." Now, however, I found myself following Zheng Manqing's approach: "Put the qi and the heart-mind in the dantian as much as possible."

The awareness directed toward a hostile environment is no different from the awareness of the qi in the dantian; only the direction is different. Reflecting on Laoshi's words, insight suddenly came to me in regard to the MMA fighter: he was merely acting in exactly the same manner as I would have a decade or so earlier.

A little later I confessed my newfound perspective to Laoshi. "That arsehole isn't just my friend, Laoshi. That arsehole used to be me."

Laoshi laughed. "So . . . on the path of integration at last, I see."

Chapter 28: Step Back and Listen

One of the comedian Jimmy Carr's gags goes like this: "Someone once said that people don't really listen to each other—they're only waiting for their turn to talk. At least that's what I think he said. I wasn't really listening."

左
分
腳

He might have been talking about push-hands, not just because in our desperation to win we usually ignore our teachers' instructions to remain sensitive, but also because the push-hands exchange is very much like a normal conversation—which is to say nobody really listens to anybody else. We respectfully allow other people to bore us; in return, they allow us to bore them. It is similar in push-hands. We pay little attention to what our partner is actually doing, focusing instead on what we are doing as "pusher" or "neutralizer."

Wang Lang said a person with good keqi (manners) would be a good push-hands player; Laoshi's view was that someone who is a good listener would be a good push-hands player. It amounts to the same thing.

On the same theme, I recall Laoshi telling us about a conversation he once overheard among some tai chi students while he was attending a workshop in London. "As we were milling around, waiting for the teacher," Laoshi said, "I seized the opportunity to take the measure of the other students. This was my first workshop with this teacher, who was doing introductory seminars in his particular style. I did not know any of the other students, so I drifted around from group to group, unashamedly eavesdropping as some bragged and others listened. The hierarchy was being established.

"My attention was particularly drawn to one fellow who was explaining to a small group of fellow students how his school no longer took a shoulder-width stance when pushing hands. 'We all stand with one foot in front of the other now—like this,' he said, demonstrating. 'We have given up on the shoulder-width stuff.' 'Why?' asked one of his audience. 'Because a while ago we had a visitor who came to push hands with us and he kicked one of the guys in the balls. See? Standing with feet shoulder width, you are just too open, so we all changed.'

"I moved on," Laoshi added.

Asked to say more about this episode, Laoshi smiled. "The fellow took the wrong lesson from the incident," he said. "He is like the guy who refused to cook, claiming cookers were dangerous because he once burned his backside when he sat on one."

He continued on a more serious note: "Some people think push-hands is a fight. This is a common delusion. When have you ever seen people fight this way? Push-hands is an exercise we practice in order to learn something about conflict; it is less like a fight and more like a conversation. In conversation, there are certain formalities we observe: for instance, only one of us talks at a time. We position ourselves neither too close nor too far away. We moderate the tone and volume of our voice as circumstances dictate—and we don't punch each other in the face if we hear something we don't like. Not in normal circumstances, anyway.

"In fixed-step push-hands, kicking someone means you have to move at least one foot off the ground, which is to change the whole nature of the practice. You have altered the parameters of the encounter without reference to the other person. You have changed the rules without telling anyone. The usual excuse is, 'You should be ready for anything,' but if you were to take that idea to its logical conclusion, you might as well just hit him when he bows or walks into the room— or, better still, ambush him as he gets out of the car. You get the point.

"This is why it is so difficult when visiting another school and joining in with their push-hands. They may have their unique ways of doing things, which seem strange to us. It is as if they speak another dialect—if not a whole other language."

This is why Laoshi advised us to closely observe everything that is going on when we visit other tai chi schools. "It is impolite to go into someone else's space and proceed to tell him how he should be doing things," Laoshi said. "This would be like visiting another country, trashing their culture, and installing our own. This may have been the way in imperial times, but it is arrogant and narrow minded. Similarly, when a visitor comes to practice with us, we don't begin by telling him what he is doing wrong. This would be like laughing at a foreigner who is taking his first steps in learning a new language. Instead, we take time to see what is similar and what is different. We take the measure of the other. Good martial artists do this before a contest. Kanazawa Sensei assessed opponents even as they warmed up. He would warm up prior to entering the arena so he could watch his opponent for any signs of injury or weakness. The renowned MMA fighter Anderson Silva spends the first few minutes of a contest assessing the range, rhythm, and movement of an opponent before getting serious. Such assessment is a focused form of listening."

Laoshi's words reminded me of my own informative experience when visiting a tai chi class while on holiday. The players appeared to listen to each other, follow the peng-lu-ji-an form scrupulously—until they came to the final push. It was a sudden, violent, unskilled shove, followed by an equally sudden retraction of the hands. Watching, I was astounded by the contrast between the lead-up play and the climax of the push. Laoshi had often told us the push itself should maintain the same quality as the rest of the push-hands form. Laoshi quoted Wang Lang on this: "When you finally push, don't use anything you didn't bring to the party."

Back in the tai chi class, I was wondering about the sudden and severe retraction of the hands. When I began pushing with one of the seniors, I soon found out. These students had developed a collective habit of grabbing the arms of anyone attempting to push them. So ingrained had this practice become that I was left with bruises on my upper arms after class. Unable to yield and neutralize correctly, they simply grabbed the pusher's arms in order to survive, or else drag the other off balance as he fell—a pyrrhic victory of sorts, but not in the spirit of tai chi, I thought. Didn't Zheng Manqing say there is no grabbing in tai chi? In this class, however, the response developed by the students in the role of "pusher" was to deliver a lightning-fast push, before ripping their arms free from the grasp of their opponent.

This was not unlike my own early days pushing hands in Glasgow, where faith in principle was a scarce commodity, soon exhausted and quickly replaced by grunting and grappling. The problem faced by all thoughtful tai chi players is how to act with principle when our partner does not. All too often the response we develop in the face of rough-and-ready technique is equally inappropriate.

Grabbing and holding your opponent and ripping your arms free from his grasp are examples of what Laoshi liked to call deviations—departures from correct form. You might also describe them as examples of insisting or not listening. However, when faced with deviations such as grabbing, most of us tend to respond with a deviation of our own. In other words, a fault in our partner generally elicits a fault in us. Many students are frustrated by their inability to remain soft and sensitive when their partner is hard. The entire experience becomes one of escalation, as each responds to the hard energy of his partner with hard energy of his own. This sorry state of affairs continues until one gives up and opts out of the whole scene, justifiably reasoning the process is pointless.

I experienced such an exchange myself once, when attending a workshop with an American teacher who had studied extensively in Taiwan but was returning to the States via Europe. Toward the end of the workshop, we were allowed some time to practice free pushing. Physically imposing, very tall, and well built, this teacher had a good reputation both in baguazhang (八卦掌) and tai chi, having studied with famous teachers in Taiwan. In particular, his tai chi teacher was known for his soft style of push-hands.

During the free pushing session, he moved from student to student, staying perhaps five minutes with each. After around twenty minutes it was my turn. Taking up our stances, we began the feeling-out process gently and softly. After a minute or so I began to wonder how he would respond if I became a little bit more physical. I was curious as to how someone steeped in a soft approach to push-hands would deal with a more forceful attitude. When the answer came, it was a genuine disappointment: as I grew harder in my energy, he simply matched my level of force. I tried a little escalation; he responded in kind. Before long, we both abandoned any pretense of observing the four-ounce principle, and, at some point, he attempted foot sweeps and joint locks as we struggled for dominance.

Our exchange managed to remain friendly enough, no doubt because we both recognized we were being childish—but we were enjoying it nonetheless. It was akin to getting into a food fight with friends, only with a lot less cleaning up afterward.

One of the lessons of our push-hands practice is in its ability to clearly demonstrate our tendency to respond in kind when we are confronted by childish behavior. Emerging from an immature encounter with someone, thinking, "That guy is an ass," is one thing; the capacity to think, "We are both asses," is probably a great deal healthier. My favorite line from the novelist Raymond Chandler captures the dilemma facing the sincere push-hands player: "Down these mean streets a man must go who is not himself mean." Push-hands practice offers us the glimmer of an idea as to how to walk those streets.

Though the process brings us greater familiarity with failure than success, each failing nevertheless throws some light on the dispositions of others. Zheng Manqing once said: "As soon as I put my hands on someone, I know him." Perhaps he meant something subtler, but there is still great value in seeing how a man's nature will manifest in the melee that is often push-hands.

Laoshi often talked in these terms when describing the relative merits of his teachers' push-hands. He said of Wang Lang's push-hands that he tended to be "Soft, soft, soft—until you got too close; then, with a sharp pull, he would rip you off balance. This was like saying, 'I'm soft up to a point, but if you cross me, I'll dump you.' Interestingly, he treated people in much the same way in real life: affable up to the point where he judged that you, inadvertently or not, had crossed his sense of correct behavior. Then, 'Wham, you're finished with me.' This led to a kind of cultish behavior among his students, who were fearful of getting on the wrong side of him, fearful of potential ostracism. One of Wang Lang's favorite sayings was, 'Fool me once, shame on you; fool me twice, shame on me.' There was a lot of repressed fear in his school.

"To be fair," Laoshi added, "Wang Lang's push was more educated than his yielding. To me, this too was a reflection of his character—he was far more generous in his 'giving' than forgiving in his 'receiving.' That his uprooting skill far exceeded his neutralizing was not unknown to Wang Lang: he was not without considerable self-awareness. There was a sweet sensitivity to his push, which was echoed in his capacity to be very tender with those students he did not find overly challenging.

"Master Lin's neutralization, on the other hand, was of an entirely different order," Laoshi noted. "Prior to meeting him, I had heard he was the softest of the soft, like smoke or the proverbial 'empty jacket on a hanger.' Such descriptions led me to seek out Master Lin, but they also, initially, led me to an erroneous view of superior skill in push-hands. The moment I pushed with him, I realized there was a good deal more to Master Lin's push-hands than his simply being soft. After all, in conversation, if I can return to the metaphor, true listening does not mean simply being empty or vacant; there is an active component. When pushing with Master Lin, there was an exquisite feeling of my push not only being received, but guided. This was subtle but detectable nonetheless. To me, Master Lin did not feel like an empty jacket; he felt as though he had heard the nuance of my push and had connected to the heart of the matter. His soft neutralization revealed that a loss of balance is the inevitable consequence of excessive force.

"Trying to push Master Lin was like entering a flowing river. The pusher had no choice but to join with the flow of the current and be led away from its intended destination. Rather than feel forced to comply, there was an impression of consensus between the push and the energy into which it had entered.

"In fact, there was a feeling of empathy in Master Lin's neutralization. In aikido terms, we might say he harmonized with the push and led it to a place where it was no longer destructive. Importantly, there was no feeling that Master Lin was against you; there was no feeling of judgment. Instead, he instilled a feeling of rapport, with the result that, when he returned your energy by pushing—or even putting his fist in your face—you somehow felt able to 'listen,' even if the message was severe.

"I believe such a feeling of rapport translated to Master Lin's capacity to be very direct with his students, including me," Laoshi said. "He was blunt in pointing out our faults as our attempts at replicating his skill fell short. His tendency to criticize my posture at length led to my interpreter, no doubt, thinking I was getting more than I bargained for, trying to soften the blow by saying, 'Don't worry. He does this to everybody.' The fact was, however, I was appreciative of Master Lin's directness and grateful he felt I was worth the effort.

"Master Lin was remarkable in his ability to speak to us in an apparently critical fashion without creating the resentment that censure usually brings. This is the nature of the genuine push in push-hands."

As I reflected on Laoshi's experiences, I realized how far we students had to go. We could not even have a friendly push with each other without descending into an egofest—never mind utilizing the principles to conduct honest and sincere dialogue with those around us.

"Will we ever get there, Laoshi?" I asked, feeling a touch dispirited.

"Keep trying," he urged softly. "Bear in mind the stuff that prevents you from being able to do it will, in time, be the very carriage for your progress. Have you not heard the saying, 'The poison becomes the cure'? It is in the yin-yang nature of things. In other words, all things contain the seed of their opposite. In every friend there is a seed of enmity, but in every enemy there is a seed of friendship. In push-hands, the very habits that stop us from progressing are also the impetuses for that progress."

I was not entirely sure this made sense, so I asked Laoshi to explain further.

"We all know Zheng Manqing and Ben Lo were both motivated by severe, life-threatening health problems," Laoshi said. "The very fact of their respective illnesses became the seed of their great progress. Now take a look around at your fellow students: though of a lesser order, the obstacles to progress in each of them are also responsible for their progress. Look at Benny. He is aggressive and competitive. He hinders his development with his win-at-all-costs mentality—but that very same mentality keeps him practicing in spite of loss after loss after loss.

"Look at Freddie," Laoshi continued. "There is no one slower on the uptake. He plods along, making no apparent progress—but he is dogged and he never gets bored. He always attends class, and when, through sheer obstinacy, he does make a midge's eyebrow worth of progress, he savors it as a diamond or a ruby.

"Look at Stan, who overanalyzes everything. He ties himself up in knots with constant theorizing, but he watches everything assiduously and will eventually gain insight.

"All students bring their own obstacles to learning," Laoshi said. "I used to think my job as a teacher was to educate them out of their 'poisons,' but now I believe all I have to do is nurture them and allow them to transform their weaknesses into strengths."

It was a comforting lesson: our weaknesses can be transformed into strengths. I began to realize the faults I perceived in others were nothing more than the dark side of virtue.

Laoshi had a last piece of advice on this subject: "In both push-hands and dealing with people in everyday life, pay more attention to what they are doing or saying, and less attention to what you are going to do or say. Then trust the right response will arise by itself."

Chapter 29: Circles around Push-Hands

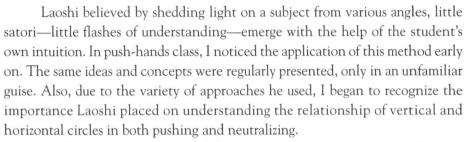

Laoshi believed by shedding light on a subject from various angles, little satori—little flashes of understanding—emerge with the help of the student's own intuition. In push-hands class, I noticed the application of this method early on. The same ideas and concepts were regularly presented, only in an unfamiliar guise. Also, due to the variety of approaches he used, I began to recognize the importance Laoshi placed on understanding the relationship of vertical and horizontal circles in both pushing and neutralizing.

Laoshi's explanations ranged from the reassuringly concrete to the genuinely perplexing. One week, for instance, he said, "When neutralizing, study the horizontal first; then add the vertical. When pushing, study the vertical first; then add the horizontal."

However, the following week Laoshi said, "When neutralizing, study the centrifugal; then add the centripetal. When pushing, study the centripetal; then add the centrifugal."

On reflection, I came to understand these statements meant the same thing.

Another time he took from his bag one of his "teaching aids," a length of string with a weight attached. Holding the string, he spun the weight around to demonstrate that it was trying to pull away, using the power of the spinning movement. This was the centrifugal effect. The centrifugal effect, however, was balanced by the length of string, which prevented the weight from flying away. This represented the centripetal force that pulled inward toward the center, where Laoshi held the string in his fingers.

On another occasion, Laoshi showed us a video clip of the yin-yang symbol spinning around. First spinning clockwise, then spinning counterclockwise. He invited us to observe that when spinning clockwise, there was a sense of expansion from the center; when spinning counterclockwise, however, there was a sense of contraction toward the center.

Laoshi talked at length about circles, using video clips and teaching aids, as he said, to "demonstrate how horizontal and vertical circles manifest in push-hands." Laoshi's own understanding of circles initially came from Wang Lang. Then, some years later, this understanding was enhanced by Master Lin's teaching. Laoshi told us: "Wang Lang first showed me the horizontal circle in neutralizing and the vertical circle in pushing. Master Lin completed my training by showing me the other way around—that is, he added the vertical in neutralizing and the horizontal in pushing."

At first I had absolutely no idea what Laoshi was talking about. Indeed, his explanation seemed nothing short of gibberish. Over time, however, as Laoshi talked about his own struggles with these concepts, it began to make sense.

Laoshi told us, "When I first studied with Wang Lang, I had already learned the peng-lu-ji-an form with other teachers, but my application of the method was crude. I was reduced to shoving people to the side as they pushed, and I really struggled with strong men who did not practice with the idea of softness. When one such fellow rebutted my protestations at his hard energy by insisting that I did not seem particularly soft either, I knew something was missing.

"When I pushed with Wang Lang, he turned his waist very effectively. I felt as if I were pushing a spinning top that was fixed to the floor. It was a bit like pushing a greased ball: when you thought you had achieved some purchase on it, you found yourself slipping off. I began to realize the secret was in the centrifugal effect of this turning of the waist. As I pushed, I was just like the string with the spinning weight: the more forcefully I pushed, the more quickly he would turn—and I would be thrown off by this rotation. As long as Wang Lang could time his turn and use the right amount of speed, I was unable to line up my hands to push him.

"After some time and practice, however, I began to see there was a flaw in Wang Lang's method: as I began to push with increased sensitivity, I noticed there was a spot where he found it difficult to turn. If I kept on this spot, all Wang Lang could do was continue to move back until he ran out of room. He then responded with an ungracious heave to pull me off balance. I realized there was also something missing in his understanding.

"Sadly," Laoshi continued, "Wang Lang and I parted company over an unfortunate incident. I was left without a teacher and with many questions still to be answered. However, nothing is all good or all bad, and I began to entertain the idea of traveling to Taiwan to seek out Master Lin. Had I not separated from Wang Lang, I might never have progressed to the heart of the matter with Master Lin. Is this coincidence—or are the fingerprints of the Dao to be detected in the matter? Who can say? All I know is Master Lin built on the understanding I had gleaned from Wang Lang and completed the picture by adding the notion of the vertical circle.

"Master Lin emphasized the need to rotate the pelvis vertically a little, dropping the lower spine in response to a push. In doing so, the feeling is one of getting underneath the push. This then allows you to 'catch' the push and, with the aid of the horizontal turn, smoothly slide the push to the side.

"Not only does adding the vertical circle create a sphere from a circle, but it also allows us to catch the incoming push and redirect it from within the sphere. The push is drawn in deeper and thus controlled."

Laoshi glanced toward me to check that I was following, then resumed. "You see, there was a marked difference in feeling between Wang Lang and Master Lin. Wang Lang's neutralizing seemed to keep you on the outside, while Master Lin's neutralizing somehow brought you in. Does life imitate art, or vice versa? Who can say categorically whether technique affects personality or the other way around? Outside of class, however, Wang Lang kept people at a distance, while Master Lin did the opposite.

"As I have said many times before," Laoshi continued, "Wang Lang's push was infinitely better than his neutralizing. His uprooting technique was sound and he continually sought to develop it further. Here too, however, Wang Lang encountered a problem: while the alignment of his body was correct and he could achieve an excellent connection from his hands all the way down into his feet to deliver a powerful push, the push only seemed to work flawlessly when the receiver was standing right in front of him. If the angle of body position between him and his partner was not favorable, his push was no longer effortless.

"In pushing, this alignment from hands all the way to the feet is the vertical circle, although 'arc' might be more accurate. You could think of a longbow being drawn, to use Ben Lo's analogy. As the bow is drawn, potential release power is being generated. To be effective, the whole arc must be connected without any breaks, as must the body in pushing. Once fully drawn, the arrow can be released in the same manner that the push is released by the pusher. Wang Lang could 'bend the bow' very well and release the power cleanly; however, he found difficulty turning to the left or right with the bow drawn. If the target was in front of him, well and good, but if not, he was unable to track effectively to the right or the left.

"This was a significant problem for Wang Lang," Laoshi mused. "He sought to solve it, in part, by insisting his students maintain the peng-lu-ji-an form to the point of rigidity. Doing so limited the amount of lateral movement and waist rotation the receiver could employ, and so left him easier to push cleanly. I always felt uncomfortable with this arrangement, as it seemed to require the receiver to collude in getting pushed.

"Unlike firing an arrow, the push does not lend itself to aiming right or left in the manner of a bow. Initially, I tried to solve this dilemma in my own way by grabbing the receiver's arm and holding him in place before I pushed. But soon I realized this was not tai chi. In effect, I was moving the target into my sights, rather than aiming where the target was. I knew I was relying on brute force, but could not fathom what to do instead.

"Again, it was Master Lin who put me out of my misery by helping me to see that I did not have only one bow, but a limitless number of potential bows arrayed in a circle around my center, each one capable of firing the arrow. To switch analogies for a moment, the push became like a ripple from a stone dropped into a still pond, spreading out until it encounters a rock peeping above the surface. The rock represents the point of resistance in the receiver. In pushing, my center would then connect with this one point of resistance and release the energy in that direction. The arms, from shoulder through elbow to hand and back to the other shoulder, formed the edge of the ripple of water, and whatever point made contact with the resistance of the receiver could release the arrow.

"From this perspective, pushing becomes more like sending out a sonar pulse and waiting for the ping that indicates an enemy ship, like in those old war movies. The torpedo is then launched toward the contact."

Laoshi must have noticed my mind visibly bulging with the effort to wrap itself around his analogies, for he smiled and said, "At the deeper levels of understanding, trying to explain the subtleties of push-hands almost inevitably requires the use of images and analogies. Imagery is our last resort when the rational mind tries to explain what the heart-mind already knows. It is the reason we practice. We are trying to understand what cannot be fully described in words; our cultural bias requires us to make the effort, however futile it seems. The danger is, of course, that the filter of the rational mind can easily distort the message."

In spite of my difficulty in comprehension, or maybe because of the challenge, I loved the whole process of discovering the meaning in Laoshi's words and their application in both life and push-hands. These were my *koan*, and they informed my development as a tai chi player, encouraging me to seek the essence in everything I attempted to learn. As a by-product of the practice, I began to feel my intuition improving and to trust in it more than I had. My own intuition now became as much a teacher to me as Laoshi. This realization called to mind an old adage: "When the student is ready, the teacher appears." The teacher that appeared was intuition.

Chapter 30: The Old Lion Gives Way

左
右
摟
膝

My father was a strong man, stronger in his sixties than I was in my twenties. He had been something of a wrestler in his youth and wrestled with me in mine. It was wrestling for fun—more his fun than mine—as his compact, powerful physique easily outmatched my skinny youthful frame. In his day, he was known for his bear hug. After cracking a man's ribs during one playful contest, however, he was a little more discriminating—a change his friends greatly appreciated. My father's hands and arms were so freakishly strong that he would have rivalled even Popeye. For the amusement of us children at Halloween, he would break the shells of hazelnuts by placing a couple in the crook of his elbow and using his powerful arms like nutcrackers, breaking the shells against each other. He could also use his first two fingers to "cut" apples as if using scissors. The cut was not exactly clean—he used his other hand to squeeze his sturdy fingers together, mutilating the apple to an inedible mush—but he could do it nevertheless.

Another of his party tricks, especially after a drink or two, was to pick up heavy wooden dining chairs by the bottom of one leg, lifting them up without tilting them. He would challenge me to do the same and laugh heartily, if good naturedly, at my failings. From time to time he would order me to flex my biceps—and I would humor him, waiting for him to feel the minor bump, which was all I could manage, before he rendered his verdict: "Sparrow's legs!" His assessment may have been accurate, but the game became old quickly, as the assessment was the same every time, and my father's laughter the inevitable encore.

In my teens I began studying martial arts, first karate, then aikido, and I grew stronger. In terms of raw physical strength, I was still some way behind my father, but I was also beginning to learn technique. My father was proud of my development and called me "Aikido Boy."

One day in my late teens, while a student and still living at home, I was practicing some *suburi* (sword cuts) with my bokken in my room. After practicing for a while, I sat on my settee for a rest, my bokken resting horizontally on my thighs. In walked my father. He noticed I had been practicing and picked up another bokken lying beside the bedroom door. My father had no formal training in sword, or indeed any martial art; having watched me a few times, however, he was holding the wooden sword correctly. He pointed it toward me as he advanced.

"Come on then. Let's have a go—you and me!" he challenged.

"Oh, Dad," I moaned. "I'm tired." I was really hoping to forego this latest contest.

My father continued to advance upon me, undaunted. As he moved just in range, with a speed of movement that even surprised me, I picked up my bokken, slapped his out of the way, and stabbed him in the stomach. The stab was not forceful, but enough to make the point: you're dead.

What happened next surprised me. My father turned around, replaced the bokken by the door where he had found it, and walked out of the room. He never wrestled with me again, never issued another challenge. He never again commented on my "sparrow leg" arms. The balance of power had shifted.

There comes a time when a young man's developing strength begins to outstrip the failing strength of his father. I realized I had reached this point.

Although my father never openly acknowledged the fact, our relationship changed from then on. In my case, martial technique perhaps tilted the equation in my favor a little sooner than would have been the case if we were only competing on physical strength.

The martial arts student may also find himself having to deal with the problems that arise when his growing ability begins to narrow the gap between him and his teacher. The teacher may feel threatened by "the natural's" rapid mastery of skills—skills the teacher had to acquire painstakingly over the course of a lifetime. Of course, the compensatory effect of the teacher's superior technique and experience may delay the point of parity; if the teacher continues in his own development through the years, that point may be delayed further. However, the point at which a student begins to surpass his teacher can be a tricky time for them both.

I wondered from time to time if I would ever reach the level of Laoshi. I wondered too if Laoshi thought he had surpassed the level of his own teachers. I decided to ask him. In response, he told me this story from the time he stayed with Wang Lang.

"In those days," Laoshi recalled, "I had a particularly close relationship with Wang Lang. He invited me to stay with him for periods of two to three weeks whenever I was able to travel to the States. No other student was permitted this privilege, and consequently, I was appreciative of the honor. It was especially precious to me because, at that time, I thought it essential to have some kind of uchi-deshi [live-in student] relationship with a teacher to really absorb all the lessons he had to teach.

"During my periods of stay we would practice every day and talk about life, tai chi, Zheng Manqing, and martial arts. The seven-year period during which I regularly stayed with my teacher was a wonderful time in my life. I was living the dream: studying an art I believed in with a teacher I respected and even loved like a father. The future was also bright, promising ever deeper understanding and, perhaps, the possibility of inheriting his position as head of the school.

"As my skill improved, however, an underlying tension developed between us. Sometimes Wang Lang would congratulate me on learning what he had learned in half the time it had taken him. At other times he would ask me if I was content with the training he could provide. I found myself growing fearful that Wang Lang was trying to distance himself from me. I tried to reassure him once, saying, 'I am totally loyal to you.'

"Wang Lang merely replied, 'Don't be loyal to me. Be loyal to the Dao.'

"I wondered what he meant but, at the time, I was unable to find the right words to get to the bottom of it.

"Then one day it happened: we reached the point of parity—in push-hands, at least. I was pushing with him at his house as one of the neighborhood children, who often came to play with his son, stood watching. Standing with my back to the wall with Wang Lang in the role of pusher, I hit the wall a few times, as usual, in response to his well-timed ti fang push. At some point, as Wang Lang was closing in to uproot me once again, I turned just the right amount, at the right time, in the right direction, and felt as if the crosshairs were no longer on me. 'I've got him!' I thought. Still unsure, however, I did nothing. He completed the pass and came with another push. I angled again, felt the same thing, and this time nudged him sideways. He staggered to the side and I immediately counterattacked, pushing him all the way across the room.

"He was not used to being pushed, and so looked ungainly as he tottered across the floor. The little girl laughed, which did little to relieve the tension that was beginning to build. He came again to push. We connected, following the form, and he pushed. Again, I angled correctly, nudged him off balance, and directed him to the far side of the room. He stumbled backward, trying to regain his balance. The little girl laughed again and called to the other kids in the next room: 'Lang got pushed! Lang got pushed!'

"There was the thunder of feet as three children burst in to watch the spectacle. They were left disappointed as Wang Lang announced to me, 'That will be all for now,' and left abruptly. He never pushed hands with me in public again. Indeed, he only ever pushed hands with me one more time, shortly before a class. I pushed him a few times before the other students started arriving.

"Living in a competitive environment, as Wang Lang did, and having a reputation as a great push-hands teacher, I had the impression he could not allow himself to be seen getting pushed. Sadly, in my opinion, his art suffered as a result—for he was denied the opportunity to experiment freely without fear of losing his mystique. His position as a direct student of Zheng Manqing and skilful push-hands player had served him well, but I suspect he had arrived at a place where further progress would have involved a considerable period of investing in loss. Perhaps he feared a temporary loss in efficacy would rob him of his students' esteem. This was a lesson I learned well, and I have tried to avoid the same mistake with my own students.

"I was not without sympathy for Wang Lang's predicament. In a case of foreshadowing, Wang Lang once told me of the difficulty Tam Gibbs faced as the number 1 student and disciple of Zheng Manqing in America. Tam was expected to 'take on' visitors who came to test Zheng Manqing in the Shr Jung School in New York. The Professor would have Tam push-hands with these challengers— but Tam was not allowed to invest in loss. He had to win."

Listening to Laoshi's experiences of the pressures that surround teachers, as well as reflecting on my own frustrations, I began to have a greater appreciation of the tension that accompanies the relationship between teacher and senior student.

In Eastern countries, the cultural emphasis on respect and obligation serves to confirm a student's place in the hierarchical arrangement with the teacher. The stories concerning O Sensei Ueshiba when he would receive periodic visits from Takeda Sokaku, his Daito-ryu teacher, are testament to this. According to some of O Sensei's students, Takeda would be a demanding guest who continued to treat Ueshiba, by then a famous teacher in his own right, as his personal servant. It seems reasonable to suggest that Ueshiba did not look forward to these visits. Some witnesses at the time suggested if Ueshiba had prior knowledge of Takeda's visits, he would run away to one of the satellite dojos. There was also a financial obligation placed upon Ueshiba, since his teaching license stipulated he pay three yen to Takeda for every new student who enrolled. If Ueshiba had neglected to send money to Takeda, or if Takeda thought money was due, he would arrive unannounced to take payment.

There may also be some truth to the rumors that masters of old martial arts schools withheld the secret techniques of the school, only passing them on to one or two students in each generation. No doubt such practices ensured a solid expression of loyalty to the master.

For Laoshi, the student-teacher relationship was less formalized, and he never condoned the practice of holding back instruction. Furthermore, he encouraged us, his students, to surpass him. The higher we reached, he said, the further we would push him.

During the time I knew Laoshi, none of his students ever managed to close the distance with him—because he was relentless in striving to improve his own understanding. Perhaps as a result of wishful thinking, every now and then, one of the senior students felt he was beginning to approach his level, but then Laoshi appeared to evolve and was suddenly as far ahead as ever. This may have bothered some of the seniors but I, for one, was relieved. The prospect of surpassing him and finding myself without a teacher was something I dreaded, even while striving toward it with all my might.

Chapter 31: Armor Fist and Elbow

進
步
栽
捶

One evening after class, Robert, one of the senior students, told me of a telephone inquiry Laoshi had received. The call came from a woman who informed Laoshi that she had learned the twenty-four-step form, Zheng Manqing's thirty-seven-posture form, and some weapons forms; she was now looking for someone to teach her the original Yang long form. "She was taken aback," Robert said, "when Laoshi said, 'You already know enough forms. Why do you want to learn another?'

"Laoshi is not a supermarket," Robert added. "You don't go in and buy a form off the shelf."

I understood the mild irritation I detected in his voice. The expectations of the consumer, when applied to martial arts and spiritual disciplines, can lead to frustrations on both sides. As Zheng Manqing pointed out, some of us might fall into the trap of thinking that following a spiritual or martial discipline is the same as buying a soda: "You pay your fifty cents, and if you don't like it, you buy another."

No doubt, as a result of the unquestioning consumerist point of view, many would-be students approach the search for a tai chi teacher in the way they would buy a soda. It seems there are a number of forms available, with an approach and style to suit everyone.

The downside, in the opinion of many, is that the purity of the art is tainted by marketplace preoccupations with price or convenience; the quality of the teaching is no longer the critical factor. On the other hand, things have never been so good for the discerning student with some idea of what he wants from the art. More teachers are available—some excellent, some less so—and if the student is prepared to travel, he can find a pretty good fit in terms of approach. Teachers are also prepared to travel—some with messianic zeal—to spread the word of true tai chi to the faithful.

It was against this backdrop that a few serious students invited Laoshi to teach workshops in Europe. They were beginning to question the approach inherent in the styles they had first learned, and, having read of Zheng Manqing and his approach, were keen to sample his method and compare it to the various styles available locally. For Laoshi, this was an adventure: he was acting as Wang Lang's representative in Europe, and over a three-year period, traveled abroad thirty-six times, variously staying with his teacher, attending his teacher's summer courses, and instructing at fledgling branches of Wang Lang's school. For a while it was a lot of fun. There was a growing enthusiasm around the school and a yearning for the teachings of Zheng Manqing around Europe.

Though Laoshi enjoyed teaching form and push-hands workshops, he was particularly savoring a weekend course in sword form and fencing in northern Spain. He knew the students at the Spanish school well from previous visits and was not surprised to learn many had commissioned a local carpenter to make a wooden sword especially for this, his first sword workshop. On an earlier visit, Laoshi had left the Spanish students a template as a guide to the type of sword he favored for tai chi.

When he arrived, however, the swords he encountered were a little surprising. They were made of a particularly lightweight wood—not the

American cherry or maple he had recommended—and so lacked any kind of substance. Laoshi felt that a heavier sword was better for beginners but, appreciating that Zheng Manqing would reputedly practice with a feather duster, he accepted that they would have served their purpose well enough—if it were not for the hand guards.

He was not prepared for the variety of hand guards. They were certainly unique, with each one bigger and more grandiose than the last. At first Laoshi suspected that, since the size and shape of the blade were more or less defined, the carpenter or the student wished to express his individuality by shaping the guard in styles ranging from slightly exaggerated to wholly grotesque. However, when Laoshi questioned the purpose of the variety in the guards, he was informed that the students heard the hand is a major target in tai chi fencing, so they had taken steps to gain an advantage. Having discovered an apparent weakness in the traditional sword design, the students had instructed the carpenter to increase the size of the guard to compensate for the hand's vulnerability.

Commenting on the matter, Laoshi told us, "You have to realize that my understanding of fencing at the time was still a little green, and I found fencing with some of the more experienced students more challenging than it should have been. Countless times, their sword hilt saved them from my sword's edge, and while my defense did not desert me, my angles of attack were nullified to a great extent."

Laoshi found himself in a quandary. "As you know," he continued, "I do not like to tell people to drop a deviation from the purity of the technique simply because I cannot defeat it. I prefer to find the weakness in the deviation and demonstrate the inherent limitations of straying from clean technique.

"I have to admit, though, on this occasion I had no idea what to say. After all, what kind of teacher tells a student, 'You have to change your sword in order to let me win'? The sword workshop began on Friday evening with an introduction to sword form for the less experienced, and basic fencing principles for the more experienced, but I was distracted as I pondered the problem with their sword guards. Even when I was focusing on the sword form, the problem did not leave my mind.

"In fact, the question of the sword guards remained with me through the night, and I returned to the hall for the second day of the course, still unsure what to say. Then I had a moment of inspiration. I knew how to proceed. 'I see many of you have opted for large hand guards on your swords,' I said, addressing the students. 'From a certain point of view, it makes a lot of sense—but why stop there? Why not have a sword with a basket hilt like a Scottish broadsword—the kind where the hilt wraps around the whole hand? Then you will not have to worry about attacks to your hand.

"'But then, if you have a basket hilt, why stop there? Why not have arm protectors? If you have an arm protector, you will not have to worry about someone cutting your arm.

"'But then again, if you have arm protectors, why not have a breastplate? And a helmet and leg armor? You see the problem?'

"It was a rhetorical question, and I was unsure that the students did in fact see the problem. So I continued: 'If you are armored, or even if you just have a large hand guard, the style of your fencing will change. In time you will become reliant on the armor and incorporate it into your fencing. You will stray from using your own movement to avoid your opponent's sword—relying on the guard, or helmet, or whatever for blocking.'"

"How did that go down?" I asked, knowing people get very defensive about the shape of their swords, especially if they had a hand in the design.

"Well . . . they understood the point, I think," Laoshi said. "They were there, after all, to learn tai chi sword. Mind you, it is easy enough to trim some of the wood off a guard. It might have been a different story if I suggested they had to get new swords made!"

Listening to Laoshi, I remembered a fellow student asked Billy Coyle, my aikido teacher, "Why do we not wear armor when practicing sword?" Billy's reply was characteristically succinct and definitive: "Our movement is our armor." He had a way with words.

Reflecting now on Laoshi's words, I see their wisdom. He advocated the use of the traditional hand guards to encourage correct movement—using the whole arm, rather than blocking using wrist or fingers to manipulate the sword. The more armored we are, the more likely we are to block and hack, losing much of the delicacy available to us with a softer fencing style.

However, Laoshi's experience foreshadowed a new trend in Chinese swordplay. Some aficionados of the Chinese sword have become dissatisfied with the limitations implicit in trying to hit someone with a wooden sword without causing actual harm. While one prominent teacher has responded to this limitation by using swords made of soft plastic, others have developed a type of competitive sword fighting that requires long padded coats, as well as gloves and helmets, for protection.

I asked Laoshi what he thought of this development, although I anticipated his response. "It is a matter of the personal philosophy you subscribe to," he said. "When at a crossroads, some make one choice, some another. Speaking for myself, when faced with the emergence of armor, as happened with those Spanish students, I prefer to take away to reveal the essence of principle. Others—such as those you describe who use armor—prefer to add something to overcome the limitations they feel bind them.

"It is the same with other sports, including tennis and golf," he added. "In golf, the evolution of the club means the ball can be hit farther and harder with the result that the hazards are no longer in the right place to challenge the mammoth hitters. In tennis, the change from wooden racquets to graphite meant the game would never be the same again. While it is true we all benefit from technological advances, I remain 'old school' and favor tradition over technology, especially in matters relating to tai chi. I prefer improving the technique to changing the rules of the game. You might say I am old fashioned, but I feel there is more to be learned by refining the man, not the equipment. On a deeper level, for me, it is a spiritual question: do we seek to change the world or to change ourselves?

"I cannot help but feel that by hiding ourselves under a coat of armor, we lose something of the original spirit that made the art worth studying in the first place," Laoshi said. "Just as in push-hands, you cannot simply remove the difficulty to make it easier for people without cheapening the process. The difficulty is part of the majesty of the art. To paraphrase some wise words, 'What does it benefit a man to gain technical advantage, only to lose the spirit of the art he pursues?'"

Laoshi paused for a second and looked at me. I could see the twinkle in his eye. "Besides," he said, "those who want to hit each other with wooden swords should go practice kendo—if only for aesthetic reasons."

I had known Laoshi long enough to sense when he was inviting me to question him. I played along. "Why is that, Laoshi?"

"Well," he answered, his smile broadening, "at least if you practice kendo, you look like Darth Vader. If you practice Chinese swordsmanship with those long coats, you look like Columbo."

And with that remark, Laoshi got up and left, chuckling to himself. I felt a smile spreading across my face. I liked to see Laoshi happy. Our relationship was deepening and he felt increasingly like a father to me. It was only natural to want the best for him.

I did not think much more about the subject until a few weeks later at sword class. Laoshi called a halt to our fencing practice when two of the students were enjoying a particularly stormy session. The sound of wooden swords clashing had increased over the course of the class—never a good sign in tai chi fencing, when all you should hear, according to Laoshi, is "the sliding of wood against wood, and shoes on the floor." The mood between the two students was becoming heated. This was something Laoshi would tolerate to a limited extent in push-hands, where tempers sometimes threatened to leak out, but never in fencing: the consequences could be too damaging.

Laoshi addressed us. "Do any of you know the name Mike Winkeljohn?" None of us did.

"He is a particularly fine martial arts teacher in America. He was world champion in kickboxing and muay Thai, and now teaches professional MMA fighters. That means, in case you have any doubt, he is really good at what he does."

Laoshi's gaze swept over us, ensuring we were listening, before continuing. "A couple of years ago, Mike was holding pads for one of his students. In a very rare moment of decreased focus, he got too close to a kick and was hit in the eye. At first he felt liquid welling around his eye and thought he was cut, but when he asked his student to verify, he received an answer that shocked him to the core. 'No, coach, it's your eyeball.'

"His eyeball had been sliced open by the toenail of the student performing the kick—a freak accident, but one that left him blind in one eye. The liquid he felt was the inside of his eye leaking out."

It was a gruesome story, and one Laoshi chose not to sanitize by sparing the details: "The lens fell out of the ruptured eye and, despite the best medical treatment available at the time, he was blinded in that eye. I have never heard of such a thing happening before, nor since, but that is no consolation to him. True to his art, he still teaches, but now he wears a pair of protective goggles, just in case.

"As you know, our tradition is one of fencing without protective equipment, but when I heard about Mike Winkeljohn's accident, I began to wonder if I should insist that you all have protective eyewear for fencing. Since we try to not let force build up on our swords, thankfully, injuries are few and far between—the worst being a crack on the fingers. That is acceptable. But the real vulnerability in fencing is the eye. It would not take much to severely damage so delicate a part of the body with grave consequences—not just for the person who lost his eye, but for all of us.

"So, it may seem that protective eyewear is a good idea, and if you want to buy some, then be my guest—but I will not make it compulsory. Why? Because sometimes the more protection you add, the more recklessly people behave. Instead of adding to the situation, it would be better that we never lose awareness of the potential dangers of our practice—better that we bear responsibility for ourselves, and those around us, and not act recklessly."

I understood Laoshi's point completely. For not only does protective equipment change the spirit of a practice, but it can also encourage reckless abandon within that practice.

I recalled watching a television documentary about road safety. It featured a particularly dangerous level crossing in a Canadian forest that had seen more than its fair share of accidents. In an attempt to address the situation, a large number of trees were cut down so drivers could see the trains approaching earlier and stop in time. But the result was an increased number of accidents. By making things seem safer, people perceived that they could take more risks. In other words, the important factor is not the actual risk, but the perception of risk. One contributor to the program suggested if we make cars safer, people will only drive more recklessly. His tongue-in-cheek solution to the problem was to make cars with huge petrol tanks on the front and a six-inch spike protruding from the steering wheel toward the driver.

All this got me thinking. A little later, during one of our talks, I asked Laoshi, jokingly, if we ought to fence with live blades in order to improve our awareness. Instead of laughing, Laoshi cocked his head to one side and replied, "You know, of course, that some masters say iaido should be performed with a live blade. They believe that without the potential danger of using a live blade, it is impossible to develop the correct attitude. Your idea is interesting, but I think we will have a problem with liability insurance."

Chapter 32: Embrace Tiger, Return to Energy

玉
女
穿
梭

Laoshi had a fondness for a passage in Gerda Geddes's *Looking for the Golden Needle*. He would sometimes read this passage aloud in class:

> The tiger, in China, is an ambivalent animal; it can be either yin or yang. When it is yang, the tiger depicts authority, courage, bodily strength, and military prowess. It is often painted on warriors' shields to frighten away the enemy. It terrifies demons and spirits. When the tiger is in conflict with the yang celestial dragon, it becomes yin, the quality of earth. To the tai chi performer, the tiger represents all forms of energy, and it is with these energies that we have to learn to deal. We have to direct our energy in such a way that the natural healing process of the body can be enhanced.

Laoshi was especially taken with this passage because it suggested a nonjudgmental view of yin and yang energies, an idea at odds with our cultural preference for labeling things as either good or bad. Laoshi felt that habitually defining an experience in polarized terms encourages us to confuse yin and yang with good and bad, an attitude leading inevitably to a philosophy of conflict: man versus nature, life versus death, material versus spiritual. To Laoshi, this was an unnecessarily antagonistic view of the world, where one side seeks the utter annihilation of the other.

An alternative view, one suggested by the embrace-tiger posture and tai chi practice generally, is that man and nature, life and death, material and spiritual are all part of one process, two sides of the same coin. To foster one at the expense of the other is both futile and damaging to our physical and mental health.

Laoshi observed that many of his students' tensions were rooted in the habit of labeling certain energies, attitudes, or opinions as good and others as bad, leading to an internal war of suppression against parts of their own psyche. Our ability to deal with inner conflict, to accept our natural expression of "human beingness" was hampered, Laoshi felt, by a common view of tai chi. As he once said, "Tai chi is often characterized as a peaceful and gentle exercise, particularly suited to the elderly or the spiritually aware; its physical and mental properties are said to lead to calmness, serenity, and nonviolence. In short, tai chi players are nice people."

In Laoshi's view, this was patent nonsense: tai chi players are not "nice," but neither are they "not nice." He would often say, "Tai chi players are appropriate."

To illustrate this point Laoshi told us of a newspaper story he had read some years before: "One evening in the emergency room of an American safety net hospital, the night shift was struggling to deal with the usual combination of assault victims, accident casualties, overdoses, and drunks in a neighborhood where medical insurance was a rarity. As usual, two armed security guards were on duty, as confrontation was commonplace.

"The waiting room was overcrowded with people waiting their turn for treatment. Suddenly, the front door crashed open as a young Hispanic man stormed in, wearing nothing but a pair of underpants. He charged straight across the foyer, passing the reception area, and headed for the glass door leading to the treatment rooms. Such was the young man's speed, energy, and aggressive intent that neither security guard seemed able to respond as he blasted through that door into the treatment zone. He returned minutes later, dragging a shocked young doctor in his wake. As those waiting to be treated looked on at the unfolding drama, the front door burst open again and a young woman, wearing only a nightdress, hurried into view, carrying a baby whose face was blue. The young man hauled the still-shocked doctor over to the baby and shouted, 'Fix him!'

"The point of the story," Laoshi continued, "is that in this case, with a baby's life hanging in the balance, the normal, polite approach of filling in the forms and sitting patiently to wait your turn would not have been appropriate. The need for speed superseded the usual procedures, if fatal consequences were to be averted.

"The lesson for us," Laoshi concluded, "is that we need to be able to use whatever energy or take whatever action is appropriate to the circumstances we find ourselves in, including responding in a highly yang way.

"Many people who come to study tai chi have been indirectly taught from a young age that expressing yang energy is wrong, and so they repress this energy, both in themselves and in others. This does not mean the potential expression of yang energy simply disappears when repressed; it tends to resurface in various unhealthy ways. It disguises itself and emerges as passive aggression, depression, or other health problems. Because it is part of who we are, yang energy does not cease to exist if its expression is thwarted. It stays with us because there will be times when it is needed. Rather than deny our energy, we would be better off to become friends with it, to understand its place, or it may well destroy us.

"As the posture directs, we must embrace both the yin and yang within us—embrace our tiger—in order to return to the mountain, the mountain that represents wholeness and health."

Who knows how many students identified with this particular aspect of Laoshi's teaching? Certainly, some of us experienced a major sense of relief and a feeling of liberation on hearing Laoshi's views. Over the years I have met many people who, urged by the directive of teachers, parents, and clergy to "be nice," have found themselves the victims of abuse and manipulation at the hands of those who identified them as easy targets. To me, the misguided notion that nice people should be happy to turn the other cheek merely compounds the internal struggle. I began to understand the violence I was perpetrating on myself by constantly biting my tongue and refraining from asserting my rights or asking for my due. I found it easier to demand that other people be treated with justice, but I suspect that my parents and teachers conditioned me early on to feel guilty for standing up for myself. They instilled in me a dread of being perceived as selfish, and coached me in denying my true feelings, suppressing the hurt and anger that resulted from turning the other cheek in the face of the casual injustice of the world around me. Perhaps unsurprisingly, part of me shut down; then in my early teens, I became easy prey to those flimflam men who skewed every arrangement in favor of themselves.

I was aware of my dilemma and sought out martial arts to empower the part of me that had atrophied as a result of my childhood conditioning. It might be argued that the hard-style variants to which I found myself drawn worked almost too well in encouraging my repressed feelings. I became overly proficient in the opposite direction, hostage to a resurgent yang energy that was reaping revenge for its imprisonment in the name of niceness.

Realizing I was once again veering away from balance, I tried to repress the yang qualities that had emerged from my confused psyche and once again found myself shackled by niceness. I was imprisoned by the approval of my "betters," who concluded I had been going through a phase and had settled down again. Once again, I found myself alone with my internal struggle.

Through my study with Laoshi, I began to reawaken the tiger that had lain repressed in my psyche, but in a more measured way. I felt the surge of energy being released—relieved of its duty of guarding me from myself. It is true the tiger within me still had to learn when to show its teeth and when to retract its claws, but the journey toward wholeness seemed to bring me more energy, creativity, and well-being borne of personal integrity.

I was curious, then, when I heard of another teacher's assertion that the embrace-tiger posture is akin to the biblical quote, "First take the log out of your own eye before taking the speck out of your brother's eye." I asked Laoshi what he thought of this particular interpretation.

Laoshi's reply was interesting. "It amounts to the same thing," he told me. "The quotation speaks of the danger inherent in judging others, when we ourselves are blinded by our own distorted view of life. It is about the separation of yin and yang caused by our being judgmental. As the *Xinxin Ming* [信心銘] says, 'Make the smallest distinction and heaven and earth are set infinitely apart.' The very act of being judgmental sets us apart from the one integrated reality, from the universe itself—and, in the process, alienates us from our spiritual home. embrace tiger is about healing that separation."

Laoshi was careful to draw a distinction between the habit of being judgmental and the need to defend ourselves against another's unreasonable behavior. "You are not being judgmental," he said, "but of course, you can still wave a stick about when necessary. It is about dealing with energy, not judging it."

For Laoshi, embrace tiger, return to mountain contained lessons concerning maintaining personal integrity in the face of pressure to conform to the norms of society.

Physically, the posture requires that from a position looking north, we take a 135-degree step around to face diagonally, to the southeast corner. This movement is easy to perform badly but extremely difficult to accomplish while remaining single weighted, with a shoulder-width step and with a straight spine—all key principles of our tai chi. Most of us do not have enough flexibility in our hips to reach the southeast corner, if performing this movement correctly. We simply cannot get around far enough.

At this point many students succumb to the temptation to turn the upper body toward the southeast, even though the lower body has not managed to get around far enough. Laoshi always corrected this fault: "Whatever direction your foot is facing, that is where you are. Maintain the integrity of your posture. If you cannot reach the diagonal with the lower body, do not make up for it by twisting the upper body to make it look as though you have. The integrity of your bodily structure is more important than the dictates of direction. Do not twist and distort your body to fit the posture. This applies in life as well: do not contort who you are simply in order to fit it."

Perhaps the message was old fashioned, as Laoshi would concede. Nevertheless, he firmly believed in putting substance before style and exaggerated the point for effect by portraying himself as a hoary ancient, valiantly championing the virtues of honor and character in a superficial, materialistic, fame-obsessed world. The fact that Laoshi was younger in years than many of his students did not seem to prevent him from making the point: worldly fashions may change, but integrity does not. When some of Laoshi's older students jokingly remarked about such old-fashioned virtue in a younger man, Laoshi merely smiled and replied, "Just because the leaves are green, it does not mean the tree is not old."

Returning to considerations of the posture, Laoshi believed there is a still deeper message contained within embrace tiger: "It was for a long time a characteristic of some schools of religious thought that the lower body housed the base, animalistic instincts of the human being—instincts that needed to be suppressed. The prevailing attitudes against sexual expression condemned the regions below the waist as libidinous badlands, which threatened to defile the wholesome purity of the heart and mind. Is it an accident," he asked, "that this posture contains within it the temptation to twist the spine so the upper body conforms to an abstract notion of the right direction, even though the lower body cannot reach as far? This twisting of the spine effectively cuts off the creative energy of the lower body from its right and natural expression in the upper body. We are separated from our true power, the power of the ground acting in concert with the heart-mind through the auspices of the qi."

While Laoshi often teased my brain cells with his explanations, I was also quietly impressed by his ability to marry ideas. Here he had explained to me the subtleties of embrace tiger in both spiritual and energetic terms. Laoshi held the spiritual notion of not demonizing yang energy. He also advocated the energetic notion that the base of our power lies in the lower body, which serves us best when not disconnected from the upper body.

Often, Laoshi summed up the lessons of embrace tiger with a quote from Wang Lang: "It took me a long time to realize tai chi is not a yin art; it is a yin and yang art."

Chapter 33: Easy Is Right

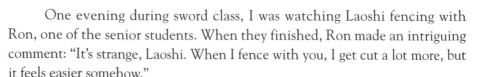

上
步
七
星

One evening during sword class, I was watching Laoshi fencing with Ron, one of the senior students. When they finished, Ron made an intriguing comment: "It's strange, Laoshi. When I fence with you, I get cut a lot more, but it feels easier somehow."

"Compared to what?" Laoshi asked.

"Well, compared with everybody else."

"That is because the principle is easy," Laoshi replied, "but nobody uses it."

It was a curious little episode, and I thought about it at length afterward. I understood almost immediately that Laoshi was not using the word "easy" in its usual sense. The principles he described were anything but easy—simple, perhaps, in the sense of not overly complex, but certainly not easy to put into practice.

A quote from the Daoist sage Zhuangzi came to mind: "Easy is right. Begin right and you are easy. Continue easy and you are right."

Zhuangzi also noted: "When the shoe fits, the foot is forgotten. When the belt fits, the belly is forgotten."

I felt there was an important lesson here, so when an opportunity presented itself, I asked Laoshi if he would elaborate on what he meant by "easy," and whether it had anything to do with the passages from Zhuangzi.

"Indeed, it does," Laoshi replied. "This is about the purity of the practice. When Ron said fencing with me is easy, he was trying to describe the exquisite feeling that goes with pure technique. There is no forcefulness, no reliance on speed or strength. There is no yang against yang. There is no clash of sword against sword.

"In a real sense, the training you are undergoing is less about improving technique, and more about understanding what pure technique feels like. When you reach the point where your technique is becoming distilled toward purity and you are no longer relying on speed and strength, then that very feeling will become your teacher. You could say it is easy, or you could say it is joyful—but once attained, you will not want to lose the feeling by returning to hardness and forcefulness.

"Too many of us are only concerned with winning, and we pay little attention to how winning feels. Even worse, we presume to instruct others, since we assume because we are winning, we must be right. Zhuangzi, however, points out that easy is right; he does not say, 'Forcing is right,' or even, 'Winning is right.' Zhuangzi is talking about the principle of *wu wei* [無爲]—doing without forcing. Our fencing is purest when it embodies this quality—but we find such a virtue elusive because we cannot let go of our desperate need to win. In the middle of vigorous push-hands or a spirited fencing exchange, it is all too easy to forget the words of Zheng Manqing: 'Small loss, small gain; big loss, big gain.'

"Letting go of the desperate need to win is problematic enough, but even worse is our reluctance to allow our classmates to let go of their own need to win."

"I don't understand that, Laoshi," I interrupted. "How do we prevent other students from letting go of their need to win?"

"It is a subtle and mostly unconscious process," Laoshi said. "Ironically, a classmate who is not using force does not automatically become a source of inspiration and emulation; rather, he may become a threat to our view of ourselves—for if he is right, then we must be wrong. Our egos cannot tolerate inferiority. Faced with such a threat, most of us do not aspire to a classmate's superior level but, instead, seek to drag him down to our inferior level. The ego frequently prefers all of us to be wrong rather than someone else to be right. It is a peculiarity of the human condition. As a result, instead of letting our classmates go through the process of losing big in order to gain big, we often instruct them in how to lose small so they only gain small. This serves nobody."

Ruefully, I recognized the truth in Laoshi's words, having several times been on the receiving end of an uncultured shove by a fellow student who, straining and grunting with the effort, then assumed the role of teacher. Not content with winning by pushing me over, he would also seek to instruct me how I should be losing.

Laoshi reiterated his point. "It is more important to learn how purity of technique feels. When the feeling is right, pushing or cutting the other person in push-hands or fencing will not only be a simple matter, but it will be rooted in principle."

"It seems, Laoshi," I commented, "that this is a particularly difficult idea to cultivate, even among your own students. I guess Zheng Manqing was right: we have no faith."

"Correct," he replied. "Zheng Manqing usually turns out to be right—a lesson in itself, as it is so easy to doubt your teacher. However, it is also a matter of time and perseverance for the student."

"Because it is so difficult to learn?" I interrupted.

"No," Laoshi replied, furrowing his brow in mock irritation. "No, the technique is easy. Didn't we just establish that?"

"Then why does it take so much time?" I asked, confused once more.

Laoshi sighed in mild exasperation. Then he smiled and returned to an attempt at explanation. "There is a story about a tourist walking along a country road in the southern states of America. He comes upon an old shack with a porch. On the porch is an old-timer sitting on his rocking chair, smoking a pipe and watching the sun go down. Lying beside him on the porch floor is a dog, quietly whimpering. The tourist approaches the old-timer, who is rocking gently to and fro, paying no attention to the dog, and says, 'Say, what's wrong with your dog?'

"'Aw, nothin',' says the old man. 'He just lyin' on a nail is all.'

"'Why doesn't he move?' asks the tourist.

"The old man replies simply, 'Well . . . it ain't hurting bad enough yet.'

"For most of the students, the foul taste of 'winning' isn't bad enough yet. It takes time to realize that winning, of itself, is a waste of time—because losing follows in its wake, like yin follows yang. You are better to win with principle or not at all.

"I learned this lesson myself when I studied with Wang Lang," Laoshi added. "I had become ferocious with the sword. I could dominate most of his students by forcing their swords where I wanted them to go. I thought my method superior to Wang Lang's and his students', and I even tried to fool myself into thinking it was a credible method by giving it a name: Sword Domination.

"I could win most of the time—but I began to tire of winning, as it left a bad taste in my mouth. I was using force to control my opponents and found no joy in what I did. I was also creating a growing resentment in those whose sword I dominated. The whole approach was empty of the Dao; there was no benefit in it. When I realized this, I abandoned my skill, such as it was, and began all over again. It took a long time with many false dawns before the feeling of joy began to emerge, but eventually emerge, it did. I must confess, I found it immensely difficult to let go of the need to win, to abandon what I thought I knew in order to pursue something I didn't even know existed.

"The abandoning of petty, crude technique is the hard part, as is finding the faith to follow the heart-mind in its joyfulness, wherever it may lead. This is where the time is needed. We need to get to the point where we are sick and tired of winning and losing, tired of playing for peanuts."

Hearing Laoshi relate his own experience, I began to make sense of his habit of only offering a few corrections when teaching push-hands or fencing. Instead, he simply outlined the principles in their purity from time to time and left us to struggle with our resistance to his instructions.

Now and then, however, Laoshi would become frustrated with our failings. On one occasion, Gordon, a fairly seasoned student, asked Laoshi about a point of technique. Laoshi replied, "Why are you asking me? Why not ask your teacher?" He nodded in the direction of Duncan, one of the worst exemplars of pure technique, who, nevertheless, was very successful at pushing people with a mixture of trickery and physical force.

"But, he is not my teacher," Gordon protested, visibly a little upset.

"Then why are you doing what he is doing?" Laoshi countered.

The allure of easy victory continued to prove enticing for many students, and we all bumbled down the road of forcing and straining for a long time in order to satisfy our egos. Fortunately, Laoshi remained remarkably good humored in the face of our ineptitude, only occasionally reacting to our failings as he did with Gordon. His customary method was to allow the need to win to run its course until we tired of butting heads with each other. Over time, most of his students became aware of the feeling he was encouraging us to experience, but there were also those students, like Duncan, who never changed and remained a challenge for us in our attempts to "continue easy."

When I complained about the seeming insensitivity of the Duncans of the class, Laoshi simply replied, "Be grateful to the Duncans, as they sacrifice their own progress for you. The challenge they offer is what helps you grow. They are a kind of bodhisattva."

Chapter 34: Conserving the Qi

退
步
跨
虎

Laoshi often talked about Wang Lang on a personal basis, as well as the instruction he received as a student in Wang Lang's regular classes and periodic workshops. Laoshi appeared to analyze everything Wang Lang said and did, and he found meaning in apparently insignificant details of word and action. He kept notebooks full of technical instruction, as well as pages of opinions, stories, and quotes from Wang Lang, which he treasured.

I enjoyed hearing about Wang Lang, and Laoshi's other teachers, even if I was only basking in the glow of their understanding conveyed through Laoshi. However, one of Wang Lang's personal idiosyncrasies as described by Laoshi troubled me a little. According to Laoshi, although Wang Lang was approachable at home and talked at length about tai chi, at the beginning of a workshop, he always stipulated that tai chi–related questions should only be addressed to him during the regular teaching sessions. He did not want to be drawn into extramural sessions with well-meaning students. Questions were to be put to him in the regular sessions.

Wang Lang's stated reason was his need to "conserve his qi." He did not want to be worn out by being "on duty" twenty-four/seven, and he hoped students would respect his wishes. Naturally, in the main, his students did just that and there was never a problem in regard to the matter.

Although I did not ever meet Wang Lang, I felt this attitude regarding his qi was a strange one. It did not tally somehow with the things I had read about tai chi—most notably, the idea that qi energy, whatever it is, is inexhaustible, that the more you use, the more is available to you. Furthermore, all I had read seemed to imply that it is better to use as much qi as possible in order that the flow through your body will be all the greater.

I asked Laoshi what he thought of Wang's reluctance to engage with his students in a more informal way outside of regular class time.

Laoshi's answer was, as usual, considered and intriguing: "There is a larger view of qi and a smaller view of qi; more accurately, you might say we can think of qi in terms of the universal or the personal. Different people take a particular view depending on their own experience, or interpretation of their experience.

"When I first began studying tai chi, I was told that the dantian acts as a sort of savings bank for qi. Each time you do a form, or other qi-related exercise, you deposit qi into the qi bank. Your daily activities are fuelled by this qi, which is gradually depleted over time if you withdraw more than you put in. The idea is to bank as much qi as possible, and either spend it cautiously or lavishly, depending on how much you are prepared to work to replenish what you spend.

"It did not surprise me," Laoshi continued, "when I found that Wang Lang's approach had something in common with this view. Wang Lang often told me, 'You need energy in order to relax.' To him, it made sense to husband his energy in order to get on with the serious business of relaxing. You might say this is the personal approach to the notion of qi, wherein your individual qi is limited and not to be wasted on trivia. You nurture it as best you can by avoiding overtaxing yourself and by adding to it at regular intervals—not allowing yourself the luxury of missing even a day of replenishment.

"Later on, however, I came to understand that there might be another approach. This also uses the bank analogy, but with significant differences. Your 'account' is already filled with as much qi as you can possibly use, and every time you make a withdrawal, your account is topped off from the universal source. The only problem is that you have forgotten your PIN, and so you are trying to rediscover it by practicing the form or other exercises.

"This is the universal view of qi and the realm of people like Zheng Manqing, who they say only slept four hours a night and worked continuously on his five excellences—tai chi, medicine, painting, poetry, and calligraphy, alongside his other interests. Zheng Manqing's schedule was exhausting by normal standards, but he maintained it until his death. O Sensei Ueshiba seems also to have accessed an inexhaustible kind of energy. He was immensely strong and worked tirelessly in pursuit of his goals; he also seemed capable of summoning energy to practice his aikido and perform demonstrations even when seriously ill. There are stories of him being carried to the dojo, appearing miraculously revived during the practice, only to be carried back to his sickbed once the practice had finished.

"The implication we might draw from the examples of Zheng Manqing, O Sensei, and others is that there is a way of tapping into an energy source outside of our ordinary day-to-day resources. Zheng Manqing even talked about 'borrowing qi from the universe,' although he also suggested that we should not be greedy about it and limit the amount we draw down for our use, or else we might end up bouncing around like a basketball. He also warned, 'If you borrow too much qi, you won't be able to move. . . . It's only useful when qi can actually circulate inside.'"

"So . . ." I said carefully, "are you suggesting, Laoshi, that we start out by adopting a personal view of qi and developing our practice until we reach the point where we can command the universal energy to flow through us?"

"I don't think that is the way to look at it," Laoshi said, shaking his head. "Such a view puts us on another treadmill where the only thing that matters is the gathering of more and more qi. A 'more is better' approach may appeal to our consumerist, materialistic society, but I suspect it may be better to consider our particular need for qi as a personal preference or even a practical function of our destiny. For instance, Laozi says, 'Without leaving my room, I know the whole of the universe.' What need has Laozi for unlimited energy? His mission in life is modest and personal, and so is his need for energy. You might think of energy as manure: more is not always better. If you have a small garden, you don't need a truckload of shit. It would just smell. On the other hand, a farmer cannot get by on one shovelful. The particular approach you follow is perhaps best related to who you are."

"Laoshi," I said, "what approach do you take?" It was the inevitable question.

Laoshi considered for a minute. "One of my old teachers used to say, 'Imagine you have just come home from work and you are really exhausted after a hard day. All you want to do is sit on the sofa and slump in front of the television. While you are sitting there, the phone rings. You pick it up sleepily and hear the voice of someone you really like inviting you to go out for the evening. So keen are you to spend time with this person, you suddenly don't feel tired anymore, and off you go. So, the question is: were you really tired or not?'"

"So . . . then," I said, searching for the right words, "does that mean you want to be able to summon as much energy as you want, when you want?"

Laoshi shook his head before saying, "Not really. It is not a case of my wanting limitless energy, but instead trusting that the right kind of energy, in the right amount, will be available at the right time. Harmony means just this. Bear in mind, too much energy may be more damaging to balance than too little."

Laoshi's words reminded me of what Ed Young, one of Zheng Manqing's disciples, said about push-hands: "I think the key is doing the right thing, in the right direction, at the right time." I concluded that even in searching for the gifts of tai chi, there needs to be balance. After all, recalling Laoshi's analogy of manure, we do not want to stink of qi any more than the Zen student wants to "stink of Zen" by being overly pious.

The reported sayings of Zheng Manqing are a rich vein of material for tai chi players to mine. Some are simply charming, leaving a smile on the face—like his assertion that, as winter approaches, bears make a home for themselves in the ground, complete with a little window, and go to sleep. During the winter, if they wake up hungry, they lick their right paw and go back to sleep.

轉
身
擺
蓮

Other comments merit regular revisitation, for they contain the seeds of universal truths highlighted from new and interesting angles, filtered, as they are, through the lens of a different cultural experience. Zheng Manqing's comments are multifaceted, delivering fresh insights as we are ready to receive them.

One of the Professor's most famous pronouncements concerns the reason none of his students ever approached his level in push-hands. He clearly expressed the view that it was a question of faith.

On first reading of the role of faith in push-hands, I assumed I knew what Zheng Manqing meant. Since I had learned by this stage, however, that much of what seems obvious at first glance frequently proves anything but obvious with further examination, I decided I had best check out my understanding with Laoshi.

"Laoshi, when Zheng Manqing said his students lacked faith, did he mean they did not believe strongly enough in their push-hands ability? Was his own outstanding ability in push-hands and fencing due to the fact that he simply believed he could do it?"

I thought this was a reasonable enough question, so you might imagine my disappointment when Laoshi responded with a sigh and a roll of his eyes. Although he often said, "There is no such thing as a stupid question," there were times when I seriously doubted it. This felt to be one of those times.

Laoshi quickly relented, however, and sought to answer the question. "You are confusing faith with belief," he said firmly. "They are not the same thing. This is a common mistake in our part of the world. What Zheng Manqing is talking about here is faith in the sense of trust, rather than belief in whether an idea or theory is true or not."

"Er . . . I'm not sure I understand the difference, Laoshi," I admitted.

"Hmm . . . let's see how best to explain this," Laoshi said, searching for a suitable analogy. "I once saw a BBC documentary about a Buddhist monk in Japan who kept honeybees. He would care for them lovingly and harvest the honey in a respectful way. Things went well until his hives were attacked by giant hornets from a nearby valley. These hornets were not numerous but were large and too well armored for the honeybees to kill with their sting. The hornets were also very aggressive: a small group of thirty or forty of them could wipe out an entire hive of thirty thousand honeybees before plundering the larvae.

"The monk, whose name was Yamaguchi, would visit his hives in the morning and find some of them completely decimated. It was heartbreaking for him to see his bees lifeless in the tens of thousands.

"Yamaguchi knew where the hornets were coming from, and it would have been easy enough to locate their nest and kill them to protect his bees. But he did not do so because, as a Buddhist, he revered all life as sacred. It would have been against his religious beliefs to kill the hornets.

"Do you see?" Laoshi asked. "This is about a man's belief. He put his trust in the balance of nature and took no action against the hornets, in spite of discovering a new hornet queen among his orchids at the end of the summer. He feared what this might mean for the following year, when the hornet queen established a colony of hornets right in his backyard—but he continued to put his trust in nature. This is an example of faith."

"So what happened the next year?" I pursued, eager to discover the happy ending in Laoshi's little morality tale.

"I don't know," he said. "The documentary ended there."

"What?" Absurdly, I felt myself outraged. "So the hornets continue to kill his bees? What on earth is the point in having faith then?"

"Exactly," Laoshi replied. "That is why so few people possess it. Faith does not offer guarantees. It is of the heart-mind. You have to feel that an action is the thing to do. If you do not have a well-developed sense of your heart-mind, then the rational mind will find all kinds of reasons why you should abandon faith."

It was all rather disappointing. My sense of "how things should be" required a happy ending. What was the point of relating a story about faith when it seemed that having faith led nowhere? I grasped, at least, that Laoshi was making just that point: having faith can mean following a path that may seem to offer no profit. We follow it simply because we feel it is the thing to do.

I glimpsed a small smile on Laoshi's face and figured he knew exactly what I was thinking.

"Am I missing something?" I asked.

"Not really," Laoshi said, "but you are wondering what the point of the story is. Am I right?"

He continued with his tale. "A few years after watching the documentary, I read a story in the *Guardian* newspaper about Japanese hornets invading Europe, killing European honeybees just as they had killed the Japanese honeybees on the other side of the world. There was concern that the hornets would eventually make their way to Britain and gradually spread northward. Our British bees had no defense against the hornets. Crucially, however, the article related that European bees had not yet learned how to defeat their attackers in the way the Japanese honeybees had.

"I reread that paragraph. Indeed, it was true. The Japanese bees had worked out a way to kill the marauding hornets. Unable to penetrate the thick armor of the hornets, they had changed strategy. Instead of ineffectively stinging the attackers, they formed a massive ball of bee bodies around the hornets and killed them by causing them to overheat. Nature had found a way to restore balance.

"Interestingly—incredibly even," Laoshi continued, "the honeybees at the center of the ball of bees do not themselves overheat. The honeybees are able to withstand a higher temperature, while the hornets' ability to withstand the heat is diminished by the carbon dioxide that builds up in the middle of the ball.

"It seems Yamaguchi's faith in the balance of nature was justified, even though there was every appearance that all would be lost.

"Zheng Manqing urges us to put our faith in principle: the principle that four ounces can deflect a thousand pounds; the principle that the soft can overcome the hard; the principle that wherever there is strength, there must also be weakness. The difficulty of his method does not lie in the hours of practice, nor does it lie in accepting that the principle exists. The difficulty lies in having enough faith in principle to deny ourselves the use of force when things are not going as we would wish."

The lesson seemed relevant beyond the immediate concerns of the push-hands player. When we consider our responses to life's challenges, it is easy to see how, when things go against us, many of us either try to force the issue, or else sulk—because it's not fair. To be able to accept the trials of life and metaphorically push hands with disappointment, to embrace loss and failure and to rediscover within ourselves our trust in the balance of nature—this is one of the major lessons of our tai chi.

Laoshi told us that Wang Lang often said the Chinese character for the word "crisis" is composed of the characters for "danger" and "opportunity." Change, which we fear so much, is never only loss or gain; it is always loss and gain. We have only to gain clarity on how the balance is being altered in order to rectify our own balance in response. In a very real sense, our push-hands, fencing, and form are all about maintaining balance in the face of change.

Like the bear licking his paw and waiting for summer, we have to trust that, when the time is right, we will know what to do. The only thing that can go wrong is that our lack of faith will turn our hearts to stone and we will sabotage ourselves with our own fear.

As Laoshi had concluded his story about the bees, I recalled an incident at one of the tai chi and meditation courses I had attended at a Buddhist retreat center before I met Laoshi.

The center was located on the side of a hill, overlooking a beautiful valley. The building was old and venerable, as was the old Tibetan *geshe*, the learned monk, who lived and taught there.

One year a colony of wasps moved into the attic space of the old house and caused mayhem at the retreats and courses over the summer. Great care had to be taken, as the wasps found their way into every nook and cranny of the building. Naturally, in a place of Buddhist belief, the practice of nonviolence applied to the wasps, since they were regarded as the reincarnations of angry souls. The customary solution of gassing the wasps was, therefore, out of the question. The geshe's solution, however, was certainly unique. Any wasps that entered his room were captured in an empty jam jar. The geshe would then chant at the bees, invoking them to return to the nest and persuade the entire colony to leave. I never did find out if the wasps left, or were driven out, but I told Laoshi of this incident.

Laoshi smiled. "Ah," he said, "he is like Yamaguchi: a man of belief and faith."

Chapter 36: Embrace the Sword That Does Not Shine

彎
弓
射
虎

During one of my ventures into the wider world of tai chi, I attended a workshop in the American Midwest. The workshop attracted a couple of dozen tai chi players from various countries, one of whom was a big, friendly middle-aged man from North Dakota. He was one of the senior students of a well-known teacher who had studied with Zheng Manqing in the Shr Jung School in New York. The fellow, perhaps due to the twenty-year age difference between us, seemed keen to take me under his wing and help me settle into the student dorms where we were staying for the duration of the workshop.

My new acquaintance seemed an amiable fellow and we chatted pleasantly while waiting in the main hall for the teacher to arrive and formally introduce the weekend's itinerary. I was happy to have someone sociable to talk to since I was in a strange city far from home and my usual comforts. I suspect in hearing my accent my new friend surmised I was from some godforsaken tai chi hinterland, and so proceeded to "mark my card" as to the state of play on the American tai chi scene: "Yeah, so there are some good teachers over here like Ken, Bataan, Barbara, and the like, but there are a lot who are just not doing it right at all. Their push-hands is just force against force. You would be best to avoid them. I'll tell you who they are so you will know to give them a wide berth."

While respecting the well-intentioned motivation of this kind of help, I prefer to make up my own mind about teachers and the various approaches they favor. Furthermore, it was not as if I were unaware of the point he was making, and so I was less than keen to discuss the matter at that time. I thought I would tactfully deflect his comments with a little humor and wit: "Well, maybe it's not that they aren't doing it right," I said with an impish smile. "Maybe it's just that you aren't able to deal with them."

I hit a nerve. My would-be companion's friendly countenance disappeared. He became more than a little flustered before blurting out, "That's what they say, but they are wrong."

I was taken unawares by the strength of his feeling on the matter. He began to defend his position with growing vigor, while I looked on, trying to find a way to defuse the situation.

Fortunately, the teacher appeared and we returned to the relative calm of learning a set of exercises known as the *kugong* (苦功)—bitter practice. I hoped my conversation with the big man would not leave him with a bitter aftertaste, but my hopes were dashed later that evening at dinner, when he managed to find a seat near me and picked up where he had left off. I listened patiently for a while before assuring him that I had only been joking when I said what I did. I understood and respected his position. But he was not so easily placated, and I spent the rest of dinner hearing why he was using superior technique against uncultured force when engaging in push-hands.

Of course, the subject under discussion was not new to me. It is the common experience of all who have even a passing acquaintance with push-hands that the issue of force—and who is using too much—is a much-argued topic. The usual recriminations pass back and forth, as both parties blame each other for being too forceful, insensitive, or misguided.

Perhaps the situation arises due to the various interpretations of Zheng Manqing's admonition that we use no more than four ounces to push, nor allow more than four ounces of force to build up on us. Zheng Manqing's words have been interpreted liberally over the years and can be used to justify just about anything. One of the more extreme interpretations I have come across is that we should only use four ounces of force more than our opponent. In effect, this means if our partner can muster four tons of pressure, we are at liberty to apply up to four tons and four ounces against him. Another interpretation is that the four-ounce rule only applies to force placed directly onto our partner's body; on the arms, the amount of force applied can be as much as we can generate.

At first I thought it was only in the West that we had such a varied view of what four ounces meant, but Laoshi's experiences in the East made me think again.

"When I was in Taiwan," he said, "I was invited to a tai chi competition one Sunday afternoon after regular practice with Master Lin. By chance, my visit coincided with the tournament, and I was keen to see what the local scene was like. The venue, a large gym hall, was packed with competitors, supporters, and assorted other bodies, including my traveling companion and me. I was feeling slightly self-conscious because I was down to my last clean T-shirt—black with a giant yin-yang symbol on the front. It looked like a giant circular target. Interest, however, was fixed not on me, but on the competition, which was in full swing.

"At one end of the hall, near the stage, where the invited dignitaries were sitting, was the form competition—exclusively the Zheng Manqing thirty-seven-step form. At the other end, the rowdier push-hands tournament was underway. There were maybe half a dozen teams all wearing their school T-shirts—none with yin-yang symbols to trouble mine—surrounding a foam mat with a circle drawn on it measuring about ten yards in diameter. The combatants in the center were attempting to push each other out of the circle, or else throw each other to the floor.

"It seemed to me most of the competitors were not just using a little more force than perhaps they should; instead, it seemed physically impossible for them to use any more force than they did. Each bout seemed only to outdo the one before in the epic nature of the struggle. The competitors routinely grabbed each other by the arms and thrashed around as violently as they could, straining every fiber, urged on by their screaming teammates around the sides. There was next to no evidence of 'four ounces' on display."

"So, Laoshi, did you think they were doing it wrong?" I asked, hoping to pin him down to a precise answer. I should have known better.

"A friend of mine came to push-hands class for a while," he replied. "He had some martial arts experience and I thought he might enjoy trying out what we were doing. He only lasted a few weeks before giving up. When I next met up with him, I asked him why.

"'It was too much like golf,' my friend complained.

"'In what way?' I asked him.

"'Nobody can do it right, but it doesn't stop anyone from telling you what you are doing wrong.'"

I saw what Laoshi was getting at, having played a little golf myself. There seems to be no shortage of swing doctors, who, unable to hit a decent ball themselves, are nevertheless happy to reveal the faults in your technique.

Laoshi continued with his answer: "Simply declaring that a fellow push-hands player is 'wrong' turns out to be a pointless exercise; worse still, it is an example of very limited verbal push-hands. To a great extent, push-hands is about not showing your hand until you know what the other person is doing—

hence the advice to only use four ounces, since the more physical you are, the less sensitive you become. We are encouraged to be soft in order that we can remain sensitive to what our partner is doing. Softness in itself is not the goal; rather, by being soft, or only using four ounces, we can feel more, which should be an advantage. As the saying goes: 'If you are talking, you cannot be listening'—and how we love to talk."

I was not overly impressed by Laoshi's answer. At the time I was struggling more than usual with my own push-hands. Despite the encouragement of Laoshi and the assurances of the senior students that my skill was improving, I was having a frustrating time when confronted by forceful fellow students.

One of the disheartening aspects of studying push-hands, I was realizing, is that even after years of "progress," the crude, rough and ready beginner is dispiritingly difficult to deal with while adhering to the idea of softness we are encouraged to apply. I wanted someone to tell these unrefined blunderers they were wrong.

Periodically, I would recall my brief acquaintance with the man from North Dakota and sympathize with the position in which he had found himself—the same position, I suspect, in which I now found myself. I was hoping the voice of authority would, once and for all, thunder from the heavens the verdict that those bullish, overly physical students were wholly wrong, thus validating me.

Lacking any prospect of divine intervention, I desperately wished Laoshi would make the pronouncement and condemn those who disregarded the four-once principle. This, of course, did not happen, and so, for me, the question remained: what to do when you are more sensitive than your partner, but he, due to greater strength and willingness to use it, still pushes you over?

This very question presented itself a little while later. Phil, a Londoner, began to attend Laoshi's push-hands class every fortnight or so. He was in Glasgow with work and wanted somewhere to keep up his practice. He had studied for twenty years or more in the London area with all the main teachers, so he did not want to learn any more forms, but he was keen to continue with push-hands. I was surprised when Laoshi allowed him to come to push-hands without learning our version of the form.

It would have been easy to be intimidated by Phil, since he was a big man. He was about six inches taller than Laoshi and maybe three stone heavier. However, on first meeting, he appeared to be a very nice fellow, and he talked about the vital importance of softness and sensitivity in push-hands. Once on the floor, though, it was another story: he was a demon. He would employ a wide stance and shove, pull, and grab mercilessly. If you did succeed in deflecting his force, he would simply employ the "grand piano technique"—

he would fall on top of you, in a bid to take you down with him. He was a nightmare.

Most of us found him impossible to deal with at all, and I would secretly watch when Laoshi took his turn to push with him, looking for clues as to how to deal with this monster. I hoped to see Laoshi handling him like a baby and bouncing him around at will, but this was not the case. Laoshi was only able to neutralize him half the time. I had never seen anyone give Laoshi so much trouble in class. Laoshi himself did not seem very concerned when he was pushed, but I and some of the other students were secretly disgruntled that our teacher could not deal with this interloper. Indeed, some students lost faith and left, reasoning that if Laoshi could not deal with the guy after all his time practicing, what good was this art?

I mentioned to Tony, one of Laoshi's longtime students and an assistant instructor, my disappointment at Laoshi's failure to deal with Phil. He was one of Laoshi's earliest students and loved him dearly. I wanted to know what he thought about the situation. His reply was informative.

"Have you ever noticed the floor around Phil when he has finished pushing with Laoshi?"

"Er . . . no," I admitted, bemused by his reply. "I was not looking at the floor."

"Well, next time have a look and you will see dozens of drip stains from his sweat forming a nice little semicircle around where he has been standing. Then you will notice that he goes over to his kit bag, breathing heavily, to fetch a towel to dry off. Then he has to change into a fresh T-shirt because the one he is wearing is wringing with sweat.

"Next, have a look at Laoshi. He is wearing his customary T-shirt and sweatshirt, yet he never even breaks a sweat. When he is finished, he looks as if he has been sitting down for the last half hour, rather than battling with a behemoth. Phil uses huge amounts of force yet cannot dominate Laoshi, who is still practicing with softness. It's true Phil can hold his own with Laoshi—who uses more root than maybe he would like—but look at what Phil has to resort to, to push Laoshi."

Although I appreciated Tony's insight, I was still not convinced. Surely, I thought, if the principle is so wonderful, it should be able to deal with whoever, whatever, whenever. I could not contain myself and determined to talk to Laoshi about it when an opportunity presented itself. One evening, when we were alone, I seized my chance.

"Laoshi, so . . . when Phil comes to class and uses that much force—and pushes everybody—is he wrong?"

Laoshi was silent for a moment. "Do you want to do what he does?"

Here we go again, I thought. He never gives a straight answer to this question. I knew there was no point asking why he answered a question with a question.

Laoshi did not wait for my reply. He continued: "For my father, there seemed to be almost something sacred in the process of sharpening a knife or his open razor in preparation for shaving. As a boy, I would watch as he stood in the bathroom at an ancient leather strop, honing the edge of his razor until he was ready to test it by plucking a hair from his head and cutting it cleanly with the edge. At other times, he would go outside to the stone step by the front door and use it to sharpen his favorite knife. He would work the edge till it became so sharp that it would not shine. He once told me the edge of a truly sharp blade looks dull, since it is too sharp to reflect the light. The knife was decades old and showed the effects of a lifetime of persistent sharpening.

"The point is that the hard and unyielding stone is there to hone your sharpness. If there were no hard, unyielding stone, you would never become sharp. The difference is that the stone never changes. It will always be a stone—but the knife becomes sharp. Phil is like a stone. We 'use' him to hone ourselves. It is up to him whether he wants to be a stone or a knife. It is not for you to judge. It is for you to make yourself sharp.

"Bear in mind, however, as my father said, the edge of a truly sharp knife does not shine. In your practice, you are becoming sharp, but you still want to shine. To really 'get it,' don't worry about shining, and you will get there. The stone wears away your ego, expectations, and attachments to reveal you—the you that does not need to shine."

Slowly I began to see push-hands as the process through which I might refine my awareness of who I really am. This was the lesson I gleaned from watching big Phil push with Laoshi—the lesson that made sense of Zheng Manqing's statement, "If your idea is to push or not be pushed, it is not tai chi."

Chapter 37: The Greatness of the Qi

Not long after I began studying aikido with Billy Coyle, I attended a conference at Glasgow University entitled "The Samurai and Japanese Culture." It was a full weekend of talks, martial arts demonstrations, and movies related to the samurai arts and their place in Japanese culture, both past and present. I loved it. This was my introduction to the famous Kurosawa movies *Yojimbo* and *Sanjuro*, starring Toshiro Mifune. Local and national martial arts instructors treated us to excellent displays of the fighting arts and a lecture by Stephen Turnbull, an authority on the samurai and their culture, was first class.

合
太
极

The highlight for me, however, was Billy's talk. Though not a highly educated man in the academic sense, he had a natural ability in aikido and was an outstanding teacher and communicator.

I can still picture the scene. Even decades later, I can remember a great deal of his lecture. Such was the impression it made on me. A receptive if modest-sized audience greeted him with polite applause as he entered the lecture theater carrying a pair of sword bags. He opened the bags and took out two swords, which he unsheathed and held up for our inspection. He asked the audience whether we perceived any difference between the two swords. It was a rhetorical question, as none of us was qualified to offer an opinion on the subtlety of Japanese swords. His point was that, to the naked eye, the two swords looked almost identical—but one was an iaito and the other was a real sword.

An iaito is a metal practice sword used in iaido—the art of drawing the sword. It is a good idea for a beginner to use an iaito, as it reduces the risk of injury that accompanies drawing a sword and returning it to its scabbard in the formal, ritualized manner at the heart of iaido. It looks real enough and feels closer to the real thing than a bokken; it is, however, not the real thing. It is an imitation.

Billy proceeded to extend the analogy from sword to man. He compared the process of making a real sword with the training of a martial artist. He was making a point about the soul of a sword and the spirit of a human being. The implication was that the soul of a true sword is the same as the soul of a true man.

The samurai regarded their swords as sacred, possessing a power of their own. Through training, the spirit of a man could be forged and polished in much the same way in order to fashion a man of the highest ideals.

Billy continued with the analogy, more or less, as follows:

In order to make a man or a sword, you must first seek out good raw material. Then you must go through the process of removing the impurities. In men, these impurities are arrogance and selfishness. The process of removing impurities is similar for man and metal. It is a process of "heating up and beating up." Once the raw material has been purged of impurities, it is then fashioned by training or shaping until it becomes a sword or a man of potency and integrity. It, or he, becomes an instrument of power, capable of affecting the world.

The critical moment in the process comes when the sword is tested. The red-hot blade is immersed in cold water and it takes on its final shape. This is a tricky time. If the steel has not been prepared properly, or if any impurities remain, then the sword will break and all effort up to this point will have been wasted. If the sword survives, however, it is then refined, polished, and dressed in its furniture—handle, hilt, guard, and scabbard. Similarly, when the time is judged to be right, the man is also tested, sometimes by circumstance, and if he is not broken, he will move on to the next phase.

Although Billy did not belabor the sword-man connection, the analogy was clear: the stages required in fashioning the sword correspond to the stages in training the human spirit.

Billy did, however, spend more time talking about an additional fascinating feature essential to the strength of the sword. Clay is applied in a wavelike pattern to the cutting edge of the sword before cooling. When immersed in water, the cutting edge takes longer to cool, thus making it harder. Combined with the softer, more flexible back of the blade, the sword now possesses the twin attributes of hardness and softness. Now, in Billy's words, "When the sword meets something softer than itself, it cuts through, but when it meets something harder than itself, it cuts through to the point where it will break—then bends slightly so it can cut deeper." This was one of the most important principles in Billy's approach to martial arts: the ability to meet and cut through that which is stronger or harder than oneself by being able to yield a little when required.

Billy then held up the sword and the iaito before our gaze once more, impressing on us the visual similarity. "They are both curved," he noted. "They both have *tsuka* and tsuba—handles and guards. They both have a *hamon*, the wavelike pattern separating hard and soft—but the iaito has no edge. It cannot cut and, even if it could, it would shatter the moment it encountered anything harder than itself. It is an imitation. It has not gone through the process."

The lecture was well received, including by those with a chiefly academic interest in martial arts. It was only much later that I wondered if Billy had deliberately chosen this topic in order to highlight the difference between him and the intellectuals with whom he shared the platform. By the time I thought about it, the opportunity to ask him had gone—but I still recall the talk as being one of the most memorable and important pieces of instruction I ever received.

All through the following years, I strived to remain true to Billy's teaching, viewing martial arts training as a forging of the spirit in order to live a life of strength and integrity. I was acutely aware that my spirit desperately needed training. My own particular impurities, including arrogance, were born out of insecurity and self-doubt. For much of my youth, I felt myself to be a fraud, unable to meet the demands that were placed upon me—but my one ally throughout this time was the notion that I could "cut through" by harnessing my spirit, and I could keep on going. Each New Year, we—Billy's students—engaged in mysogi, or cleansing practices: thousands of sword cuts, followed by hundreds of iai kata, followed by aikido throws—to the point of exhaustion. I kept on going, in the company of tough men. Billy was twice my age, but he led us all, never faltering, always demanding one hundred percent, and always giving the same.

And yet, I continued to feel like a fraud. In my twenties, I went through a period of testing myself against anyone I felt was dishonoring me. I lived like a gunslinger, ready to react to the slightest provocation—and in those days, provocation seemed to find me everywhere. I began to have a nagging suspicion that I was drawing it to me. Still unwilling to look closely at myself, I faced down all perceived challenges with the resolute spirit of the dojo, engaging my hardened spirit in order to intimidate those who treated me disrespectfully.

One rainy afternoon, for instance, I was returning home from a routine visit to a local supermarket. I had no car at the time, so I was obliged to trudge through the sodden Glasgow streets, laden plastic carrier bags cutting into fingers numbed with the cold. In those days I wouldn't have been caught dead wearing gloves.

On the route home, there was a stretch where the sidewalks were not very wide. As I made my way down the street, I came alongside three young men who were ambling along, enjoying each other's banter and good-natured teasing. As I was about to pass on the inside, the middle fellow nudged his pal walking nearest to me, and I had to take a large step to avoid a collision. My foot had only one place to land: in a deep puddle. Cold rain water immediately filled my shoe and the force of my step caused me to splash icy water over my other leg.

The young man with whom I had nearly collided witnessed what had happened and started to laugh. To be fair, he appeared to be in a joyful mood—not necessarily laughing directly at my mishap. Nevertheless, as I continued past him, I grunted, "Who are you laughing at?"

"Och, don't take it like that," he said smiling in an attempt to calm the air.

I stopped dead. Standing about three yards from him and his two companions, I turned to face them, dropped my shopping bags, and spat out, "Who the fuck are you to tell me how to take it?"

I was in full fight mode, glaring menacingly at the young man but including all of them in my vitriol.

They were not looking for confrontation, however, and moved swiftly along. As they did so, I squatted down in the rain, shook the water off my sliced loaf, and returned it to the bag alongside the split carton of milk, which left a milky trail all the way home.

In those days, I had the ability to calm down as quickly as I was able to ramp up my energy and, as I plodded along, I admonished myself wearily, "You know, you really will have to stop doing stuff like that."

Of course, there were times when the role of gunslinger seemed justified. One Saturday afternoon, a friend and I were traveling to his place in the east end of the city. As neither of us had a car, we were obliged to take the bus. It was a busy afternoon—Celtic was playing at Parkhead and the support was out in force. Our bus arrived at the stop and we squeezed in with half of Glasgow, so it seemed, for the thirty-minute journey.

There were no seats left on the lower deck, so, reluctantly, we climbed the stairs to the upper level. I was not keen to sit upstairs as, in those days, smoking was permitted on the upper deck. Still, half an hour standing on the lower level in cattle-truck conditions did not appeal either, so we made our way up top.

There were only two vacant seats, just in front of the long back-row seat at the rear window. As I approached the back of the bus, I was dismayed to discover that more than half a dozen youths were boisterously amusing themselves on the long backseat, the one next to where I had to sit.

My friend and I sat down and a sense of foreboding enveloped me as I waited for it to happen. The exact form was yet to be revealed but, having spent years working with youngsters in their late teens, I knew it was coming.

Sure enough, over the next twenty minutes, the laughing, swearing, and abusing of other passengers escalated into "soggy ball" attacks. A soggy ball is a piece of paper, chewed enough to be soggy and then thrown as an unpleasant if harmless missile—either at a wall, where it sticks or, as on this occasion, the back of someone's head.

The several passengers who were now becoming victims of these attacks said nothing and endured. They did not want to tackle a mob of unruly, loutish, and unpredictable teenagers. I suspected it was only a matter of time before they got around to me. I was proved right. Smack! A soggy ball hit me on the ear.

I turned around in my seat and directed a steely gaze at one of the young lads: "What the fuck are you doin?" I snarled. This was my standard opening line in conflict situations.

"It wasnae me!" he said, laughing in mock protest, clearly feeling the safety in numbers.

"I don't give a rat's arse who it was," I hissed. "If anything hits me again, I'm comin' for you, you little shit. I'm bigger than you, harder than you, and definitely more evil than you. Understand?"

There was instant quiet as he and his hooligan comrades made an assessment of my person. Now, I was a big lad. So was my friend. The teenage mob suddenly became unsure. Silence reigned and I slowly turned my gaze forward once more. After a few minutes, one of the youths began talking quietly again—but no more soggy balls were thrown.

As a strategy, it was not without risk: if the randomly nominated youth was intimidated enough, he would have to protect my back or face the threatened consequences. On the other hand, there was always the chance that one of his buddies would call my bluff, or else be twisted enough to enjoy watching his mate dealing with those consequences. The key to it all lay in how unhinged and, therefore, unpredictable I could appear, making any action on their part inadvisable. Mind you, I was well enough on the way to becoming unhinged at the time, so perhaps I did not have to rely on any great acting skill.

The ten remaining minutes of the bus journey passed without significant incident and I got off the bus without a backward glance. Reviewing the situation later, I consoled myself by thinking I had done a public service. But I was still uneasy. Was this me? I did not truly feel it was.

All through this period in my life, somewhere inside, I knew I was afraid. I used the sword edge of my spirit to survive in challenging environments and heard the words of Billy encouraging me when I faltered: "Cut through. Cut through." But I was becoming exhausted living on the edge all the time. I realized I was slowly killing myself.

I took a step back from aikido and dabbled half-heartedly in Shotokan karate for a while before meeting Laoshi. I recognized immediately that there was something of the forged steel about Laoshi but, somehow, he combined the steel with a compassion I was unable to find in myself. I wanted to know how he could be the way he was, combining cutting edge with genuine human warmth. It took some time, but finally I reached the point where I felt able to ask him about it.

"Laoshi," I said one afternoon at his house, "you know I studied aikido and sword with Billy Coyle? Billy was very focused on the sword, and he seemed to find great similarity in the process of making a sword and making a man. Is there an equivalent idea in tai chi?"

"Hmm . . ." he said, nodding thoughtfully as he sat down on a soft chair. I could see this was going to take a bit of time to explain. "In a way there is. Your teacher was a serious man. By that I do not mean 'solemn,' but serious about his art. In other words, he was sincere—the most important quality for a martial artist. He was the kind of man who would die for his art.

"The best of the samurai were also serious. As it says in *Hagakure*, 'The way of the warrior is death.' Some argue this refers to a Zen-like death of the ego—but for many samurai, facing the prospect of impending death was a literal reality. You had to be ready to die at any time for your master.

"That is a big thing to ask, don't you think?" Laoshi said, eyeing me solemnly. "To be constantly ready to die at the whim of another? It is very stressful because it means constantly looking into the eyes of your deepest fear. Ultimately, no matter how you dress them up, all martial arts are about the problem of fear. Most of our terrors are rooted in the ultimate fear—the fear of being extinguished.

"There is a piece of film somewhere of a real fight to the death between two trained swordsmen. It is old and grainy, but it still shows enough of what happens when even skilled men engage in mortal combat. Those who have seen it and know enough to judge say these men use their swords like hammers, rather than precision instruments. What happened? Their skills deserted them at the crucial point, and they were reduced to the level of brawlers. That is the power of fear."

Zhuangzi makes the same point when he describes how, when practicing, an expert archer shoots his arrows with unerring accuracy, but when standing on the edge of a precipice a thousand feet high, the expert archer falls "prostrate on the ground, with sweat pouring down to his heels."

"Consider also," Laoshi continued, "the story of Yagyu Munemori when he was the shogun's sword teacher. A palace guard approached Yagyu to learn the art of the sword, but Yagyu would not agree to take him as student until he divulged the art he had already mastered. Mystified, the guard denied having mastered any art but revealed that as a young man he was afraid to die, and so he meditated on the matter until he came to the point where he no longer feared death. Yagyu said, 'There is nothing else I can teach you.'

"The training you underwent in aikido was designed to arrive at the same place, only using a different method. You were brought to a point where you could use the strength of your spirit like a sword to defeat your fear. The analogy here is apt: you use the razor-sharp concentration of your mind to cut through veils created by your fear. In order to do this, however, you must be able to tap into an energy that can raise your spirit when you need its power."

Laoshi was right. The thousands of sword cuts and techniques we practiced in class were partly fighting skills, but, as Billy often said, more importantly, they were "spirit exercises." Fighting spirit was prized above technique. I remembered hearing that Zheng Manqing said an indomitable fighting spirit can make up for deficiencies in technique. We were training to be able to blast through an opponent using fighting spirit.

I began to feel uneasy. I wondered if I had abandoned my path in aikido due to my own weakness. I wondered whether my fighting spirit were still contaminated by impurities. I felt like a fraud once more.

I sighed heavily. "So," I said, "was all that training a waste of time, now that I have given it up?" It was a painful notion.

Laoshi shook his head slowly, emphatically. "No," he said. "It was not a waste of time. It gave you a strong foundation, but it was just not your path."

"But, how can I know that?" I asked, unsure what exactly Laoshi meant. I only knew I was confused about the whole thing.

Laoshi continued, "I know you respected your teacher and learned a great deal from him. But did you not also feel there was a distance between you?"

It was true. Once again Laoshi's intuition was astonishing. I truly respected

Billy, but I never felt myself to be one of his inner circle of students. I dearly wanted to be, but there it was: a distance between us that I could never close. Once again, I felt it was my fault. I did not have enough commitment, not enough spirit.

Laoshi resumed: "The distance you felt prevented you from developing yourself fully. You understood the hard, cutting-edge aspect of the training, but you missed the softer, flexible part that bends when it needs to. You were always trying to prove something to yourself and your teacher by hardening yourself ever further. It is no wonder you felt you were killing yourself. All the emphasis on the hard edge cutting through was denying the yin part of you. This part is cultivated through a deepening of the connection between you and your teacher; it is learned through harmonizing with him. You have to give up the resistance to your teacher. This is impossible, of course, if you feel that he does not accept you."

I suddenly began to feel disturbed. This conversation was proceeding to a deeper level than I had intended. I felt I needed some air and so I got up, went out into Laoshi's garden, and sat down to consider what he was saying.

Some time passed before Laoshi came out to join me.

"What can I do?" I asked him. "I feel so empty."

"Breathe in the qi of heaven. Let it fill you up as if you have breathed in for the first time ever. You have become empty. This is good. Allow the energy of the universe to fill you. You are ready to become filled. Fill your dantian with the greatness of the qi."

"But I don't know how!" I blurted out.

"There is no 'how,'" Laoshi said quietly. "There is only the feeling. Remember how you felt when you raised your sword and cut through your fear? The energy is the same but more expansive than the narrow focus of a sword cut. Let the greatness of the qi fill you until you feel yourself to be as limitless as the universe. Let your mind, as Yang Chengfu taught, become 'as spacious as the universe. Become qi-ful.'"

I had heard many times the injunction to breathe into the dantian, but I had always found it to be of limited use. I suppose I imagined some sort of mystical experience would take place—that I would experience some kind of satori. Instead, what I was feeling was, well . . . fairly normal. I felt good in the same way I might when I was having an enjoyable time with friends, or doing something pleasant. Nevertheless, I thought I began to see what Laoshi was offering: a way of returning to balance when fear—whichever of its ten thousand forms—had gripped my mind.

"When we are afraid," Laoshi said, "we tend to make ourselves small. We physically shrink and empty out like a scared dog. So when you feel afraid, expand your energy. Remember the qi-expansion exercise for your hands that I showed you before? Do this—but with your whole body."

Laoshi was referring to the exercise he showed students when talking about qi, the one in which visualizing eyes on the fingertips encourages a feeling of flow in the hands. He was now suggesting that same feeling could be expanded into the whole body.

"There is a way to summon energy from the depth of our being. This energy can be used in a focused way to raise the fighting spirit—or it can be used in a more diffuse way, to fill out the body and expand the mind until the fear that confronts us becomes smaller and smaller.

"When you feel fear approaching, fill yourself from the inside. This feeling of expansive energy and the feeling of fear cannot mutually exist. One must displace the other. This is the power of tai chi."

With that Laoshi left me alone. I sat there in his garden for a long time, just feeling good and feeling my dantian subtly filling my body every time I breathed in. I thought perhaps I was just fooling myself and nothing was really happening—but then again, I thought, "I am happy anyway, so why worry about it?"

Some few weeks later, I was returning home from a café the students frequented after class. I was aware of a feeling of well-being and fullness, a feeling that seemed to come to me more often and remain longer these days—especially after my talk with Laoshi in his garden. My car felt sweet to drive and, as a result, I was probably driving a little too fast. I was in a state of harmony with the car, and I felt like we were floating along. I turned into the one-way crescent close to where I lived and where I often parked the car. As I turned in, two young men who were about to cross the road had to pull up short on the curb. It was not that I almost ran them over, but I was aware of the sudden halt in their movement.

I drove around the crescent, found a parking space, and began to get out of the car. It was then I noticed the two men had doubled back and entered the crescent from the exit side. They were in their early twenties, lean and fit, and their energy seemed to carry intent. They looked at me purposefully as they closed the distance between us with some speed. It occurred to me that they had taken offense at my driving and had doubled back hoping for an opportunity to "discuss" my maneuver. It was around midnight and this was Glasgow after all.

There was a threat in the air and I concluded I was going to have to fight. Instinctively, I began breathing into my dantian and felt my energy, my whole being expanding. By the time I was out of the car and locking the door, I felt myself to be enormous. Now, I was maybe slightly taller than each of them in actual physical height, but energetically I felt massive compared to them. There was no rush of adrenalin that normally accompanies such occurrences, and I was aware that I did not feel even the slightest bit afraid.

As the two men drew level, I noticed they remained on the pavement, on the opposite side of the car from me. There was a small hesitation before one of them addressed me: "Eh, do you know where a bar called Oblimovs is?"

The preamble to an assault is often an innocuous question designed to throw the victim off balance, or to assess his potency when the action starts. I was not worried. I felt myself still, relaxed, and secure.

"Sure, pal. It's around that corner," I replied, pointing in the direction they were going. "But it will be closed by now. It's nearly midnight."

"Aye, right," he said, a grunted acknowledgement. Another small hesitation before the two headed off in the direction I had indicated.

I stood watching them for a little while just in case they decided to return. Since they did not, I went home. Later, reflecting on the incident, I figured there were two possibilities. One, they were riled at my driving and were coming to vent their feelings, only sensing my energy, had thought better of it. Or two, they were simply looking for a bar and were lost. It occurred to me that, even if they were lost, I was not to know that. The point was that although I had anticipated an attack, I felt unafraid.

And because I felt safe, I was not emitting a hostile vibe. This was a first for me. At no time in the past had I ever felt so secure when faced with this kind of trouble. And I had faced this kind of trouble often. I would be in full fight-or-flight mode, bristling with the cutting energy I had clung to in my fear.

Could it be that Laoshi had shown me another way? I had for long years understood that one of the major questions we all must answer to our own satisfaction is whether the universe is essentially hostile or benign. For most of my life, I had experienced the world as hostile and lived my life in accordance with that view. Life was a fight. Now, for the first time, I glimpsed the truth that life could not only be benign, but joyful as well. I began to look forward to each day from then on. I had such a lot of time to make up.

I felt reborn.

epilogue

Those early years with Laoshi were a remarkable period in my life. As I became more centered, life became more joyful. The growing feeling of relaxation nurtured in me a sense of belonging: at last I was at home in the universe, and I greeted each day with enthusiasm.

It was tempting to think I had arrived. After my struggles to find the Way, I was rewarded with the holy grail of tai chi study: health, happiness, and martial skill, all built on an ever-deepening bond with Laoshi.

Alas, that is not the way it is with life—and certainly not the way it was with Laoshi. I began to discover, to paraphrase Winston Churchill, that this was not the end, nor was it the beginning of the end. It was merely the end of the beginning.

Life had plans for me—as did Laoshi. I was not permitted to rest on my laurels and watch the days pass by. There was work to be done.

And so, I found myself teaching tai chi, a role I would sooner have avoided but, nevertheless, the one I inhabited for the next two decades of my life.

How this came to pass, and the insights and lessons I learned on the way, are, as they say, another story.

bibliography

CHENG, MAN-CH'ING. *Master Cheng's New Method of Taichi Ch'uan Self-Cultivation*. Translated by Mark Hennessy. Berkeley, CA: Blue Snake Books, 1999.

CHENG, MAN-CH'ING AND ROBERT W. SMITH. *T'ai Chi: The "Supreme Ultimate" Exercise for Health, Sport, and Self-Defense*. 2nd ed. Boston: Tuttle Publishing, 2004.

COOK, HARRY. *Way of the Warrior: Essays on the Martial Arts, Vol. 1*. Prudhoe, UK: Warrior's Dreams Publications, 1999.

DONOHUE, JOHN. *Sensei: A Thriller*. New York: Onyx, 2004.

GEDDES, GERDA. *Looking for the Golden Needle: An Allegorical Journey*. London: Paul H. Crompton, 1995.

GOULLART, PETER. *The Monastery of Jade Mountain*. London: J. Murray, 1961.

LAO TZU. *Tao Te Ching: A New English Version*. Translated by Stephen Mitchell. New York: Harper Perennial, 2000.

LIU, DA. *The Tao and Chinese Culture*. New York: Schocken Books, 1987.

LO, BENJAMIN PANG JENG. *The Lectures with Benjamin Pang Jeng Lo*, four-DVD set. San Francisco: IRI Press, 2010.

LOWENTHAL, WOLFE. *There Are No Secrets: Professor Cheng Man-ch'ing and His Tai Chi Chuan*. Berkeley, CA: Blue Snake Books, 1993.

——. *Gateway to the Miraculous: Further Explorations in the Tao of Cheng Man-ch'ing*. Berkeley, CA: Blue Snake Books, 1994.

PERRY, SUSAN, ED. *Remembering O-Sensei: Living and Training with Morihei Ueshiba, Founder of Aikido*. Boston: Shambhala, 2002.

PRANIN, STANLEY, ED. *Aikido Masters: Prewar Students of Morihei Ueshiba, Vol. 1*. Tokyo: Aiki News, 1993.

SALZMAN, MARK. *Iron and Silk*. New York: Vintage, 1987.

SHIODA, GOZO. *Aikido: My Spiritual Journey*. New York: Kodansha, 2013.

SMITH, ROBERT W. *Martial Musings: A Portrayal of Martial Arts in the 20th Century*. Erie, PA: Via Media Publishing, 1999.

TSUNETOMO, YAMAMOTO. *Hagakure: The Book of the Samurai*. Translated by William Scott Wilson. Boston: Shambhala, 2012.

UESHIBA, MORIHEI. *The Art of Peace: Teachings of the Founder of Aikido*. Translated by John Stevens. Boston: Shambhala, 1992.

WILE, DOUGLAS. *Zheng Manqing's Uncollected Writings on Taijiquan, Qiqong, and Health, with New Biographical Notes*. Milwaukee, WI: Sweet Ch'i Press, 2007.